# STARTUP MYTHS AND MODELS

PRAISE FOR

# Startup Myths and Models

"In this lively read, Rizwan Virk scrutinizes popular *startup myths* and provides crystal-clear *startup models* to guide entrepreneurs on their journey. Fortify yourself on this book's rich experience and insights before you set out."

**RANDY KOMISAR**, partner, Kleiner Perkins Caufield & Byers, author of *The Monk and the Riddle* and *Straight Talk for Startups*

"Virk has been a founder, advisor, and investor in startups for twenty-five years. *Startup Myths and Models* condenses those years of experience into a set of coherent lessons about the real challenges entrepreneurs face and how to overcome them. If you are going on the entrepreneur's journey, this book is a great companion for every stage of the adventure."

**BRAD FELD**, cofounder of Foundry Group and author of *#GiveFirst* and *Venture Deals*

"When launching a new business, there's no one I'd rather have at my side than Riz Virk as a cofounder or adviser. Having his book *Startup Myths and Models* is the next-best thing. Equip yourself to win the battles that you'll encounter in your startup adventure by reading and digesting the lessons in this book. 100% results, no fluff!"

**MITCHELL LIU**, cofounder of SLIVER.tv, Theta Labs, and Tapjoy

"In *Startup Myths and Models,* Riz Virk debunks common misconceptions about life in Startup Land. Both funny and wise, this book is a worthwhile read for any entrepreneur."

**JEFFREY BUSSGANG**, Harvard Business School, general partner at Flybridge Capital Partners, and author of *Mastering the VC Game*

"Riz Virk was one of my inspirations to be an entrepreneur. My advice to would-be entrepreneurs is to read Riz's book *Startup Myths and Models*, because it contains wisdom drawn from his twenty-five years of startup battles."

**RAJEEV SURATI**, cofounder of Flash Communications (sold to Microsoft) and Photo.net

"I've founded five companies, made angel investments in over one hundred, and served on numerous startup boards—I wish I had a book like this before I started! Packed with hard-earned wisdom, this book does a great job of debunking myths and over-simple rules of thumb in the startup universe."

**MICHAEL DORNBROOK**, COO of Harmonix (makers of *Guitar Hero*), member of Common Angels, and VP of marketing at InfoCom (makers of *Zork*)

"*Startup Myths and Models* is one of the best textbooks for founders who are going through accelerators (and, of course, for those who aren't). Virk reveals secrets about starting, funding, growing, and selling your startup all while doing what's most important—staying sane and healthy. This is one of my go-to recommendations for any founder beginning or currently on the startup journey."

**PAT RILEY**, CEO of GAN (Global Accelerator Network)

"Whether you're a curious student or a serial entrepreneur, *Startup Myths and Models* is on my recommended reading list for any startup founder. Virk's use of the Hero's Journey will help you understand how answering the call to the startup adventure will forever change you for the better."

**TIM MIANO**, associate director, Harvard Innovation Labs, and cofounder/CEO, SP@CE

"*Startup Myths and Models* cuts through all the startup noise, bringing real-world experience to every entrepreneur in a super easy to access reference book."

**WILL HERMAN**, coauthor of *The Startup Playbook*, angel investor, and founder of five startups (2 IPOs)

# Startup Myths and Models

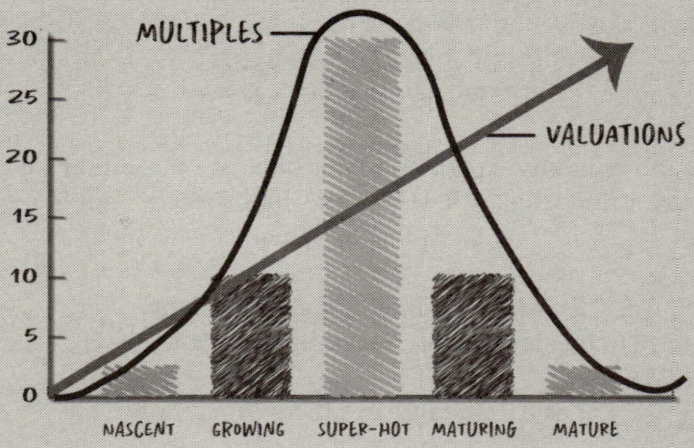


## WHAT YOU WON'T LEARN IN BUSINESS SCHOOL

RIZWAN VIRK

HARPER BUSINESS

*An Imprint of* HarperCollins *Publishers*

First published in 2020 by Columbia University Press, New York
This English-language reprint edition is a complete reproduction, specially authorized by the original publisher, Columbia University Press, for publication and sale throughout South Asia.

This edition published in paperback in India in 2021 by Harper Business
An imprint of HarperCollins *Publishers*
A-75, Sector 57, Noida, Uttar Pradesh 201301, India
www.harpercollins.co.in

2 4 6 8 10 9 7 5 3 1



P-ISBN: 978-93-5489-227-1
E-ISBN: 978-93-5489-273-8



Cover design: Lisa Hamm

Printed and bound at
Thomson Press (India) Ltd

HarperCollinsIn

MIX
Paper
FSC FSC® C010615

This book is produced from independently certified FSC® paper
to ensure responsible forest management.

# CONTENTS

# SIDEBARS

## STARTUP MODELS



## STARTUP TOOLS

# INTRODUCTION

## Who Needs This Book?

*Startup Myths and Models* is a book I wish I'd had when I started my first company. It could have saved me a lot of pain. Well, now that I think about it, I wish I'd had it when I started my second and third ventures too!

Although every entrepreneurial adventure follows different roads, the challenges that crop up along the way are often similar. And often, these challenges aren't just external—they exist in our minds and are based on everything we have heard and learned about how startups *should* work.

This book is about the challenges faced by entrepreneurs who are embarking on the startup journey. More specifically, this book focuses on the internal responses to those external challenges, each presented as a "myth"—a rule of thumb that gets tossed around in the startup world as if it's gospel, but it is actually a mental trap.

Here are some examples of these myths:

- You have to build a billion-dollar company.
- Hire the most experienced people you can find.
- Raise as little (or as much) money as possible.
- Focus, focus, focus.
- Fail fast, pivot quickly.

All of these *seem* to make sense for any startup, obviously! Correct?

Wrong. These are some of the common myths that are debunked in this book.

Each of these myths represent common wisdom that is likely to involve a very serious dilemma for you at key points in your startup adventure (whether to raise money, with whom to start a company, whom to hire or fire, whether and when to sell the company, etc.). If you simply follow the "rule of thumb" without understanding what's behind it, you may find yourself the unwitting victim of the myth.

## Myths and Models in Startup Land

These myths are prevalent in Startup Land, a mythical version of Silicon Valley that is supported by numerous blogs, residents, and success stories, all packaged for the world at large.

Startup Land comes with its own mythology about famous heroes (the founders of Google or Facebook or Apple, for example), villains (greedy venture capitalists and unethical founders), as well colorful characters who crop up around the main protagonists of startup stories.

Startup Land really consists of an ecosystem that's grown up around Silicon Valley: a large number of venture capitalists, angel investors, founders, lawyers, managers, accountants, and an endless number of consultants/advisors/mentors all gathered in one place. Like the characters in any good adventure, the colorful residents of Startup Land can either help you along your path or hinder your progress. Some may even look like they are there to help, but often have their own hidden agendas.

Of course, Startup Land reaches well beyond the geographical limits of Silicon Valley itself, and now includes places like Boston, New York, Austin, Los Angeles, and Seattle, among others. Many countries in Europe and Asia are currently trying to reproduce the innovation and dynamism in their own versions of Startup Land, albeit with a nod to their local culture, often incorporating many of the legends, mythology, and philosophy of Silicon Valley in the process.

This common mythology leads to "groupthink" on the one hand (everyone spouts the same platitudes), and on the other hand, it sometimes leads to completely contradictory advice. As a simple example, here are two pieces of advice I've heard (and sometimes given): "Raise as little money as you can" *and* "Raise as much money as you can!"

If there were academic models for how startups should work, which were backed up by real-world experience, then it would be possible to evaluate the myths against these models. You would think that given the popularity of startups today, business schools would teach some of these important lessons and Startup Models, which could help residents of Startup Land think critically about the major decisions they need to make in the life of a startup.

But they don't. So what's a budding entrepreneur to do?

## The Times They Are a-Changing: Harvard Versus Stanford Business School

In 1980s popular culture, Harvard Business School was considered the pinnacle of business thought, and many ambitious future businesspersons wanted to get admitted there (which was no easy task, since it had a 10 percent admission rate). Those who wanted to succeed in business wanted to leverage the power of the HBS alumni network and curriculum so they could become the next captains of industry, running a division of (and eventually becoming CEO of) a large company like General Motors or General Electric or Exxon, which were the most valuable companies in the world at that time. The other big ambition in the 1980s was to enter Wall Street and become a finance wizard (as exemplified in Oliver Stone's now-classic movie about the period, *Wall Street*).

As a result, most business schools' curricula were tailored to one of these goals—to produce either managers of Fortune 1000 companies or Wall Street wizards (traders or fund managers).

Even with these goals, it was generally recognized that business school couldn't teach you everything you needed to know about business. In a mark of the times, the 1984 book *What They Don't Teach You at Harvard Business School*, by Mark McCormack, was about aspects of management that were hard to teach in a classroom environment and could be acquired only through experience. It became an international best seller.

Fast forward to today.

Not only are today's most valuable companies different from those of the past, but so are the ambitions of the next generation of business leaders. The most valuable companies in the world today (largest by market cap) are all tech companies—Apple, Amazon, Microsoft, Facebook, Google—and several of these companies have surpassed $1 trillion in market cap for the first time in history. All of these companies were once startups that needed to go through all of the stages of the entrepreneur's journey that are described in this book. All of them needed to raise money, recruit travel companions, find product-market fit, and make decisions about whether to sell the company at each stage.

The ambitious businessperson today aspires not to become the next Jack Welch or Lee Iacocca or Alfred Sloan, but rather the next Mark Zuckerberg (founder of Facebook) or the next Elon Musk (founder of Tesla and SpaceX).

If the heart of Startup Land is Silicon Valley (even if you aren't physically located there), then the heart of Silicon Valley is probably Stanford University. Most concentrated areas of tech entrepreneurship are built around a leading technical university. Hewlett-Packard, Google, Yahoo!, and many other successful startups had a Stanford affiliation; even companies that were headquartered in Seattle, like Microsoft and Amazon, recruited heavily from Silicon Valley and Stanford's business school (also called "the GSB", short for Stanford's Graduate School of Business).

As a sign of the changing times, today Stanford's GSB has replaced Harvard as the most selective business school in the country (with a 6 percent acceptance rate). Moreover, if you want an alumni network and curriculum that are tailored to future founders of the world's most valuable companies, you would think that Stanford GSB would be the place to go. After attending another great university, MIT, for my undergraduate degree, I went to Stanford GSB when I moved to Silicon Valley, and I can attest that the alumni network is among the best in the world for tech entrepreneurship and venture capital.

Although I found multiple classes on entrepreneurship when I went to the GSB (and many graduates will choose to start a company or go into venture capital as a career), I was surprised to find that entrepreneurship was not one of the main options for concentration. Much of the curriculum at the GSB, even in the heart of Silicon Valley, was still geared toward producing managers of Fortune 1000 companies or finance wizards.

This book is my attempt to reconcile Stanford's position as the heart of Startup Land, and in the spirit of the classic book, teach those things which can only be taught through the experience.

To that end, the Startup Myths, Startup Models, and Startup Tools in this book are the equivalent of a startup MBA curriculum—complete with secrets and lessons that you can't really learn in any classroom.

## Startup Myths: Find the Kernel of Truth

Let's start with the myths, which are the backbone of this book. The reason I wish I had this book when I started my first few companies is not that the myths presented in this book aren't true. It's rather that they are true *sometimes*. This means they are *also* wrong *at other times*.

The myths mask a complexity that you need to understand not just about your startup—but about how startup markets evolve and change in general. If you simply follow the rule of thumb without understanding this underlying complexity, this can lead to not just a bad decision but the death of your company. This complexity obscures the kernel of truth in each myth. With this book, you can use the secret behind each myth to extract this kernel of truth and learn how to apply it to your situation.

Let's take a very common example of advice you hear on the startup journey: Myth #11: Focus, Focus, Focus. It seems pretty obvious, right? But I've seen many startups miss a great market opportunity because they had tunnel vision about what they were trying to build.

I've seen other startups go from mediocre results to great success by *not focusing*, but by keeping their eyes and ears open to ancillary opportunities that came up while they were supposed to be following their VC investors' advice to "focus, focus, focus" (good thing they didn't focus too much!).

On the other hand, a startup *does need to focus* to be successful. The real trick is understanding what you should be focused on, and when. To uncover the secret behind this myth, you'll see that the secret behind this myth is *Focus, Explore, Focus*. To succeed where others have failed, you'll need to learn how to apply this secret in your own unique situation.

## When to Follow Advice and When Not To

You'll see that these myths aren't a matter of simple "do's and don'ts"; rather, each myth in this book encapsulates a point of view that we can easily find ourselves in as entrepreneurs (and as investors, too!).

This point of view, if followed blindly, will get you into a dilemma. The *secret* behind each myth is a different way to think about the dilemma; if you do that, you might find yourself successfully overcoming that particular challenge and continuing happily on your startup journey.

How do you shift a point of view? As on all good journeys, you need good mentors and advisors to help along the path. Bilbo needed Gandalf; Luke needed Obi-Wan Kenobi (yes, I mean that "crazy old wizard, Ben").

Good mentors—usually in the form of advisors, board members, and investors—can give you advice, help you get perspective, and tell you their secrets. And more important, good mentors have a sense of how things should work in successful startups, which is often encapsulated into a mental model they can teach you to apply. But they're not always available, and unlike in mythological journeys where the mentor shows up early, in the real world, finding the right mentors at the right time can be challenging.

This book is meant to help in these situations: it can be a mentor and advisor for you along your journey and can reveal the secrets that can get you past the ogres and demons that crop up along the entrepreneurial adventure.

But don't just take my word for it. The myths that made it into this book (and their corresponding secrets) have been culled from interviews with many other entrepreneurs, angel investors, lawyers, and venture capitalists from Silicon Valley and beyond (the "experts"), who are profiled in Appendix B: Meet Our Cast of Characters and Startups.

## Startup Models: What They Should Teach at Startup Business School

In addition to the myths themselves, this book will introduce you to several important Startup Models and Startup Tools, which can help you to make sense of the lessons inside each myth.

When I was at the GSB, we learned many models of how economics and finance worked. Of particular interest to me were the supply and demand curves that economists use in both macro- and microeconomics. Unlike financial equations that rely on precise numbers, these models provide ways to think about the world of economics, which apply equally to markets of goods as well as money markets, showing how supply and demand create an equilibrium point.

I remember my professors telling me that the *direction* of the curves was the most important thing—they helped us to visualize what was going on in a particular market, and helped us figure out how things might change over time.

I lamented that there was no corresponding set of formal models for startups that would help entrepreneurs and investors figure out what was happening not just to a particular startup, but to a market as a whole.

The Startup Models in this book are conceptual frameworks for thinking about startups and startup markets, which account for the fact that startup markets follow different rules than mature markets. There are two kinds of models presented in this book:

- *Startup Market Lifecycle.* In this model, which is fully developed through the course of the book, I've put together my observations of how startup markets evolve. This is based on what I've seen in my twenty-five–plus years of founding and investing in startups: that very different startup markets evolve through very similar stages. These stages aren't just theoretical; investors and acquirers intuitively base their valuations and put their money into companies completely differently depending on what stage the market is in. Many of the myths (and corresponding bad decisions made by entrepreneurs) derive from not understanding this model and where in the model a particular market is.
- *Mental Models for Startup Challenges.* These are models that help you think about different aspects of your startup experience—including hiring, firing, pivoting, and even selling your company. Two examples of these models are the Four Quadrants of Pivoting and the Four Quadrants of Hiring. Some of these models have been passed down from advisor/investor to entrepreneur, and I learned them from my mentors. Others I have put together in the course of mentoring entrepreneurs as a way to explain how they should think about today's fast moving startup markets.

## Startup Tools You Should Dig Into

In addition to the models, many chapters include Startup Tools—checklists and questions that can help you recognize your priorities and biases about important aspects of starting and growing a company.

For example, Startup Tool #1: Prioritizing Founder Motivations, and Startup Tool #2: Uncovering Founder Expectations, can be used to explore the motivations of your cofounders as well as the implicit expectations that each of you is carrying into your startup adventure.

These tools aren't just academic checklists—the answers to these questions can change the direction of your startup. They can make the difference between a founding team breaking up or staying together, and they can make millions of dollars of difference in an acquisition. I've used them myself in the Play Labs startup accelerator at MIT, which I founded recently. I refined them based on my own experience in working with entrepreneurs.

## How This Book Is Organized: The Hero's Journey

Joseph Campbell, the well-known American professor of literature and a student of Carl Jung, analyzed the mythology and heroic epics of many different cultures. He found that although no two adventure stories were exactly the same, the heroes of these myths went through similar stages in their journeys and faced similar challenges.

He outlined these stages in his book, *The Hero with a Thousand Faces*. He dubbed these the stages of "the Hero's Journey" and this became a great way to think about adventure stories. These stages made their way into more modern adventures, like *Star Wars* and *Lord of the Rings*.

I've always held the point of view that a startup journey is like an adventure. Like all good adventures, no two startup journeys will be exactly the same, but the heroes may go through similar stages and face similar challenges.

Like all good adventurers, every entrepreneur has to find their own way through these stages, just like in the old myths. Like all good adventures, the hero (or heroine) will be joined on the journey by colorful characters, some of whom are there to help, some who are there to hinder, and some who have hidden motivations.

Thus, I've chosen to organize this book by adapting the stages of the Hero's Journey to the most common stages of the Startup Journey. These stages make it easy to organize, read and digest the myths in this book:

1. The Call to Adventure: Myths About Starting a Company
2. Fuel for the Journey: Myths About Raising Money
3. Travel Companions: Myths About Hiring and Management
4. The Road of Trials: Myths About Going to Market
5. Acquiring the Treasure: Myths About Exiting Your Company
6. The Underworld and the Return: Myths About Life and Death in a Startup

In each stage, I've chosen the top few "myths" based on my own experience as an entrepreneur, the numerous startups I've invested in and advised, and through consultation with some of the top venture capitalists, angel investors, and entrepreneurs in Silicon Valley (the experts that I interviewed for this book). Unless otherwise indicated in a note, the quotes from these experts were taken from direct interviews I did with them, or in some cases, from their writings. The experts' advice is featured in the text and in sidebars after many of the main myths.

## The Biggest Startup Myth

In addition to these individual myths, there is an overriding myth about startups that is prevalent in Startup Land and beyond. It comes from the fact that in the press we usually hear only about the standouts—the startups that have become famous because of their success: Microsoft, Apple, Oracle, Google, Facebook. This "Big Startup Myth" goes something like this:

1. Entrepreneur comes up with great idea, quits job to start company;
2. investors believe in entrepreneur's idea and invest;
3. small team completes product quickly;
4. product is released and is a big success;
5. company experiences straight-line growth, year after year.

Of course, shortly thereafter, the company has an IPO or is acquired, and as a result everyone is fat, rich, and happy!

You'll notice that this modern myth is missing some of the key elements of the Hero's Journey—namely, the negative ones: the "refusal of the call" (where the hero turns down the adventure), "the road of trials" (where the hero must slay monsters or overcome serious hardships), and the "trip to the underworld" (where the hero faces mortality and becomes a different person). Ignoring these challenging times is perhaps the biggest myth of all; this book is all about how to navigate these difficult stages.

## My Own Startup Journey

I started my first company well before I went to business school. As a fresh graduate from MIT in the 1990s, just before the dot-com revolution,

I certainly believed this "Big Startup Myth" when I cofounded my first startup with my college roommate, Mitch, and my brother, Irfan. We didn't need any outside investment initially, and we built the product ourselves in a few months.

At first, it seemed like everything was proceeding according to plan. We released the product and it was a big hit! All the computer magazines wrote about us and we had more leads than we could handle. All in all, over a thousand companies adopted our first product, which was a link between Microsoft's Visual Basic and Lotus Notes (which later became a part of IBM).

Venture capitalists took note, and we thought we were on to the rest of the growth curve that appears on the left side of figure 0.1. But then, as inevitably happens on the startup journey, we came face to face with our own "road of trials" as the market changed and our growth slowed well below our (overly) optimistic projections. Our burn rate had increased and we were suddenly in danger of running out of money, facing our own startup's mortality, our own personal "trip to the underworld."

That's when I realized that any realistic startup journey really looks more like the right side of figure 0.1—with lots of unexpected twists and turns.

I went on to create multiple startups, including both enterprise software companies and direct to consumer companies, some of which went on to be sold successfully, and some of which failed. Ironically, I learned just as

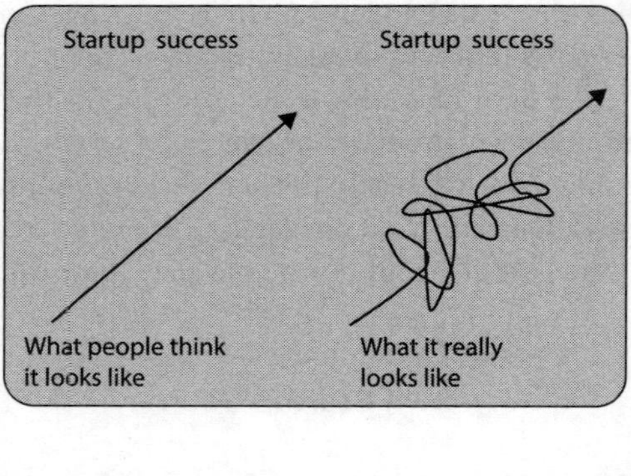


Figure 0.1
What Success Looks Like. This popular internet meme applies to startups perfectly! Recreated by the author

much (if not more) from the failures. It was through seeing the same lessons apply in different markets to different entrepreneurs over many years that I started to develop the frameworks in this book.

In particular, the mobile gaming revolution that kicked off with the release of the iPhone in 2008 was a time when I really started to see patterns based on previous startup markets I had been a part of. I started to see how startup markets evolve similarly, and I learned how to ride this wave. My cofounders (Mitch and Irfan again) and I created one of the top games in the early days of the Apple iTunes app store called *Tap Fish*, which had over 30 million downloads. I then went on to invest in many other startups, including some that went on to be worth billions, and others that looked like they were going to be big successes but had their own "trip to the underworld" and unexpectedly died.

Years later I found myself teaching many first-time (and sometimes repeat) entrepreneurs the same lessons I had learned on my startup journeys—lessons about founding a company, gauging the market, launching a product, building an organization, and selling a startup. I traveled back to MIT in the summer to start my accelerator, Play Labs, so that I could work with groups of entrepreneurs, many of whom were going on the entrepreneur's journey for the first time, and I battle-tested out the lessons in this book.

The hard truth about entrepreneurship is that most startups fail. Even those that succeed must still go down their own "road of trials" and have their own "trip to the underworld." By arming yourself with the Startup Models, tools, and the secrets behind each Startup Myth, you can give yourself an edge by learning from the success and failure of many who have gone before you on this adventure.

## Bonus Myths

In my research and writing, I found many more myths and secrets than I could fit into this book. Practical considerations required me to choose the top few myths for each stage of the Hero's Journey. In some cases, I felt the myths we needed to cut were important enough to deserve a mention, even if I wasn't able to include a full text. I have included these in the "Bonus Myths" supplement to this book, which is available online to download on my website (www.zenentrepreneur.com). Over time, this supplemental material may grow, so you may want to sign up to the mailing list. After all, Startup Land is always growing and evolving—so why wouldn't the myths, models, and tools also grow and evolve too?

## How to Use This Book

I decided to write this book to encapsulate the lessons I've learned across multiple startup markets and many startup adventures. I believe the best way to summarize these lessons is not through a set of rigid rules; rather, it is by explaining the Startup Myths and models presented here. Any rules that you have been told about startups will need to be adjusted depending on the context (stage of the market, stage of the company). You might be surprised to learn that any rules in Startup Land also have to be adjusted based on the strengths and weaknesses of each founding team!

In the ancient Greek stories, Odysseus and Hercules were both known as "sackers of Troy." Each had very different strengths—Odysseus succeeded through cunning, using the Trojan horse, while Hercules was endowed with superhuman strength and simply used his club to beat the Trojans into submission (this episode happened many years before *The Iliad* and is briefly referenced by Homer).

The myths, models, and tools presented in this book will help you figure out the best solutions for you, given your own strengths and weaknesses, in your startup journey.

You can read the book all at once (though that's quite a lot to digest, so I don't recommend it), or keep the book on the shelf and pull it out when you and your band of adventurers are at a particular stage of the journey.

I have yet to meet an entrepreneur who didn't become a very different person by the end of their startup journey. Like Frodo and Samwise (not to mention Merry and Pippin) in *The Lord of the Rings*, you will return to your own Shire as a wiser and stronger person, ready to apply what you've learned to your own little corner of Middle Earth.

I applaud you for hearing the "call to adventure" and not refusing it.

May your journey be fruitful, inspiring, and life changing!

# Stage 1

## The Call to Adventure

## *Myths About Starting a Company*

### Introduction to Stage 1

The hero can go forth of his own volition to accomplish the adventure . . . or he may be carried or sent abroad by some benign or malignant agent as was Odysseus, driven about the Mediterranean by the winds of the angered god, Poseidon. The adventure may begin as a mere blunder . . . or still again, one may be only casually strolling when some passing phenomenon catches the wandering eye and lures one away from the frequented paths of man.

—JOSEPH CAMPBELL

Crossing the threshold: This is the point where the hero actually crosses into the field of adventure, leaving the known limits of his world and venturing into an unknown and dangerous realm where the rules and limits are unknown.[1]

—JOSEPH CAMPBELL

1. The wording describing this stage of the journey comes from "Hero's Journey" on Wikipedia. See https://en.wikipedia.org/wiki/Hero%27s_journey.

The first stage of the entrepreneur's journey, like many mythical adventures, might be full of excitement or fits of doubt and uncertainty. More likely, it includes all of these emotions. There are as many startup origin stories as there are startups.

Sometimes, an entrepreneur has an idea in a moment of insight, as did Jeff Taylor, founder of Monster.com, who saw the new job-search website in a dream in the middle of the night. He woke up, and sketched out all the screens he had seen, and had the beginnings of his product.

More likely, your startup adventure might creep up on you slowly over time. Or, it might even come as a complete surprise, as happened to Bilbo Baggins when he hosted an unexpected party including the wizard Gandalf and the twelve dwarves. He found himself in the middle of an "adventure" when it was the last thing he thought he wanted!

In some cases, as with my first venture, you may see an opportunity that your employer is not chasing, but which seems obvious to you. This process accounts for the beginning of many startup adventures. When I thought of the idea for the product for my first startup, I was working for Lotus Development Corporation (later part of IBM), which was one of the largest software companies in the world. It was the work I was doing there that convinced me there needed to be a bridge between Microsoft and Lotus products. Since Lotus wasn't going to pursue this opportunity, I convinced my roommate to start the company with me, and within a few months we had over a thousand companies using our product!

In the case of Service Metrics, which I helped cofound during the dot-com boom, Rajat Bhargava thought of the idea when he was running his first startup, net.Genesis. But that company decided not to pursue the idea, so Rajat looked for a way to launch the product as a separate company.

Sometimes a big client, sponsor, or investor comes calling. This isn't unlike what happens in most Indiana Jones films, which start with a government official asking our academic hero to go on an adventure. In the startup world, this usually comes in the form of a client asking you to build something for them, which you realize could then apply to a whole bunch of other customers. Or it could be in the form of a venture capitalist or investor recruiting members of a team to attack an opportunity they can't resist.

However the call to adventure comes, Joseph Campbell found that a "refusal of the call" was one of the common themes in many mythological adventures of antiquity, and it is still common today. Bilbo Baggins refuses to go on an adventure when Gandalf first asks him, saying that adventures are bound to make him "late for dinner," which is a no-no for Hobbits (and many employees of big corporations too)!

In these mythical stories, after the refusal of the call, the hero is often forced into "crossing the threshold" to start the adventure. Luke Skywalker initially refuses the call to adventure, telling Ben Kenobi that there is no way he can follow him on some "damn fool" trip to Alderaan to rescue the princess. But as often happens, destiny comes calling when Imperial stormtroopers end up murdering Luke's family, leaving Luke "no choice" but to go with Ben. Thus kicks off *Star Wars*, one of the most famous adventures of all time.

In the startup world too, there are many reasons to "refuse" the call to adventure, and most of them revolve around risks. Anyone with a mortgage knows that suddenly finding yourself without a paycheck, without an office to work in, without a boss, can be like taking a leap of faith over a cliff into the abyss. Or, like Bilbo, you may just not want to be "late for dinner!"

But most entrepreneurs, just like the heroes in the old stories, find that destiny pulls them into their adventures, despite any initial objections they might have had. They find themselves "crossing the threshold" into this new world beyond the safe world they once knew. Most entrepreneurs are glad to have gone on the journey, whether or not a literal treasure is acquired in the end.

## *Overview of the Myths*

In this first stage, we look at some of the common challenges and misconceptions about why entrepreneurs do or should (or don't or shouldn't) chase a startup idea. These include how big the opportunity needs to be, whether you have to be first to market, who you should (or shouldn't) cofound a company with, and whether it makes sense to jump into a particular startup market now or later.

We also explore the complex motivations of not just one, but multiple cofounders. When different team members have different values, expectations, and hopes for an outcome, there is a tendency for the team to break apart at some point in the adventure, often resulting in ruined friendships and relationships. While we can't guarantee that your startup team won't break up some day, it doesn't have to be that way. If each of you is clear about your motivations up front, it is much less likely that you'll get into crisis mode because of this important factor.

We introduce one of the most important models in this Stage Startup Model #1: The Startup Market Lifecycle, which can be useful in helping guide you throughout your startup adventure. This model—based on what I've learned in my twenty-five-plus years of watching multiple startup markets evolve—is a useful framework for making decisions that are ordinarily gut-wrenching much more understandable and rational. Should you or shouldn't you jump into a market? Should you or shouldn't you raise VC money? Should you or shouldn't you sell your company? Although at this stage we'll utilize the model to understand the complexities of jumping into a startup market, we'll develop the model further in subsequent chapters to gain insights into later stages of the startup journey.

If you are reading this and are contemplating founding your first startup, or if you are already in a startup, or even if you are thinking of doing another one, I commend you on your interest in going on this unique journey. To paraphrase the wizard Akiro (played by actor Makoto "Mako" Iwamatsu) from the *Conan the Barbarian* movies:

Welcome to the days of high adventure!

# Myth #1

## Build a Billion-Dollar Company

Somewhere along the line, entrepreneurs in Startup Land (not to mention tech reporters and investors) got obsessed with the word "billion."

I don't know when this happened exactly, but I believe it was at some point after the dot-com boom of the late 1990s. Before that, the rule of thumb was that to raise VC financing you had to show a plan that got "50 in 5," meaning VCs wanted to invest in companies that could get to $50 million in revenue within 5 years. At some point, VCs insisted they wanted to invest in entrepreneurs building the next billion-dollar company, and they would invest only if you were attacking an appropriately sized multibillion-dollar market!

I blame this in part on Justin Timberlake, who portrayed a fictionalized version of Napster cofounder Sean Parker in the 2010 movie *The Social Network*, about the founding of Facebook. In the movie, he gives a famous line about *one million* no longer being cool; *one billion* was cool!

This trend was accelerated by the focus in the tech press on "unicorns," a term that many attribute to my MIT classmate Aileen Lee, who had been a partner at Kleiner Perkins Caufield & Byers, one of the top VC firms in Silicon Valley, and left to start Cowboy Ventures. She defined a unicorn as a startup or private company that has rapidly grown to have a *valuation* that is over *one billion dollars* and was less than 10 years old. She observed that such companies were "rare creatures" and came up with the term. In fact, historically, most private companies would have gone public well before they reached a billion-dollar valuation.

However, after the financial crisis of 2008 and its accompanying regulations, private valuations of startups began to balloon as companies chose to stay private longer and longer.

As many of these private companies became valued in the billions, everyone suddenly became obsessed with building the next "unicorn." In fact, today, unicorns seem anything but rare in Startup Land—you can read about a new one in the trade rags every week! It became the prevailing wisdom that if you were pitching to venture capitalists anything less than the next billion-dollar company in anything less than a multibillion-dollar market, they would send you home because you weren't "ambitious" enough!

The reality is that most *successful* companies in Silicon Valley never reach the billion-dollar threshold (either in revenues or in valuation), and many "hot" markets never evolve to be as big as their outlandish projections. Even though there are more unicorns than before, the total percentage of all startups that achieve this valuation is still relatively small.

Moreover, by focusing too much on big numbers like this, it's possible that you'll miss out on the most fulfilling part of the startup adventure: that of building a company with a product or service that people want and are willing to pay for. Most startups never even get to a valuation of more than $100 million, but that doesn't mean you can't build a great company with happy customers with a much smaller market cap. The most money that I and many of my entrepreneur friends made from a startup happened from a company that sold for way less than $1 billion, but we were all very happy with the outcome!

Like most myths, this one does have *some* truth in it. Venture capitalists do want to see a significant market opportunity for your startup. But for some investors (myself included), you can actually hurt your chances of raising money by taking this myth at face value and spending all your time focused on the *b* word.

I remember a few years ago, an entrepreneur pitched me his idea for a billion-dollar opportunity in mobile local payments (this is when "local mobile" companies were suddenly becoming hot). Every other word out of his mouth was "billion"—as in why Andreessen-Horowitz (a well-known VC firm) thought it was a billion-dollar idea and how big the market was going to be.

I wasn't impressed.

It isn't that mobile companies couldn't be worth billions (I believed they could be, eventually), it was just that this guy was too focused on the *b* word, and not enough on the winding path that a startup usually takes to get from here to there.

That's when I came up with the *b* rule: The quickest way to recognize a *b*ullshit artist in Startup Land is when they are too focused on the *b* word—*billion*—whether it's a multibillion-dollar market or how their company is going to be worth a billion dollars (or more) just a few years down the road.

Now, I'm not saying that you don't want to attack a big market opportunity or that you don't want your company to be worth a billion dollars or more—of course we all do! It's just that the path to get there is in some ways more important than the end point.

## The Best Way to Build a Billion-Dollar Company

Let's explore a story that I think illustrates the more likely way a multibillion-dollar company comes about.

When I was a student at MIT in the early 1990s, we had a program that sent a select number of students to Japan for a summer internship. While there, we often met American students from other universities. I went to Japan one summer, and the next summer, my MIT classmate, Mitch (later a cofounder of several companies with me), went to Japan on the same program. While there, Mitch told me that he met a Stanford student named Jerry who was also there via a similar summer program.

Jerry was working on what seemed like a podunk startup idea that had extremely limited business potential: It was a catalogue of sites on something called the world wide web. Since the internet, in those days, was used mostly by universities, and primarily for email and for usenet groups, it didn't seem like a very big market opportunity at all.

It is very possible that if Jerry were pitching today's VCs, he'd be told that he was attacking a market that was too small, and that he wasn't being ambitious enough, because no one recognized at this early stage that the web would become the cornerstone of the internet in the years to come!

Of course, that idea did eventually grow into a well-known business, Yahoo!, and the student was Jerry Yang, one of its cofounders. Yahoo, as we all know, eventually became worth many billions of dollars (its later troubles in the Google era notwithstanding) and was one of the leaders during the dot-com boom.

I think this story about Yahoo illustrates many important points about startup markets, how they emerge, grow, and evolve, and how companies become perceived as leaders in new markets. I think it also illustrates a good way to think about building the next multibillion-dollar company: Don't. Find a market that is small enough that you can become the leader, which *you believe* will grow but other people have doubts about.

If you'd asked Jerry Yang in those early days what the business was going to look like, it's unlikely that he would have been boasting in every other sentence about how he was going to build a billion-dollar company!

If he had, not only would you have thought he was nuts, but you might also have concluded that if he really wanted to build a billion-dollar company, he should be doing something else, not focusing on a nascent, fledgling market like the "world wide web," which nobody had heard of in 1991.

The same is probably true of most companies that have gone on to be worth multiple billions of dollars: The founders weren't focused on starting a billion-dollar company or what it would take to have a billion-dollar exit. Rather, they were just focused on trying to bring some product or service to market, exploiting some trend that intrigued/obsessed them to no end.

## Some Famous Examples

When Bill Gates and Paul Allen were in Boston writing BASIC for the Altair computer, which led to the founding of Microsoft, do you think they were thinking about building a billion-dollar company?

Unlikely.

There might have been some recognition that personal computing was the next big thing and that they wanted to dominate it, but nobody in those days would have said that writing BASIC and development languages for emerging personal computers was a billion-dollar market. In fact, Apple and other high-flying personal computer companies didn't want to build BASIC themselves, so they just licensed it from Microsoft. You might say that Gates and Allen filled *a small hole* that people who were high flyers in the PC revolution didn't want to fill, and they dominated that little niche, becoming the de facto standard for BASIC. It would take many more products (MS-DOS, then Windows, and then Microsoft Office) before Microsoft would have a chance to become a multibillion-dollar company, but these opportunities might not have arisen if they hadn't taken that first step of becoming the go-to guys building BASIC, a much smaller market opportunity that they could dominate and no one else seemed too concerned about.

Even Google, which was a search company started after search had already been shown to be a multibillion-dollar market, was almost sold to Excite for a million dollars. But Excite wasn't interested in buying, even though Larry Page and Sergey Brin, the Google founders, were interested in selling. Anyone who is willing to sell their company and idea for a million dollars clearly isn't too preoccupied with building a billion-dollar company.

How about Facebook? Do you think that when Mark Zuckerberg built his first Facebook site, he was thinking about building a billion-dollar company? No—he was thinking about creating a site to link Harvard students together. Of course, Zuckerberg would famously turn down a billion-dollar offer many years later—but that's a different story about a different stage of the startup adventure.

One of the first companies I personally invested in that became worth more than $1 billion was Discord, one of the most popular chat applications, which now has over 40 million users, having become a unicorn in its own right. When I first invested in the company, Jason Citron, the founder who had successfully sold his previous company for $100 million, was looking to build a game company.

We'll talk about Discord in the context of pivoting later in this book ("Stage 4: The Road of Trials: Myths About Going to Market"), but one important point to note is that the mobile game market had become extremely crowded and competitive by the time the company released its first game, *Fates of Fury*, in 2014. Even though the company was started by an experienced, successful entrepreneur who knew the game industry well, it was just too difficult to make it work. Like many games at this stage of the market, their game wasn't successful (see Startup Model #1: The Startup Market Lifecycle for more information on how the mobile game market evolved). Recognizing that the market was difficult, they leveraged their chat tool (which, as hard-core obsessive gamers, they had built into their game) into a standalone app, and that was what propelled Discord to become a billion-dollar-plus company.

## Starting When the Market Is Very Small

The key to becoming a multibillion-dollar company may just be to get into a very small market that you are obsessed with, long before "everyone" recognizes it as a big market. By the time most investors and others recognize a multibillion-dollar market, you should already be one of the leaders.

Let's take a look at two startups that got into their markets when it was easy to get in and to become a player but hard to raise money, because these weren't yet recognized as multibillion-dollar markets.

Jud Valeski was a cofounder of Gnip, a company that sold for $175 million to Twitter—an exit that made everyone, including the VCs, happy. Gnip was a service that allowed enterprises to build multiple social networks into their applications with a single API.

Jud says that this market was incredibly small when they got started. The idea that anyone needed to connect to multiple social networks with APIs was not a popular one: "At the time the social networks were radically different. Twitter existed, but barely, Instagram was not there, most of the social networking services were not what they are today, and so we made this bet that social networks were going to continue to increase in relevance and significance."

Let's look at another example of an entrepreneur who got into a market when it wasn't very big. In fact, it was so small that it was hard to get investors interested because the market size was not in the billions.

Alex Haro, cofounder of Life360, which is a mobile app that lets family members keep track of each other, went on to great success with hundreds of millions of downloads. Alex says, "The number one text message in the world, even today, is 'where are you?'"

The problem was that smartphones were not prevalent when Life360 made their first version of the app in 2008. It's pretty obvious in hindsight that that the number of families in which multiple members had smartphones was pretty small, and the idea of a "mobile family app" wasn't on most investors' radars.

It wasn't until 2010, when it became common for more than one family member to have a smartphone, that Life360 started to see some momentum. The app suddenly became super useful for tracking where family members were.

Alex reminds us that people didn't think a new model for a mobile app was needed when the company first started: "At the time, I don't know if you remember in 2008, everyone was saying: Facebook's been successful. Let's create Facebook for dog lovers, and Facebook for game lovers, and Facebook for families. But we looked at Facebook and said this is everything families don't need. We went against the trend."

They started on a new platform, mobile smartphone apps, with a very small market size (since there were almost *no families* in which multiple members had smartphones), but which they thought would grow.

As the number of smartphones grew, the company was able to attract investment, and the app has become one of the most downloaded apps of all time. Life360 went public in 2019.

## The Secret

***Focus on a small market opportunity that 1) you can become a leader in, 2) you are obsessed with, and 3) you expect to grow, even if others don't.***

To rephrase this secret, the real rule of thumb might be: *If you really want to build a billion-dollar company, don't try to build a billion-dollar company*, and certainly don't spend all your time boasting about how you're going to build a multibillion-dollar company.

Instead, focus on a small, emerging market opportunity where you can be one of the key/dominant players, and build a kick-ass product that meets your customers' needs in that small but growing market. Prove yourself to your market and you will find yourself a market leader, especially if the market is small.

If your product becomes a leader and the market grows like wildfire, or if you end up inventing a new market that no one believed was going to be big, *you could very well become the next billion-dollar company*.

While some markets will produce multiple billion-dollar companies, it's a mistake to be too preoccupied with big numbers in the early stages of a startup. Don't focus on billions. Yes, a market has to eventually become a multibillion-dollar market for VCs to say they are interested. But the truth of the matter is that many VCs would be very happy with an exit of $100 million or $400 million, despite what they say on their websites. Gnip's exit for $175 million is the kind that most entrepreneurs would be ecstatic to have. We'll talk more about exits in "Stage 5: Acquiring the Treasure: Myths About Exiting Your Company."

The key is to find a market that is in a stage where you can make a major impact. This could be a totally new market, or one that's been around but has been nascent for a while, or it may be a small segment of a bigger market that has a need that's not being met.

The key to understanding how this works is to look at how startup markets *evolve* over time, which is Startup Model #1: The Startup Market Lifecycle.

## Startup Model #1: The Startup Market Lifecycle

There are, of course, many models of how technology markets evolve. The model we will use for this book is my own, based upon observing how multiple startup markets have evolved in my 25-plus years of building, investing in, and advising startups.

The core observation that led to this model is: *all startup markets go through stages*. I call this model the "Startup Market Lifecycle," and it traces the common stages that a startup market will go through if it successfully evolves into a "real" market that can sustain multi-billion dollar companies. While not every market will make it through all the stages, the insights that go with each stage are so important that we'll return to this model again and again as we look to uncover the secrets behind the myths.

Usually, a new startup market begins in the *nascent* stage, and then as the market gets recognized as the "next big thing," it enters the *growing* stage. Often there is a period in many startup markets where everyone goes crazy, which we'll call the *super-hot* stage. At this stage, companies that have missed this new market scramble to get into it, and valuations become irrational. As the market heats up, many more would-be entrepreneurs jump in looking to make a quick buck by capitalizing on this "hot trend." It's only afterward that many of these same entrepreneurs find themselves in the market but realize that market has changed. Unfortunately (for entrepreneurs, anyway), the *super-hot* stage only lasts for a short period of time.

At some point, the pool of potential acquirers dries up because there have been too many entrants into the market. Consolidation starts to happen, but no longer at outrageous valuations. We call this the *maturing* stage, where some market leaders have already been established, and much of the early consolidation has happened, leaving many funded startups in the space that are not in a leadership position without a viable exit and with a market that is difficult to raise follow-on funding for.

Finally, at some point, the market is considered *mature*, with one or more public companies in the market. At this stage, those companies are subject to the rules of mature markets—and they are measured on profitability. This is the stage that most of what we learned in business school is all about, and the laws of weighted capital and future cash flows and price/earnings ratios all start to take effect! Understand this model and you can save yourself the cost of an MBA, unless you want to join companies in markets that are in the maturing or mature stages.

Sometimes a market stalls before it gets past the nascent, growing, or super-hot stages. Often, the nascent market gets absorbed into another market and becomes a feature of it, and is no longer considered a separate market (example: groupware and sales force automation were considered separate markets in the 1990s; then they were were absorbed by other areas, including email, the web, and customer relationship management [CRM]). Alternatively, as a new technology goes mainstream, sometimes a single startup market fragments into multiple markets (example: the web, which isn't really a single market but was seen that way when it first emerged—which evolved into multiple separate markets, such as search, e-commerce, social networking, etc.).

## The Stages of the Startup Market Lifecycle

Figure 1.1 shows the stages graphically and shows some important preliminary curves which are part of this model. The stages are specific enough that anyone who has lived through startup markets will recognize them, but general enough that they can be applied to different "emerging" startup markets. This model was equally applicable to the world of personal computers, client server computing, the web, mobile gaming/apps in recent years, and going back to radios and automobiles long ago.

The valuation curve is what gives the shape to the overall model—but of course, some markets are hyped and get to the super-hot stage right away, while others stall out completely and never mature, while yet others mature over a much longer time frame. Thus, the valuation curve in any given market needn't follow the exact bell-curve shape that is shown in figure 1.1—it can go through some twists and turns, which we'll cover in variations of the basic model in future Myths.

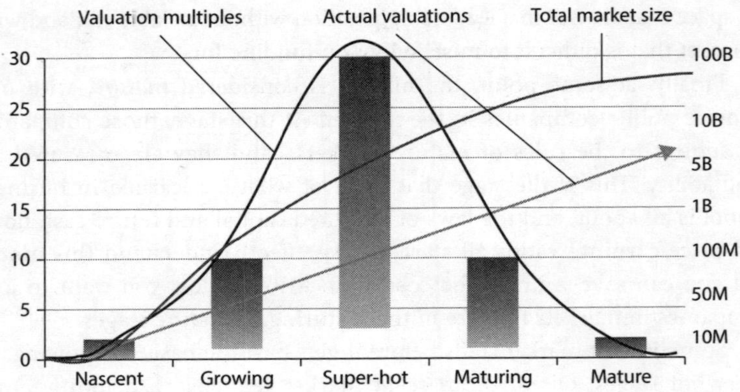


Figure 1.1
Evolution of Startup Markets and Valuations (The Startup Market Lifecycle). Created by the author

Let's look at the stages in more detail:

- *Nascent*. Most startup markets begin in what I call a "nascent" stage. This means that there is an interesting new technology, being played with by hobbyists and researchers. Generally speaking, during this stage the new technology hasn't yet hit the radar of venture capitalists and professional investors en masse and is not yet recognized as the "next big thing." During this stage, while it's great to get into a market and become a thought leader, you generally have to be able to support yourself doing something else or find innovative ways to fund the company, such as by providing consulting services. If you present a company in a nascent market to a VC, they'll probably react: "I've heard of this technology, but let's see how/if this develops into a *real market* over the next few years." Using the world wide web as an example, this stage would be when the first web browsers were being developed in Urbana-Champaign in the early 1990s.
- *Growing*. When one or more startup companies start to experience rapid growth, it is usually accompanied by an "echo chamber" in the tech media about how this market is the "next big thing" in Startup Land. Many companies that eventually become dominant players actually started during this stage. There is, as this stage progresses, a rush from big companies and VCs to put money into this space or to

plug the hole in their product lines. This leads to aggressive valuation multiples (three to five times revenues isn't uncommon), and if the market overheats beyond this, then the market has become *super-hot*. Many VCs started to invest in web-related companies after 1993, looking for ways to commercialize the world wide web. The surest sign of this stage is that multiple VCs either have invested in this space or are all trying to find an investment to add to their portfolios.

- *Super-hot*. Some markets make it to the mainstream quickly, some do it over a longer period of time. But there is an unusual period in high-tech startup markets, where big players and VCs alike realize that they are "behind the ball" and have missed out the early investment opportunities. Someone high up decides the company *desperately* needs to get into this market. This is when outsized valuations happen—I have seen 100-plus multiples on revenues during exits in this stage. The transition from *growing* to *super-hot* sometimes happens based on a particular liquidity or financing event (the Netscape IPO in the web in 1995, or the sale of ngmoco for $400 million to DeNA in mobile gaming in late 2010, the acquisition of Oculus for $2 billion by Facebook in Virtual Reality in 2014). The reasons for the outsized valuations during this phase are often more emotional than rational. In the super-hot phase, investors and big companies, afraid they will miss out, will put money into and acquire companies quickly because they are afraid that if they wait, valuations will go up even more and they will miss out (this is FOMO—the fear of missing out).
- *Maturing*. At some point, rationality comes back into a super-hot market, and there are visible signs that it is maturing. Usually this is when people realize that companies have been overvalued, and the valuations start to come back down to earth, sometimes slowly and sometimes with a thud. There is still a great opportunity to make money during the first part of this stage, but if you wait until the latter part, acquirers and VCs take on very different behavior patterns. Many acquirers have already placed bets in this space, while other acquirers want to see how you actually perform and are usually willing to give only decent multiples rather than outsized multiples. Multiples generally come back down to three- to five-times revenues (as they were in the growing phase), but the direction is different—valuation multiples are going down. As a result, acquirers are actually better off to wait during this stage—there is no longer FOMO. Venture capitalists are hesitant to make any more bets in this space, since the market already

has multiple leaders, unless a company has unusual traction. This stage often begins after some acquisition event brings rationality back into the market, or there are some clear winners. For example, the dot-com crash in 2000 during the "internet market," the dominance of Google in "search," the mobile gaming crash that happened after Zynga's stock plummeted in 2012, all represent times when a market went from super-hot to maturing. Sometimes there is no single precipitating event, but acquiers realize that they are seeing multiple "good" companies and there is no reason to "freak out" and acquire a company quickly, when they can just wait and see how the companies do with real metrics.

- *Mature*. As a market matures, the emphasis shifts from growth to profitability. Not only are there well defined market leaders, but these companies start to be valued based more on profits than on revenues. When I was at Stanford GSB, most of what we learned was tailored toward companies that are in this stage of the market—the rules of big companies don't apply to startups at first. Eventually, investors in game companies or internet companies start to look for profits, and they valued the companies based on those (sometimes nonexistent) profits.

The simplest way to figure out which stage a market is in is to look at valuations in the market. If there is M&A activity, the best way is to compare the valuation multiples to the ranges of the *valuation curve* in figure 1.1. We'll explore in much more detail how valuations evolve for both financings and exits in "Stage 5: Acquiring the Treasure: Myths About Exiting Your Company."

As shown in figure 1.1, the reality is that the actual market size is growing during all of these stages (assuming the market actually makes it through all these stages and doesn't peter out). It may not actually be a multibillion-dollar market until the beginning of the *maturing* stage.

The total value of companies in this market, as shown by the *market size curve*, actually starts off modest on the left, and although growing more rapidly from a percentage perspective, may actually be growing more in absolute dollar terms in the mature stage, even though the slope is smaller.

Similarly, valuations of market leaders still go up as the market matures, even though in the right half of the market lifecycle, multiples of revenue and profits are *going down*. As markets grow and mature, the remaining market leaders take up bigger chunks of these bigger numbers.

## Example of a Startup Market: The Mobile Gaming Market

How can you use this model to your advantage as an entrepreneur? Let's look at one specific market that I was intimately involved with. It's also a good one to look at because it started off as a modest market (in 2008 when I got into it) and by 2016 (when I sold my last company in this market) it had matured and was considered a multibillion-dollar market with multiple billion-dollar-plus valued companies. As such, it is an almost perfect example of the stages that startup markets can go through.

This market evolved from a *nascent* market in 2007 when the iPhone was released (actually 2008, when Apple opened up the iTunes app store to third-party developers), to being recognized as the "next big thing" (the growing stage) in late 2009 and early 2010.

In those exciting days, it didn't take that much money to build a mobile game, and it didn't take that much to market the game. I cofounded Gameview Studios in 2010 and we built our first game, *Tap Fish*, for under \$25,000. We marketed the game for less than \$25,000 and it shot to the top of Apple's iTunes app store and stayed there for many weeks, getting millions of downloads. It eventually went on to have over 30 million downloads and topped the Google Play store in top grossing when they came out with in-app purchases as well.

By early 2011, the mobile gaming market started to look as if it was becoming super-hot (which coincided with the acquisition of companies like ngmoco by DeNA for \$400 million, and *Words with Friends* by Zynga for a rumored \$100 million-plus).

This stage lasted for a little over a year, and then starting in the second half of 2012, the market started to mature. What happened?

For one thing, it became very difficult and expensive to get users. To launch a game, if you didn't have *at least* several hundred thousand dollars (and soon millions of dollars) to spend on marketing, it became almost impossible to get your game above the noise. When we released Tap Fish, there were maybe 10,000 apps in the app store. By 2016 there were several hundred thousand and within a few years, there would be over a million!

For another, valuations started to come down. Zynga, the first company to go public in this market, was overvalued, according to investors. This in turn led to lower valuations on companies getting acquired, since Zynga was one of the premium acquirers bidding up valuations.

One company that sold during the maturing period was Funzio, which sold to GREE (another Japanese public company) for over $200 million. This seemed like a large amount of money, but Funzio's revenues as publicly disclosed at the time were in the neighborhood of $50 million, so this valuation represented only a 4× multiple on revenues. While a good multiple, it was nowhere near the 10× that companies were getting when the market was super-hot.

With Zynga no longer able to pay top dollar, and with many of the Japanese companies who had been scrambling to get into the Western smartphone market no longer paying premiums to buy startups (DeNA and GREE were the two main offenders), valuations started to come down to earth.

Consolidation still happened throughout 2012 and 2013; by 2014, there were many mobile gaming startups that were failing and no one wanted to buy them. Too many had been funded in the growing and super-hot phases. Remember, the definition of the super-hot phase is when "everyone and their mother is jumping in and getting funded" because it looks like easy money.

Note that by 2015, mobile gaming had become a much bigger market than it had been in previous years—it had in fact become a multibillion-dollar market sporting several billion-dollar-plus companies. It had also become much more difficult for new entrepreneurs to go out and raise money for a mobile gaming company because there were so many dominant players—including companies like Super Cell (makers of *Clash of Clans*), King.com (makers of *Candy Crush*), Rovio (makers of *Angry Birds*), and others.

These were sure signs that the market was maturing:

1. the cost of getting into the market had gone up significantly,
2. valuations had come down to "reasonable" levels, and
3. there were established "leaders" doing well.

While there were still some gaming startups that began after 2013 and did well, the number and percentage were down significantly from the "boom" years and they required significantly more capital. More gaming startups were failing than succeeding during this time. It also became very difficult for firms that had raised some money to keep going. A perfect example of this was Bionic Panda, which made a game called Aqua Pets, which was similar to Tap Fish but several years late. While they had over

7 million downloads on Android, they were unable to raise their next round of financing.

In 2016, Niantic released *Pokemon Go*, which became a huge hit and shot to the top of the app store. What most people don't know was that the company had already raised $30 million before the game was released and became a big hit. Around that same time, another leader, Kabam, makers of many original games that had done well (Kingdoms of Camelot) also switched its strategy to licensed properties, including Lord of the Rings and Marvel's Contest of Champions. They publicly revealed that they wanted to do "less games" and the average cost of producting a game had gone up to over $10 million. So, in the six years after we released *Tap Fish*, the cost of building a top-performing game had gone up from twenty five thousand to many millions of dollars, as did the cost of marketing a game!

## Innovation in Mature Markets

Once a market has passed super-hot, in the "maturing" and the "mature" stages, it is very difficult for a new startup to make an impact with a small amount of money. The amount of capital that it takes to build a company in a maturing/mature market, when there are established leaders that are hard to push aside, is significantly more than it takes when companies/markets are immature.

To understand the universality of this model, let's look at a totally different kind of market: the auto market. We don't think of the auto market as being a startup market, but when automobiles were new, it was "the next big thing."

Many of the brands that we know (Dodge, Oldsmobile, Buick, etc.) were small auto companies started in the 1920s to compete with Henry Ford and his model T. Many of the small companies were innovative, and many of them were gobbled up by General Motors or Ford or Chrysler. Fast forward many decades and a new kind of car—the electric car—seemed like it was on the horizon.

Let's take two prominent examples of startups in this new market for electric cars: Tesla and Fisker. These two innovative car companies wanted to disrupt an already mature market (the auto industry) with their innovations: a unique hybrid model for Fisker and a complete electric car for Tesla. Fisker and Tesla both ran into problems, and both had questionable futures. According to public accounts, Elon Musk put in $180 million of his own money to get Tesla to where it is, and according to insiders, the company was *still* on the brink of failing. If it hadn't been for a government loan of several hundred million dollars (from the Department of Energy), neither company would have survived. Both companies tried to get the loan, but only Tesla actually got the money. As a result, Tesla survived and went on to a very successful IPO, and Fisker died for lack of funding. Compared to what happened in the 1920s, these days, starting a car company literally in your garage isn't likely to work without some major funding!

## The Myth and the Secret

So, if you want to build the next billion-dollar company, the chances of doing it by attacking a niche in a new, nascent market that's not already been exploited are a lot higher than by attacking a mature market like the auto industry. Assuming you don't have $180 million of your own money to put in, you want to find a market that is capital efficient! Even markets that looked like they were capital efficient (like mobile games, which could often be built with one or two developers) had long passed this phase by the time the market entered the maturing phase.

For everyone else, it's best to show how you are an innovator in a small but rapidly growing market. If you do it right and build a kick-ass product, you will become a leader. If the market grows as predicted, you might just find yourself having built the next billion-dollar company!

Congrats! But do me a favor: Don't brag about it until *after* you've done it, rather than before, as many residents of Startup Land try to do.

# Myth #2

## Founders Start Companies to Make a Lot of Money

This myth, which is undeniably true some of the time, delves into the motivations of startup founders. It's about how two (or more) founders can be on the same team, at the same stage of their careers, and yet have very different motivations for going on the startup journey.

Do motivations really matter when choosing your founding team?

You bet they do. I read once that the number one reason couples break up is money trouble. The same is probably true of startups—money is one of the biggest issues for startups and probably the number-one reason why founding teams break up. After all, if a company runs out of money and fails, that's a pretty good reason for a founding team to stop working together, no matter how much they wanted to work together in the first place.

But if you look deeper, you'll find that some startup teams work together again and again, even if the first startup was a financial failure. Yet other startup teams, despite having great financial success, swear they will never work together again.

One way to save yourself lots of headaches is to have an explicit understanding of what motivates each member of your founding team *before* you start on this arduous journey.

Looking back to mythology, there are many reasons why the merry band of adventurers set out on (or join in) the journey. Luke Skywalker wanted to rescue Princess Leia, Ben Kenobi wanted to fulfill obligations he had to Leia's father, not to mention he also wanted to train Luke as a Jedi. Han Solo, on the other hand, had only one motivation: money.

What is your primary reason for wanting to go on the startup adventure? Is it to make a lot of money? Is it to create something new? To be your own boss? To simply have the freedom to build products? To be a "player" in Silicon Valley (or whichever incarnation of Startup Land you happen to be in)?

Rarely is the answer to this question exactly the same, even when asked to two members of the same founding team. You might think there are as many different types of founders as there are heroes in mythological tales, and you'd be right.

## An Overview of Founder Motivations

While no two founders are exactly alike, I've found that their motivations tend to fit into general categories. More important, what is really unique about a particular founder (and eye-opening to his/her cofounders) is the *priority* of their motivations.

This brings us to our first tool. Startup Tools are featured throughout this book and are useful checklists and questions to help you figure out where you stand on important issues that might affect your startup.

Startup Tool #1: Prioritizing Founder Motivations, and Startup Tool #2: Uncovering Founder Expectations are useful not just for yourself, but for your entire team. Taken together, they amount to a conversation that many founding teams should have, but rarely do until they are well along on their startup adventures!

Let's start with the general categories of founder motivation—you'll no doubt find that some of these are more important to you than others.

- ***Money Driven.*** In recent years, I have to say I've seen an increasing number of what I would call "money-driven" entrepreneurs. These entrepreneurs are involved with startups primarily to get rich. Those who are very short-term minded I like to call "coin-driven" (that is, they want to get rich as quickly as possible), and those who are long-term minded I like to call "wealth-driven" (that is, they want to get really, really wealthy over a much longer period of time). More on these two variations later.

- ***Creativity Driven.*** I have found that some entrepreneurs just want to build things, usually products. They want to be sure they have enough money to keep building new products, and that's one of the major reasons they got into the entrepreneurial game in the first place. When a new product is being built, they are very excited. As an investor and advisor, I can usually see their excitement when they talk about the product. Creativity-driven founders are happiest when they are designing and building new features or new products, regardless of whether that activity is the best use of their time. These founders typically get bored once the company has a product that is accepted by the market generally don't like the to transition from building products to building an organization, which many founders have to undertake as a startup grows.
- ***Technology Driven (or Market Driven).*** Some entrepreneurs really have an attachment to their market (or technology area) and have made it their life's work. They would never do a startup in a field that isn't related to *that* market (whatever that market happens to be). Some entrepreneurs just love a particular new technology or emerging market, and because of this they develop deep expertise and a reputation in that technology or market. While they may be aware of (and not immune to) decisions involving money, they are more driven by the need to play with this technology and/or to be experts in their field. I've grouped these two together because the primary motivation is to work within a certain area.

  Compare this to entrepreneurs who are mostly money driven—they almost don't care which market they are in or what technology is used to build the product—they just want to be in any hot startup market that will make money. That's not to say that tech-driven people stay with the same technology always—they may want to simply jump into a new, hot tech market to see what all the hype is about, but more often are associated with a technology trend or market over a longer period of time.
- ***Fame Driven / Respect Driven.*** Some entrepreneurs really want to make a name for themselves and want to be known. They could be known for their work on a particular startup or for becoming a guru in their chosen market. Perhaps they're even trying to become a *startup guru* rather than becoming a guru in a particular product or technology. This kind of entrepreneur is usually very visible in the market, likes to give talks and seeks attention in the press. Some of these founders

can get what they want even if the company goes out of business, as long as they are seen as experts in the field and their startups get a lot of press coverage. They often become authors and speakers (or very visible venture capitalists). It's not that these entrepreneurs aren't interested in making money; it's just that money is not their driving force. When I asked an early Play Labs group to identify founder motivations, they identified a variation of the Fame Driven motivation called Respect Driven. These founders started companies so they would be respected in the tech world and have influence over others in the industry. It's a subtle distinction but an important one.

- ***Independence Driven.*** The founders in this category really like to be their own bosses; independence is their primary motivation for starting a company. They don't really care what anyone else thinks, or whether they are getting any accolades in the press, or whether their company is growing faster (or slower) than anyone else's. They also may not care so much about the money they are making; they just don't like anyone else telling them what to do. They usually do feel a strong sense of ownership in the company, and are not likely to give up more than a small portion of their company to investors because they don't want to take orders from anyone!
- ***Empire Driven (or Competition Driven).*** These entrepreneurs really like to *win* and want to build something big and dominant. This is an instinct in all entrepreneurs, of course, but some *really* can't stand the thought of losing even a single deal to a competitor. These entrepreneurs tend to be very competitive in their assessment of startup success—if any of their business school classmates, for example, sold a company for $100 million, they want to be the one who sells his company for $200 million. If someone they know raised $5 million from a well-known VC, they want to raise $10 million from a better-respected VC. The fame and the money that comes with doing so are secondary (though important) considerations.
- ***Mission Driven.*** Some startups are created from the founder's deep desire to help a particular community or to further a cause. This is especially true for socially/environmentally conscious startups—those that are working to clean up the oceans or the environment, for instance. Are you starting a company to serve an underserved community that has particular meaning to you—say, inner city residents, or the LGBT community, or immigrants? You would think that social causes motivate most startup founders in Silicon Valley, but this is often untrue.

To help you discover your own motivations, think of other entrepreneurs or cofounders you have known in the past. Sometimes other people are better at gauging our motivations than we are ourselves because of our tendency to sugarcoat our *real* reasons for wanting to go on a startup adventure or to give socially acceptable answers to personal questions.

So as not to put anyone on the spot, let's look at a couple of well-known entrepreneurs:

- ***Bill Gates.*** Most people from the early days of Microsoft will say that Gates was very competitive, and that he believed Microsoft should own the PC software market. He saw himself very much associated with that market, and was a technical guy himself. But examining his motives more closely, he was probably empire-driven while he built up Microsoft, crushing the competition again and again. Some in the nineties even called Microsoft the "Evil Empire" because of the emphasis they placed on winning at all costs. By contrast, Gates's cofounder in Microsoft, Paul Allen, was much less empire driven, according to all accounts.
- ***Steve Jobs.*** Jobs was also very competitive, but he was much more product- and creativity-driven than many other entrepreneurs. His focus was on creating great devices, and then garnering the attention and money that came from that. Although some might consider Apple to be Microsoft's successor as an "Evil Empire," there is no doubt of its dominance in the product areas that Jobs drove in his second stint as Apple's CEO—the iPod, the iPhone, and the iPad. By contrast, Jobs's cofounder, Steve Wozniak, also was product driven, but with much more focus on creativity and technology, and less on "being the best."

This brings us to our very first Startup Tool, which you and your cofounders can use to identify your primary, secondary, and tertiary motivations. The hard part of this exercise is being honest with yourself. Your assessment of your cofounder, and his or her assessment of you, may actually be more accurate than your assessment of yourself!

Also, motivations change over time. In Star Wars, although Han Solo joined the adventure simply to make some money, his motivation changed as he developed an attachment to the people and the cause of the Rebel Alliance. It's wise to repeat this exercise every year to see if your priorities have changed.

### Startup Tool #1: Prioritizing Founder Motivations

To use this tool, think about your top three motivations for launching your startup, and have your cofounders do the same. Then, before you share your insights, see if you can guess the primary and secondary motivations for your cofounder(s) and if they can do the same for you. Then compare notes. The answers may surprise you.

STARTUP TOOL: PRIORITIZING FOUNDER MOTIVATIONS

DATE:

FOUNDER NAME:

*Instructions: Rank your top three motivations from 1 (most important) to 3 (less important), and answer any supporting questions for the ones that you check.*

_______ Money/Personal Profit *(short term, medium term, long term)*

How much money would make you happy? __________

_______ Technology/Market Interests

_______ Fame/Becoming a Guru/Being Respected

_______ Empire Building/Competition

_______ Independence/Being Your Own Boss

_______ Mission (specify mission or community)

_______________________________________________

Notes:

_______________________________________________

_______________________________________________

_______________________________________________

### The Importance of Expectations

Why do you need to spend time digging into one another's motivations? If expectations are misaligned, one of the founders is likely to leave early.

As an example, if one founder wants to shoot for the moon and grow a huge public company or achieve a big exit of more than $100 million, while another would be happy to make $1 million to $2 million dollars in a few years, then expectations are misaligned.

In a real-life example, I remember a founding team of MIT alumni, all of whom were experienced entrepreneurs. Two of them knew each other, and a third, who had just moved back to Boston from Silicon Valley, decided to join them in their next startup. The third cofounder had had a nice exit from his previous startup (the VC-backed company sold for more than $50 million, and he wanted to do something bigger and better).

It turned out that these founders' expectations weren't exactly aligned—two of the three had one set of expectations (to build the company without outside financing, to profit or at least break even, to keep control, and to sell the company for a few million dollars a few years down the line), while the other founder had come from a reasonably well-financed company and wanted to do something bigger, to raise VC money, and to grow into a very big company and get a substantial exit.

After a few years of running a bootstrapped company that was doing well but not taking off super fast, the third founder decided he'd had enough.

The third founder decided to leave and join a better-financed startup to have a more stable income and be part of something bigger. I know this because it was my own company, CambridgeDocs. Clarifying our expectations and making sure we were in alignment might have served all of us better (and might have convinced our third founder not to start a company with us).

### A Misalignment in a Very Successful Startup

A mismatch of expectations can lead to a breakup even if the company is starting to do well. The following is another example of mismatched expectations.

Gnip, founded by CTO Jud Valeski and CEO Eric Marcoullier, worked with social networks as a middleman. After spending a year trying to get social networks to pay them to use their solution, they realized that their initial strategy wasn't going to work (more on this in "Stage 4: The Road of Trials: Myths About Going to Market"). So they decided to pivot to solving a problem for enterprises that needed to access data on social networks. Because there were so many different social networking APIs at the time, they discovered that enterprises were having problems keeping up with the various versions of all these APIs.

Then, just as this new business model was starting to get traction, Eric decided to leave the company, leaving Jud (unexpectedly) in the CEO slot.

Jud says, "Being CEO was never on my bucket list. It was kind of a surprise one evening that he was leaving . . . and we decided either we can kill the company or I could drive the boat just at the moment we were starting to get some traction.

"But one of the frustrating things for me is that I said, 'Eric, dude, we're just now finally getting some revenue. Why bail now?' The short answer there is we were becoming an enterprise software company and Eric just didn't want anything to do with that. It wasn't his interest."

Jud adds, "I applaud him for actually being clear about that because we ultimately became exactly what he did not want. That actually turned out really well."

It was a good thing that they didn't kill the company when the founders broke up, because Gnip was sold to Twitter for $175 million a few years later.

## Uncovering Founder Expectations—How Would It Feel?

The only *real* way to know how your cofounders will react in stressful situations is to go through stressful situations with them—that is what adventures are all about, after all! If your cofounders react well in stressful times, this is probably a good indication that your team might stay together across multiple startups.

Of course, it's difficult to know ahead of time how someone will react. Many startup teams break up because their cofounders (including their partners or spouses) act completely differently than expected during a stressful situation. You can run through hypothetical scenarios in Startup Tool #2, to better understand how each is likely to react.

All of these scenarios are ones that I have seen happen in some of the many startups I've been involved with. There are, of course, many other questions and scenarios you can run through as well.

When I ask these questions of founders and potential founders, I try to pay attention to not just what they say, but how they say it, and what their body language reveals when they are thinking about the hypothetical scenario.

It's important to do this exercise when it's just founders around and not any investors. Why? Because the answers will be more honest and less rehearsed (as in, "I'll stick with it until the startup is successful no matter what!", which is often said but rarely true). It's also worth taking a few minutes visualizing yourself in each scenario before answering.

Would you enjoy being in each scenario or would it be a living nightmare? Another approach is to ask how a founder's spouse or significant other would feel in each of these scenarios. Or better yet, ask each founder to actually run through these scenarios at home with their partners. A startup adventure is so all-encompassing that it affects every member of your family, so they should also have a say in how you proceed.

## Startup Tool #2: Uncovering Founder Expectations

Directions: Here are some scenarios to visualize. Ask yourself how you would feel in each scenario.

- What happens if the company doesn't raise money in six months? What if it doesn't raise money in five years? (1 = not happy, 2 = indifferent, 3 = happy)

| UNHAPPY | ← | 1 | 2 | 3 | → | HAPPY |
|---|---|---|---|---|---|---|

- What if someone offers to buy the company for $5 million before the product is even released? Would you sell?

| NO WAY | ← | 1 | 2 | 3 | → | YES |
|---|---|---|---|---|---|---|

- What if you were offered $5 million in another company's stock vs. $5 million in cash?

| NO WAY | ← | 1 | 2 | 3 | → | YES |
|---|---|---|---|---|---|---|

- What if your startup became the most popular company in Silicon Valley, raised $25 million or more, but eventually flamed out. How would you feel?

| UNHAPPY | ← | 1 | 2 | 3 | → | HAPPY |
|---|---|---|---|---|---|---|

- What if your company started out as direct to consumer, and you ended up pivoting to a b2b company dealing with an enterprise sales cycle (or vice versa)—would you be happy in this scenario?

| UNHAPPY | ← | 1 | 2 | 3 | → | HAPPY |
|---|---|---|---|---|---|---|

What if you are still running this company ten years from now, it's profitable and surviving but not really an acquisition target?

| UNHAPPY | ← | 1 | 2 | 3 | → | HAPPY |
|---|---|---|---|---|---|---|

Extra Credit Expectations Exercise: Come up with one scenario that would make you happy and one that would make you unhappy. Then see how your cofounders would score each of those scenarios.

## Friends First—A Tale of Two Breakups

In Startup Land, many startups are created by two or more friends. They figure that because they get along well, it will be great to go on this adventure together.

There are, of course, many famous examples of two friends who started very successful companies together—Microsoft was started by Bill Gates and Paul Allen, who had been high school friends in Seattle. Apple was started by Steve Jobs and Steve Wozniak, who were also high school friends long before they cofounded Apple. And the quintessential Silicon Valley company, Hewlett-Packard, was started by Bill Hewlett and David Packard, who were friends from Stanford before they started their company.

My first company was started with one of my best friends from college, Mitch Liu, and my brother, Irfan, Even though that company wasn't successful, all three of us worked together again and we remained friends.

So, it was a surprise to me when I met with two founding teams recently, both of whom I had invested in and both of whom had been friends before founding their startup, only to find that they were both going through bad breakups.

CoinMkt was a Bitcoin company started by two friends, Travis and Ola, who had known each other for some time. They had often talked about doing a startup together, and as the Bitcoin market looked ready to take off in early 2013, they jumped at the opportunity and created CoinMkt, one of the few U.S.-based exchanges for buying and selling Bitcoin. Angel investors (including myself) invested in them because Bitcoin was rising fast (from $100 per Bitcoin to over $1,000 per Bitcoin), and it looked like the "next big thing" in tech. But in 2014, the Bitcoin market became much more complicated, with more regulation, and the price of Bitcoin fell back to earth and stayed there for several years. A few months later I visited the founders and they were at loggerheads—each had a completely different idea of where the company should go and how, or if, it should pivot. The company was out of money, but the two friends were so frustrated with each other that I had to come in as a mediator.

They were so much at odds that I wondered if they really had been friends before they started the company. They assured me they had been, and this puzzled me.

Only a few weeks later, I met with Saurin Shah, who had started Sift Shopping, a mobile app that offered products from different retailers through a unique new app user interface, with his friend (let's call him Raj). Saurin was frustrated that his cofounder and CTO one day just decided to get up and leave the company, leaving Saurin in a bit of a lurch.

"But I thought you guys were friends and knew each other well before starting the company?" I asked Saurin.

To make a long story short, within a few months, both CoinMkt and Sift Shopping were out of business. Although the state of the market and the ability to raise money contributed to the startups' demise, the founders' mismatched priorities and expectations about where to take the company and what they needed to stay with the startup were major contributing factors.

As I dug deeper, I found that although the cofounders of these startups had been friends, they had never worked together previously and had never had to weather a stressful situation together. Once they found themselves in a tough situation, they had very different *expectations* and *motivations*.

### Date First Before Getting Married?

It might seem obvious, but getting together for a startup journey is a little like getting married. You wouldn't want to get married without dating first, would you? Well, you'd be surprised how many startup founders do just that!

If you are considering doing a startup with someone, especially if that someone is a friend (or a spouse or family member), I strongly recommend working together on a project first, before jumping into starting a company.

If you look at the three famous examples that I gave about friends starting companies, you'll notice that they weren't just friends, they had actually worked together on technical projects *before* they started a company together. Bill Hewlett and David Packard worked *for a year* in Bill's garage, creating machines and inventions before starting Hewlett-Packard. Apple's two Steves had worked on several technical projects together before starting Apple. And Bill Gates and Paul Allen had worked together and coded a big city highway project for the city of Seattle before Microsoft came into the picture. These friends all knew they worked well together before they took the plunge.

If you and your potential cofounder are both programmers, you can do a software project to see how you work together. If one of you is a product manager/marketing specialist and the other is an engineer, it'll be eye-opening to see what it's like to design a product together.

It's best if this trial project offers as little compensation as possible for both of you in the beginning, because not having money involved uncovers what's *really* important to each of you. If one person works very hard on the project, and the other person doesn't, because they are devoting more time and energy to what's bringing them income, that shows you something that you might not have learned otherwise about the potential cofounder.

In my own experience, when Mitch, one of my best friends from college, and I began our first startup, we had quite a bit of experience in doing software projects together at MIT. We knew that if something needed to be delivered the next morning, we would both be up programming all night, if necessary.

During that first startup's early days, when we were working in our living room just outside of Boston ("two guys and a garage" happens in Silicon Valley, but garages are too cold in the winter on the East Coast), I asked another friend of mine, Mario, to join our company, Brainstorm. Mario was someone I had worked with at Lotus. He had given us some great advice about the market, and we thought he might be one to join us to build our second product. He spent a few days with us as a trial period and decided that our priorities and expectations (work all the time, no social life), didn't fit with his priorities and motivations, and he decided not to join the company. The good news is that there was no ill will, as there might have been if he had joined the company and then quit.

If we hadn't had that trial period, it's possible that we could've damaged the company and our friendship. Mario and I remained good friends, just not business partners.

## Too Many Founders Versus Too Few

This myth is all about uncovering the motivations and expectations of the members of a founding team. One question I am often asked is, what is the ideal number of founders to create a startup?

Some people say one is the ideal number, because there is a clear vision and ability to make decisions. But many accelerators and VCs prefer teams with multiple founders, because regardless how talented a solo founder is, there's a risk that if something goes wrong in the founder's life, the company could fall apart.

Some say that the ideal number of cofounders is two—a builder and a hustler. Others say three, because it allows for tie breaking when the founders don't agree. There is no one right answer, as there have been successful companies with one, two, and three cofounders.

What about larger numbers?

In my own accelerator, we had one team that had six equal cofounders, whose equity was vested over a relatively short period of time. I told them that I didn't think that was going to work. At the very least, I told them, they needed to better define their roles and apportion equity based on those roles and contributions. They also needed to vest it over a longer period of time because it was sometimes impossible to tell which of the six would stick with it and which wouldn't. One thing I was sure of was that all six wouldn't stay with a startup. Startups are hard and any group of people will have different priorities and motivation.

I wasn't just guessing. I had seen several teams with five cofounders before, but by the end of the first or second year, a good number of them had moved on. It's difficult, I explained to them, to live on a low income and agree on each other's (relative) contribution. There will always be pressures from spouses or from inflated senses of self-worth. Since half of your founders are likely to move on after a year or two, do you really want them to hold so much equity in your company? Remember that a startup adventure can last five to seven years (or longer)!

Sure enough, within a year, the team members of this six-founder company in my accelerator had rejiggered their roles, and some of them had moved into part-time roles and others had moved on. But it was too late to fully adjust the equity. The team eventually fell apart over their inability to agree on very important questions.

## The Secret

***Understand each founder's motivations/expectations, and if at all possible, date before getting married!***

In many teams, it's not unusual for one member to have one set of motivations, and another member to have very different motivations. In fact, some might say this is healthy, as long as there is some overlap. In the Jobs/Wozniak and Gates/Allen teams, the cofounders had very different primary and secondary motivations.

As I said, it's difficult to get at the underlying motivations simply by asking what's most important to your cofounder. *How then do you know what each other's motivations are when you're putting together your founding team?*

The best way, of course, is to have long experience working with someone and seeing how they react in different (preferably stressful) scenarios. If you don't have that experience, it's worth running through some scenarios to figure out not just what each other's primary drivers are, but also what kind of timing they are looking for and how they will contribute. This is what the Startup Tools #1 and #2 are all about—you can use them to help you think through what might happen.

A startup is such an all-consuming experience that personal relationships often suffer no matter the business outcome, so it's worth doing your homework before you plunge in together on a multiyear adventure.

Of course, a startup journey is dynamic, not static, so it's very possible that your own feelings and those of your cofounders will change over time, which is why it's important to do this scenario analysis every year or so as you get deeper into the startup journey.

### Motivated by Money—Coin Driven Versus Wealth Driven

Many entrepreneurs will list money as one of their main motivations in Startup Tool #1. This is a generic reason to start a company, but it's important to figure out whether the motivation is "coin-driven" or "wealth-driven."

How do the two differ? It's useful to do a little game theory here.

Given a choice between door #1 and door #2, the first (and sometimes the only) question a coin-driven entrepreneur will ask is, How much will I make if I go with #1 and how much will I make if I go with #2? This entrepreneur will almost always choose the route that pays more, with more certainty, sooner.

This isn't a problem in and of itself, since all founders probably have some money motivation. But the real question comes when given a choice between *definitely making* $x now (short term, guaranteed) or *maybe making* $10x later (long term, not at all guaranteed).

What will this founder choose? The coin-driven one will definitely choose $x now. The wealth-driven one (depending on his risk threshold) will probably choose the bigger dollar number—$10x, even though it will come later. The difference can cause a serious conflict between members of a founding team; there is no right answer.

John Glynn, founder of Glynn Capital Management and legendary investor in Silicon Valley, talks about the motivation of money, and how it relates to entrepreneurs they like to invest in:

> We are looking for entrepreneurs who are looking to build a significant company, rather than those that are out to cash out quickly. Of course, the exit is a by-product of them building a significant company. To figure this out, you have to talk to them, both in the office, and outside the office, and get to know them. Most of the people who are looking to cash out probably don't get funded.

# Myth #3

## You Have to Be First to Market

This is one of the most persistent myths in Startup Land, and also one that is most often shown to be wrong. Still, there is more complexity here than might appear at first.

Why does this myth persist? Because there are often advantages to being first, especially if you can establish yourself as being synonymous with a newly emerging market.

Unfortunately, there are often some disadvantages, as nascent markets often evolve and merge with other rapidly emerging markets, and navigating these waters can be difficult as new competitors learn from what you have done to date.

Understanding this myth isn't so much about not being first; rather, it is about understanding the advantages and disadvantages of entering a market at a particular point in its evolution. As part of uncovering the secret behind this myth, we'll add a new curve to the Startup Market Lifecycle, called the Startup Opportunity Curve in Startup Model #2.

### Second (and Third) Movers Who Dominated

There are many well-known examples of companies that were not first to market, but that came to dominate their markets. In fact, the history of the tech industry is full of these kinds of stories:

• *Lotus*. In the early days of personal computers, the spreadsheet program that was king was Visicalc. According to *Byte* magazine in 1980: "The most exciting and influential piece of software that has been written for any microcomputer application is VisiCalc."

Then, Mitch Kapor, who had sold his first company, Visiplot, to Visicalc for $1 million, created Lotus to build a product he called Lotus 1-2-3. This was meant to be a spreadsheet, database, and word processor (thus the 1-2-3) *all-in-one*. Given the complexity of building all three of these, they decided to release just the spreadsheet part, which was built from the ground up for the newly emerging IBM PC (and its operating system, MS-DOS). This new program took advantage of its greater memory and screen size as compared to the Apple II, and the massive growth of the new IBM PC drove its rapid adoption. Lotus 1-2-3 sales soared as it became the killer app for the new hardware.

The success of Lotus 1-2-3 as the dominant spreadsheet player all but killed Visicalc. John Glynn, one of my professors at Stanford, who was an investor and board member at Visicalc, said that they were doing so well, "we thought we were on a rocket ship . . . then we were slow to adjust to the new IBM PC." In another twist, when Microsoft released Excel for its Windows operating system, it was well behind Lotus 1-2-3 in terms of market share, but it was able to become the dominant player by leveraging its integration with the operating system; thus it was Microsoft Office, not Lotus, which fulfilled Kapor's vision of an integrated suite of business programs.

• *Google*. Google wasn't the first search engine for the web. Some estimates say it was the eighteenth major search engine. Because of its algorithm, Google was able to convince customers that their search was better. But their success as a business didn't really happen until they added search-based keyword advertising. This was an idea that was already in the market (having been pioneered by guys at Idea Lab), but Google was able to build a killer business with it, effectively overtaking rivals such as Yahoo, Excite, and Altavista and more or less cornering the web search market.

• *Facebook*. Facebook wasn't the first social network. It wasn't even the first successful one—both Friendster and MySpace had considerable success (MySpace was sold to Fox for over $580 million). Both Facebook's early focus on a single target market (college students) and its ability to build network effects from those users as they graduated from college, combined with a clean UI, helped it become the dominant player in the web 2.0 world and the world's dominant social networks.

These are, of course, very famous examples that most tech entrepreneurs have heard of. In each of these cases, the eventual winners weren't the first movers, they were often the first movers that did *x*. What is *x*? It could be a product approach—building from the ground up for a new platform/hardware—or even a new marketing approach. Part of your task as an entrepreneur is to figure out what *x* is in your market.

Let's delve deeper into lesser-known examples for insights that might be useful in new startup markets.

### Path of a DiVA: A Small, Second Mover

When I first graduated from MIT, I joined one of the very first startups to emerge from the MIT Media Lab, called DiVA (Digital Video Applications). DiVA made video editing software for Apple's Macintosh computers, called Videoshop, which was optimized for working with Quicktime, Apple's new video format.

DiVA Videoshop wasn't the first video editing software that supported QuickTime. That was Adobe Premiere, which was DiVA's biggest competitor. Adobe was a considerably sized company even in those days. They had introduced Adobe Premiere when Apple introduced QuickTime, and it quickly became the dominant player in the low end, newly emerging, digital video editing market.

There was another, higher end editing platform already available on the market that was also built on the Mac—it was called Avid Media Composer, and it was meant to be an entire editing system for professional TV and film editors. Many TV show credits included the line "Edited using the Avid Media Composer." It was a very expensive solution and not for "hobbyists."

In those days, digital video was relatively new, and it wasn't clear that ordinary people would want or need to do video editing. This was well before the days of YouTube (the internet was used primarily by academics, and the world wide web was still a few years away).

Did being second help DiVA?

By not being first to market, DiVA was able to build features and a user interface that let it leapfrog Premiere, and it was able to be a player in the low end of the market, for "hobbyists." However, the company was small and underfunded compared to Adobe. It ended up selling to Avid, the high-end player in the market, just before Avid's IPO, and though the founders did well from the sale, the company never achieved market dominance. In this case, it might have been better to be first, but not having as much capital as Adobe certainly played a role in its decision to sell.

This is why the myths in this book are complicated. There are no easy answers. Sometimes, it is good to be first. Other times, it isn't.

## Advantages of Being Second

There are some considerable advantages to being second (or third). Here are three rules of thumb that are useful in thinking about not being a first mover:

- *The first mover usually does the missionary work, which is proving that there is a market and a need.* Just like pioneers in the old West, the first movers are also more likely to get arrows in their backs. Second movers usually can avoid this since they are able to see where the arrows are coming from.
- *The second successful product in the market usually finds ways to address some of the shortcomings of the first product, particularly in usability or performance.* MySpace became messy with its user interface and its focus on dating, whereas Facebook was able to avoid focusing on those aspects of social networks. Lotus 1-2-3 addressed some performance issues in Visicalc and was much easier to use. Of course when Visicalc was first created, no one knew what a spreadsheet was. By the time Lotus 1-2-3 came around the use cases for a spreadsheet were much better defined. Google addressed some of the problems that came from existing search engines, and it was easier to use. It's not just that you can often build a better product; you can see the approach that was taken initially and use a different, more appropriate approach based on information from the market.
- *The second product can claim a segment of the market.* One of the best ways to gain traction as a second or third player in a market is to tailor your product for a particular segment of the market. This obviates the need to be first, and allows you to focus on being the best—DiVA focused on the low end of the market, sidestepping Avid, which eventually acquired DiVA. Facebook focused on the college market at first, and was much smaller than MySpace for a long time. Lotus 1-2-3 was built from the ground up on new hardware. Salesforce.com used the emerging model of software as a service (which was called ASP in those days, or Application Service Provider) to leap over Siebel, which was the major player in enterprise CRM in those days, by focusing on the lower end of the market first.

## When Being First Is Actually Better

On the other hand, like most of the myths in this book, this myth is complicated. The reason the term "first mover advantage" exists is that there can be advantages to being first. It really depends on the segment of the market you are attacking, the stage of that market, whether there is pent-up demand, and most important of all, whether you really take advantage of being a first mover.

Prominent examples include Oracle, which was the first to produce a commercial database based on the new SQL specification that IBM had developed (Oracle's database got to market before IBM's much anticipated DB2 SQL database). While Oracle took advantage of being first and closed lots of accounts, it's important to note that there were actually many other successful SQL database companies—including Sybase and IBM. So, being first is a plus if you really take advantage of your position and watch how the market evolves.

In my very first startup, Brainstorm Technologies, we were the first to connect the products of the biggest PC software companies at the time, Microsoft and Lotus (Lotus later sold to IBM). There was pent-up demand, as customers had been asking Lotus for a way to use Microsoft's Visual Basic as a development platform for Lotus' popular Notes platform and ways to connect Notes to SQL databases. We beat many of our competitors to market, and this allowed us to get traction. However, over time we found that we had simply proved that there was a need for these tools to connect IBM products with other enterprise products. Seeing this opportunity, IBM eventually released their own toolkits and products for accessing Lotus Notes data by buying one of our competitors who didn't have as much market traction as we did, but whose products may have learned from what we did in the marketplace.

So, it's complicated. It depends a little bit on who the "later" competitors are, how much of a market lead you've gotten, and whether the competition is able to first match and then leapfrog your product.

In the case of Gnip, which provided a middleware API for dealing with multiple social network APIs, being first was an advantage. Later competitors that introduced similar products required significantly more capital. Gnip raised only $7.5 million on its way to a successful exit to Twitter for $175 million, while one of Gnip's competitors raised $75 million—almost ten times as much—to try to catch up to them.

This is consistent with the Startup Market Lifecycle, which says that the later you get in, the more money is required to "catch up" to existing players. Furthermore, when you raise more money, as Gnip's competitors did, you need to do it at higher valuations, which then makes it more difficult to sell the company (more on this in Myth #5: Two Guys and a Business are Better Than Two Guys and a Plan).

Being first in the market puts you in position to get acquired before you have to raise a significant amount of money. Look at Oculus, which Facebook acquired for $2 billion. Oculus was considered the "leader," and though the virtual reality market wasn't new (there had been an earlier wave of VR in the 1990s), they were really the first ones making waves in this new phase of VR. Since this market didn't work out as a consumer market, getting acquired for a multibillion-dollar exit (in Facebook stock, which was worth even more as time went on) was a great outcome for the founders and investors!

## Too Early vs. Too Late vs. Just Right

So, is it better to be first or not?

By now, you should understand that the underlying message of this book is that there is no single, best answer for every startup. The rules apply until they don't.

As we look at the stages of Startup Market Lifecycle, if the market you are attacking is in the "nascent" stage, it's possible you are entering too early. You are likely to be a pioneer (complete with arrows in your back) if you don't sell quickly or grow fast when the market enters the "growing" stage.

Meanwhile, fast followers often enter during the "rapid growth" phase of the market and are able to establish serious traction quickly (because the market has been proven). If, however, you start a company during the super-hot or maturing phases, it can be very, very difficult to catch up to first movers (or second or third movers that have displaced a first mover as a leader).

## Startup Model #2: The Startup Opportunity Curve (aka the Goldilocks Curve)

This brings us to the second Startup Model—an evolution of the Startup Market Lifecycle—which is used in conjunction with the other models to figure out the best time to enter or exit a market.

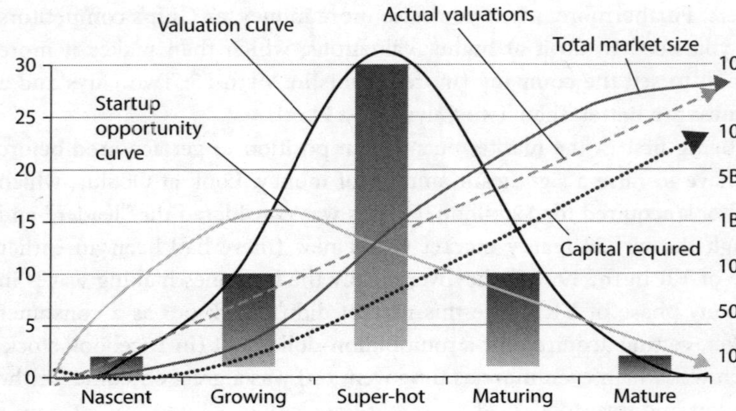


Figure 3.1
The Startup Market Opportunity Curve (aka the Goldilocks Curve). Created by the author

Figure 3.1 shows two additions to our model of how startup markets evolve and mature. As we said earlier, when the market is maturing, it becomes very expensive for startups to gain traction in the marketplace. They need to raise a lot of money. As mobile gaming started maturing after 2013, companies like Super Cell and King.com and Machine Zone started placing TV ads for their mobile games; the ads cost many millions of dollars and involved celebrities like Arnold Schwarzenegger and Kate Upton. I had looked into advertising on TV for our game, Tap Fish, in 2010 and 2011, but the market was early and there were much more efficient ways to get users than to spend millions of dollars on TV ads. Nor did the revenue of our games, which were near the top of the app store charts, justify spending that kind of money.

It is even more expensive for startups when the market reaches the *mature* stage. (Remember Tesla and how much money had be invested not just by the founder and investors, but even by the Department of Energy? Tesla was a new entrant into a mature market.) The capital required curve in figure 3.1 shows this. Similarly, the startup opportunity curve in figure 3.1 shows how easy or difficult it is for a new entrant, which may not have tens or hundreds of millions of dollars, to make an impact on a new market.

In the nascent stage, little capital is required, but the market hasn't proven itself yet. Referring back to Startup Tool #1, if you are a market- or technology-driven entrepreneur, then this may be the right time for you to get into the market, but don't expect to have a big exit quickly (and if your motivation is truly tied to the market or the technology, that shouldn't matter!).

It's in the *growing* stage that the opportunity is greatest for most entrepreneurs—this is the stage in which some capital may be required, but not too much, and in which the market is sure to be recognized by investors as lucrative.

This is the time when many *fast followers* start to enter the market.

The ideal time to enter a market is most often around the end of the "nascent" phase and the start of the "growing" phase. Why? You can get in with little to no capital, while it's still possible to make a name for yourself. Moreover, as the market moves to super-hot, you can have a higher valuation or selling price, or you can become the dominant player as the market matures.

If a startup enters early on in the *growing* stage, there is still quite a bit of opportunity to make an impact. The longer you wait, the more capital will be required and the more bets will already have been placed by investors and customers, which means it'll be harder to raise money and harder to win customers.

This is why I've nicknamed the startup opportunity curve the "Goldilocks Curve," because it shows how to get the timing just right—neither too early nor too late.

- If you are in the *nascent* stage, you may be an expert, and you are probably very passionate about the market, but you may find yourself caught in the "pioneer" trap (see Myth #3: You Have to be First to Market).
- If you join too late in the *growing* stage (which can be divided into three substages: *recognized*, *nova*, and *supernova*), just before the market transitions to *super-hot*, you could end up staying past the super-hot phase into the maturing phase—and then valuations start to go down. So even though getting funding and starting a company is not that difficult during the growing phase, it is not very wise to jump into a market during the latter part of this phase or during the super-hot stage (unless you really can claim to be the first to do it a certain way).

- If you join the market in the super-hot phase it is a very exciting time to join the market, but the savvy players have either consolidated their market position as leaders or they are selling for outrageous valuations. *Most people enter a market in the super-hot phase—which is the exact wrong time to enter!* Even though raising money is not super difficult during this phase, building the business will be difficult and raising further rounds of funding may be very very difficult unless you immediately become a leader quickly.
- Statistically speaking, joining during the *maturing* phase is a terrible time to enter the market, unless you are an experienced team with significant capital behind you, or you are focusing on a niche that isn't being served well by either the emerging leaders or the legacy large companies.

## Shall We Play a Game? If So, When?

To illustrate the Goldilocks Curve, let's take another look at the mobile gaming market for smartphones.

The market opened up in 2008 when Apple opened its platform to third-party developers, and games quickly became the most popular type of app (certainly they were the most lucrative for the first five to ten years of the app store). This market was in its nascent stage from 2008 to early 2009—only the very early pioneers entered. In fact, many other gaming companies, including those in the super-hot Facebook social gaming space (Zynga among them), were intentionally overlooking this market because it was too early and "too small" for them. I remember speaking with an entrepreneur who entered the market at this stage and quickly sold his company (which had mobile expertise) to social gaming giant Playdom for a not very large valuation.

The growing stage started in early 2010, when Apple released in-app purchases inside games. In fact, I'd say early 2010 was the post-nascent part of the growing stage, and it was a great time to get into this market.

Many of the mobile gaming companies that entered in 2010, though later considered pioneers in mobile gaming, were really more like fast followers—they were able to take game concepts that had been successful on other platforms (such as Flash portals, Facebook, Consoles, etc.) and quickly turn them into very successful, profitable mobile games.

Companies like Tapulous (makers of *Tap Tap Revenge*), Pocket Gems (makers of *Tap Zoo*), Gameview Studios (my company, makers of *Tap Fish*), and TinyCo were able to leverage this new free-to-play trend and in-app purchases to build very significant free-to-play businesses.

In 2011, the market suddenly went into super-hot mode and others started to make crazy amounts of money on mobile. Zynga and the other Facebook players, as well as traditional gaming companies, jumped into the market.

Still, it's interesting to note that it was still possible to have big hits that were introduced in the maturing phase. As reviewed in Startup Model #1: The Startup Market Lifecycle, it just took much higher production values, bigger teams, and lots of money for advertising for customers. Examples were Clash of Clans, from Super Cell, Candy Crush, from King.com, and Pokemon Go and Kabam's licensed games such as Marvel: Contest of Champions.

By 2014–16, the market had matured significantly, and it took large amounts of capital to be successful in the app stores. Why? Advertising for games, which started at twenty-five cents per install in 2009, cost as much as several dollars per install after 2012. Moreover, the app store grew to over a million apps, many of which were games. Finally, production costs were starting to approach those of big triple-A game titles. Kabam said publicly in 2016 that they expected to spend more than $10 million on each of their new titles. Only companies that did really well *and* raised large amounts of money for marketing survived and thrived in the new cut-throat app store environment. In the maturing and mature phases, bigger companies are better suited to introduce new hit products. Fortnite, one of the biggest mobile hit games, came from Epic, which was already a well-known game company.

Similarly, experienced entrepreneurs who can raise lots of money (or have lots of their own money) can usually get in even on a third wave or a mature market. For example, the founder of MySpace, Chris DeWolfe, wanted to do a mobile gaming company in 2013. This was relatively late as far as many of the mobile game pioneers were concerned, but because he had sold his last company for $580 million, it wasn't that hard for him to raise significant financing and start to consolidate the casual social market, and his company became Jam City, which became an acquirer.

## The Secret

***Being too early can be as bad as being too late to market. Remember Goldilocks. If you're early, you need to have staying power or sell relatively quickly. If you're late, you need much more capital to become a leader.***

The real secret behind this myth is that timing can help you or hurt you. Like most of the secrets in this book, applying the underlying principles regarding first-mover advantage is more of an art than a science.

In technology, being *too early* can be as big of a problem as being *too late*. Fast followers can usually watch the mistakes made by first movers and then create better products before the market is fully mature. On the other hand, if a first mover is able to leverage the initial speed into becoming a market leader that is difficult to dislodge, then being first actually can be helpful.

However, when second movers become successful they usually reach revenue levels that weren't possible in the early, nascent days of the market, and this helps them to remain one of the leaders in a virtuous cycle. They don't have the arrows from the missionary work that needs to be done by the early player in a new startup market. However, being in a set of third movers can require significantly more capital and is usually difficult for first-time entrepreneurs. This is reflected in the Startup Market Lifecycle in the Capital Required Curve, and the Startup Opportunity Curve, otherwise known as the Goldilocks Curve.

The real secret is that from an odds perspective, it's almost better to be *one of the first* entrants and establish yourself as a player, rather than being the *very first*. As the market moves from nascent to the growing stage, you're well positioned to benefit—as the old saying goes, "a rising tide lifts all boats."

### Blue Ocean Versus Red Ocean

Another way that investors and Startup Land residents like to talk about the opportunity curve—the Goldilocks Curve—is by using the terms "blue ocean" or "red ocean." A "blue ocean" opportunity is one where there aren't any clearly defined leaders and not too many competitors. A "red ocean" is where there are lots of competitors, some of whom are "sharks"—and the sharks have been eating away at the small-fry startups and at each other. Thus, a lot of blood has been spilled and will be spilled—creating the "red" ocean.

Tying it to our stages, the "blue ocean" exists in the nascent stage of the market. However, at this stage, even investors who are looking for blue ocean opportunities might not be willing to commit because the market hasn't been proven. This is where accelerators often come in. They are more willing to take a risk, admitting a startup team in a market that is relatively new, hoping that the team will figure out the market.

As an example, at Play Labs, we had a company that was building a cryptocurrency wallet inside of messengers such as Telegram—it was a company called Button Wallet. They were just getting started and it was too early for most VCs to invest. We admitted them to Play Labs and they were able to bide their time in our accelerator. Even after a few months, the market was still early. Button Wallet was then able to get into another accelerator, which was focused primarily on blockchain. After this time, about a year after I had originally heard about them, there were other companies attacking the market, and venture capital investors started to get more interested in the market. A "blue ocean" might be too early in the Goldilocks Curve—your company has to find a way to survive until the market gets to the growing stage and is recognized.

# Bonus Myth #B-1

## Start Something You Are Passionate About

*"I think passion is overrated. Passion is for the bedroom . . . I'm looking for entrepreneurs that are obsessed . . ."*

—BRAD FELD

This is one of those myths that's tossed around so often that it seems like common sense. In fact, you could argue that it's not really a myth at all; after all, why would anyone jump into a startup, an exciting but stressful multi-year odyssey, if they weren't passionate about what they were doing?

Surprisingly, it happens all the time in Silicon Valley. I would venture an unscientific guess that 50 percent of the founders I have met didn't start out super passionate about the market area they are in. It didn't, however, stop them from starting a company and making a lot of money.

That doesn't mean they aren't passionate about working for themselves or doing a startup (refer to "Startup Tool #1: Prioritizing Founder Motivations"). It's just possible that the particular product or service that the startup offers is not something they would dedicate the rest of their careers to.

▶ To read the full text of this **Bonus Myth**, including the Four Quadrants of Passion, please download the Supplement to *Startup Myths and Models* from www.zenentrepreneur.com ◀

# Stage 2

## Fuel for the Journey

## *Myths About Raising Money*

---

> With the personifications of his destiny to guide and aid him, the hero goes forward in his adventure until he comes to the 'threshold guardian' at the entrance to the zone of magnified power. . . . Beyond them is darkness, the unknown and danger. . . .
>
> The adventure is always and everywhere a passage beyond the veil of the known into the unknown; the powers that watch at the boundary are dangerous; to deal with them is risky; yet for anyone with competence and courage the danger fades.
>
> JOSEPH CAMPBELL

---

### Introduction to Stage 2

Equipping the team with the right tools is a part of the hero's journey, even if it's not explicitly called out as a stage by Joseph Campbell. This is because it's an ongoing process. Usually it begins at the very first stages of the journey and continues on as additional mentors and recruiters are brought into the mix.

Most (but not all) mythological journeys leave out the practical parts of how the team is going to finance their expedition. In real life adventures, particularly the startup kind, our hero (that would be you, the entrepreneur) is responsible for raising enough financing to start and grow the company. This was true even back in the time of Christopher Columbus, who had to rely on the financing of the monarchs for his journeys across the ocean (to what he thought was India).

When Luke Skywalker first meets Obi-Wan Kenobi, the old man gives him a light saber, telling Luke that his father wanted him to have it. Equipment granted.

But how did they pay for their journey off the planet? Luke had to sell his land speeder to have the down payment for Han Solo and Chewbacca to secure passage on Solo's ship, the Millennium Falcon.

In *The Hobbit*, when Bilbo and the dwarves start out on their adventure to go "there and back again," Bilbo famously forgets to take along any equipment, not even a pocket handkerchief! Luckily for our little hobbit, Gandalf and the dwarves are responsible for taking care of this part—"all traveling expenses guaranteed in any event"—bringing along horses, ponies, food, and supplies. In this unique case, his contract with the dwarves also specified that all funeral expenses would also be taken care of!

In the startup world, as entrepreneurs we are not as lucky as Bilbo (who, remember, was the 14th member of the expedition). While mentors and fellow adventurers are there to help, we are the ones responsible for getting the initial equipment and supplies that we might need along the way. Like Luke, entrepreneurs might have to sell some of their possessions to get enough capital to get started (or at least reduce their expenses for a time)!

Luckily for most software startups, the hardware isn't that expensive and we can just use our personal laptops and cloud servers to get started. Starting a hardware company usually requires more money up front, though both of the quintessential Silicon Valley hardware startups—Hewlett-Packard and Apple—were famously started in a garage!

### *The Mythical Trip Down Sand Hill Road*

Luckily, you don't have to pitch to kings or queens today, though in Startup Land, venture capitalists are often thought of as kingmakers and queenmakers when they choose to bet on a particularly young startup.

In Silicon Valley, it used to be that a *literal* trip down Sand Hill Road was a necessity to raise money. Sand Hill is a picturesque but sleepy stretch of road next to Stanford University (about 45 minutes south of San Francisco) that winds up to the mountains that define the western edge of the valley, beyond which is the Pacific Coast Highway and the Pacific Ocean. Traditionally, most of the well-known VC funds had offices on Sand Hill, with a few outliers in other areas. If one of these VCs wouldn't invest in you, you weren't going to be funded by VCs.

In the terminology of the hero's journey, we would say that VCs traditionally acted as 'Threshold Guardians', determining who was worthy to proceed to the rest of the adventure, with enough equipment and capital to hire the rest of the team to make it happen.

Today's funding landscape is much more diverse—both geographically and in type of investors. You don't need to take a literal trip down a road like Sand Hill Road (or its one-time equivalent in Boston, Route 128). Today, many VCs have opened offices in urban areas, since many younger startup founders want to live in the city. There are now as many VCs in the city of San Francisco proper as there are on Sand Hill Road, and this is true of other startup hubs as well—in cities like Boston, New York, Los Angeles, Austin, and Seattle.

Not only are there many more venture capital firms—there are firms with different fund sizes to cater to different stages: from seed funds and accelerator funds with less than $10 million in capital, to late stage, private equity funds with multiple billions of dollars to invest.

Because a large number of multimillionaires have emerged from tech companies like Facebook, Google, Twitter, etc., this means there are many more angel investors in Startup Land than there used to be. Although they might invest only small amounts ($25K to $100K), they are usually an early stop for entrepreneurs on the startup journey.

Both the terminology and composition of early stage funding has changed in the last decade. A *seed round* used to be the first money to go into the company, followed by Series A financing (which refers to Series A preferred stock), which is what most venture capitalists and professional investors wanted when they invested. Although it varies by industry, most startups today begin with one or more pre-seed rounds. This traditionally was startup capital gathered from the "three Fs"—friends, family, and fools! These days, it is just as common for an accelerator or incubator to provide the first funding into the company. At Play Labs, we were often (though not always) the first capital into a company, and the same is probably true for accelerators like Y Combinator and 500 Startups.

This stage is focused on the startup tradition of seeking professional investors (who are either VCs or angels or angel funds), whose full-time job it is to invest in startups. To a certain extent, they are still the main threshold guardians on today's startup adventure.

This doesn't mean that you shouldn't consider other sources of financing—like strategic investors. There are many strategic investors (large corporations who have set aside money for investment) today who are looking to invest in innovative companies. As companies grow and consolidate, they become increasingly more inefficient on the one hand, and typically less innovative on the other.

One way to keep the innovation DNA alive is to invest in startups and construct partnerships with these more agile companies. A strategic investment can enhance the reputation of your startup and give you business development opportunities. One startup I was involved with recently had the venture groups of both Samsung and Sony as early investors. Although the amount of money each had invested was small in comparison to VC investors, the name recognition of both companies provided the startup with a lot of clout and prestige they wouldn't have had otherwise. Sometimes, a strategic investment is also a precursor to acquiring a company—and there are of course myths surrounding what types of investors you should pursue.

## *Overview of the Myths*

The myths in this stage are about how you go about raising financing for your company, how much you should (or shouldn't) raise, and most important, from whom. This process is fraught with minefields that have sunk many an ambitious entrepreneur before their journey really got going.

Unlike classical adventures, where a threshold guardian lets you go on the rest of the journey if you pass their test, with VCs, you are stuck with them for the rest of your journey! Many entrepreneurs have found themselves regretting a financing round years later, and found themselves either kicked out of their company or diluted to the point of not having much ownership left, or both!

We'll start by looking at the differences between the ways VCs think about investing in companies and how entrepreneurs usually think about it. Understanding this can help you avoid making the wrong pitch—which could lead to a lack of funding. This can help you to approach the right investors and create the kind of pitch that will be successful in raising money for your fledgling enterprise.

We might be tempted to think that a VC investment from a top-tier firm ensures future success. In this point of view, we might think the reason the startup becomes a leader in its industry is because it raised the most money from the best investors. While there is some truth to this (a company that raises more money has more resources), this obscures the underlying truth: While an investment from a top-tier venture capital firm can enhance your reputation, you will be more likely to get investment at a higher valuation if your business is already *a leader* in its small, emerging market.

Sometimes, getting too much money in a round of financing can be as bad as not getting enough money! Most first-time entrepreneurs—myself included—celebrate when they close their first $1 million-plus round of financing. But, this is often because we don't realize the strings that come along with giving an investor such a big chunk of our company. More important than the visible strings (the terms of the investment) are the invisible strings—expectations that are being placed on your company both by your valuation and by the growth projections that underlie that valuation.

This misunderstanding often makes entrepreneurs spend too much time focusing on the wrong things during a financing run. Understanding the secrets behind the myths in this stage will help you not only run a better financing process, but realize when you should or shouldn't be raising financing at all!

# Myth #4

## A Great Product and a Big Market Are the Most Important Things

The first myth in this stage is really about the differences in how entrepreneurs and professional investors look at the "fundability" of a company. OK, "fundability" may not be a word you can actually find in the dictionary. Nevertheless, it's a pretty well-known concept in Startup Land, and it's important to grasp it if you plan to raise money from VCs or professional investors.

The good news is that entrepreneurs and investors generally tend to agree on the factors that make one venture more "fundable" than another. The bad news is that they usually have very different views about the *order of importance* of these factors, which is part of the complexity that underlies this myth. Adding to the complexity are different understandings of the meaning of each factor. For example, when a VC talks about a "market" and an entrepreneur talks about a "market", they might be talking about very different things. As a result, entrepreneurs often emphasize the wrong things during their fundraising pitches, which means they are less likely to be successful in raising institutional money.

### Top Down or Bottom Up?

Let's back up and look at how most entrepreneurs come up with the idea for their first startup. Over the years I've found that there are two general approaches to creating a startup: top down (market based) or bottom up (product based).

In the top-down approach, a potential entrepreneurial team starts with a market that they think is ripe. They analyze the market, interview potential customers, look for unfulfilled needs, and eventually settle on a product or service that would fill that hole. Historically, this approach was very rare as most startups were founded by product guys, but it has become more common as startups have become more popular. In a top-down approach, someone usually first decides to do "a startup," and the specific market or product is a secondary consideration. In these instances, we would say that the company was most likely started by a "business guy" who wants to get in on "the next big thing."

Most entrepreneurs, on the other hand, at least traditionally, have followed the bottom-up approach. Usually, we are already in a market: from our previous job, from our academic research, or as a user/customer who needs or wants something that doesn't exist. With this product idea in mind, sometimes entrepreneurs do a broader market analysis, but not often.

Usually we just jump in based on intuition and gut feeling and worry about market stuff later (like when we're pitching VCs). This means that most entrepreneurs, whether they are technical or not, are thought of by investors as the "product guy" (I'm using "guy" in a genderless fashion, as in "you guys").

In my first startup, Brainstorm Technologies, I not only came up with the idea for the product (based on work I was already doing at Lotus Development Corp, one of the biggest software companies in the world at the time), but I also cowrote the code and built the product with my cofounder. Although we did line up a few potential customers for our first product, we didn't really think through how big the market was or whether VCs would invest in us when we first started the company.

Our primary concern was to create a product that *some customers* would want. I was already in this market so had a feeling for what customers might want. My title in the new startup was CEO, but since I had a technical background, from the VC perspective, I was still pretty much the "product guy." True to form, as we released our first product and the company grew beyond the two of us, I was usually the one who was thinking up new product ideas. It can be difficult in the long run for a product guy to also be the one in charge of running the operations of the business, which often leads to investors bringing in a chief operating officer (COO) or replacing the founder as CEO. Sure enough, this happened to me at Brainstorm—our investors eventually decided to bring in a professional manager as CEO (this isn't always a great thing for the company, either—more on this later).

You can be the product guy even if you didn't code the original product. For example, Gurinder Sangha, a Wharton-educated lawyer working in securities filings in Hong Kong, had an idea for a product that would make his and other lawyers' lives easier. He started his first tech company, Intelligize, a legal document services company, to make it easier for legal types to create SEC filing documents.

He didn't have a tech guy, so he hired an outsourcing firm and eventually brought on a full-time chief technology officer (CTO) to help him. Even though his title was CEO, and he was a lawyer by training, he was still the product guy during the company's first few years. He was the guy who designed the product and decided which features were important to have in the first release.

When product-focused entrepreneurs raise money, they know intuitively that they need a big market, so they slap on very large market size figures, while still focusing on the product they want to build. Both of those things are fine, particularly when you are pitching to nonprofessional investors, but can fall flat when pitching to sophisticated angels or partners of VC funds.

That's not to say that a good product isn't important to VCs; it is definitely important, it's just not the first thing or even the most important thing on their minds when they're evaluating your company as a potential investment.

## Why Entrepreneurs *Think* VCs Invest Versus Why VCs Actually Invest

If I were to conduct an informal survey of first-time (and sometimes even second- or third-time) entrepreneurs about the most important factors for a partner at a VC firm to make an investment in their company, they might put the factors in this order, from most important to least important:

1. *Product*. The most important thing is a great product idea—what it is, why it's better than competitors', and why customers need it.
2. *Market Size*. Most entrepreneurs recognize the need to go after a *big market*. As we discussed in Myth #1: Build a Billion-Dollar Company, most entrepreneurs want to show that their market is

"very big" to impress investors and show them how they can build the next Google or Facebook.

3. *Team*. Entrepreneurs recognize that their team's background is important, but usually they underestimate its importance to VCs in making financing decisions.
4. *Traction*. Entrepreneurs are optimistic in nature and believe that "traction will come after we build it," so they tend to view it as less important in the fundraising process than it actually is.
5. *Everything else*.

The reality is that if you ask most VCs their priorities, they would name the same factors (product, market, team, traction, everything else), but they might put them in a very different order.

It's really important to understand the different in priorities, because it can change the way you pitch your company to potential investors, and that can increase the likelihood of success. Of course, not all VCs are the same, but it's fair to say that their priorities are usually something like this:

1. *Team*. The background of the founders is usually one of the most important considerations for a VC. This is doubly true for an early stage startup that doesn't have any (or very little) revenue.
2. *Market Opportunity*. The *size* of the market today isn't really as important as the *opportunity* for startups in the market today (this relates to the stage the startup market is in—see Startup Model #1: The Startup Market Lifecycle).
3. *Traction*. If your product has traction in the marketplace, this is very important external evidence for landing series A financing. If you don't have any traction, this will cause hesitation.
4. *Product*. The product features are important, but in some ways features are less important than the team, market opportunity, and traction.
5. *Everything Else*.

Some VCs swap the first two priorities, and consider the market opportunity the most important thing.

As the company grows, and you move from a seed round to raising a series A financing or beyond, the order of priorities usually changes. A "series A" was traditionally the first preferred stock in the company, followed by a series "B," series "C," etc. Usually a seed round is not considered in this alphabetical list because most seed investments today are done as a convertible note and not as preferred stock. After the seed (and certainly after the series A), the order of importance shifts:

1. Traction.
2. Market Opportunity.
3. Product.
4. Team.
5. Everything Else.

Why would investors put traction ahead of product and market? We'll discuss this more in detail in Myth #5: Two Guys and a Business Are Better than Two Guys and a Plan. The reality is that VCs are making a bet, usually on a market and on some people, and the more evidence they have that this is the right bet (traction), the more likely they are to make that bet on you.

In all of these cases, a good product is a given; it is a necessary but not sufficient condition for success, which is why it's rarely first in a professional investor's list.

## More Detail on What Investors Look For

Let's go into each of these factors in more detail, from the point of view of a professional investor.

***Team***. The founding team (or founder, if there is only one) is usually the first or second most important factor for most professional investors to consider in the early days of a startup. VCs look for patterns based on previous teams they have funded, and look for aspects that might make a team "fundable." If the team (and the CEO in particular) doesn't have these characteristics, many VCs will pass, even if they are interested in investing in the market.

What makes a team fundable? While there is no comprehensive list, here are a few elements that help:

1. *Credibility*. What makes a team or entrepreneur credible? You might achieve credibility from long experience in a market, but that's not always the case. Many young teams with less than a year's experience get startup funding in new markets. In this case, credibility is more about deep knowledge of the market that the product is attacking. It can come from having already launched a product in a market, or from having worked on a related academic project.

In a newly emerging market, one year of experience may be more than almost anyone else has, so if a team right out of school has been working with a new technology for a year, that may make them the most credible team on the market. When Netscape was funded, Marc Andreessen (the "product guy"), who built the first widely used web browser, Mosaic, at the University of Illinois, knew more about web browsers than almost anyone else.

In a previously used example, Gurinder Sangha, the young lawyer who started Intelligize, a very successful securities legal software firm, was not the most experienced lawyer around. He wasn't even a partner at a law firm. But the fact that he was a securities lawyer and understood the problems lawyers face gave him more credibility than a technical guy suddenly deciding that he wanted to build "legal software."

2. *Presentation Style and Excitement*. Can the team (and the CEO in particular) present the opportunity coherently, getting investors excited about the market and the team's ability to tackle the market? This has as much to do with temperament and presentation style as it does with anything else.

I once introduced an entrepreneur (who was a very strong technology guy with a PhD) to a VC, and the VC gave me this feedback: "This guy is too erratic. I don't think this guy is fundable as a CEO." The VC wasn't commenting on the entrepreneur's technical credibility (he had the technical background to build the product—he even had a patent), but rather on his ability to present the opportunity credibly to investors.

The entrepreneur's passion and general commitment to the market is also considered in this factor. Whether someone is really excited about a market comes across during pitches, and even more important, during follow-up meetings. As mentioned in Bonus Myth #B-1: Start Something You Are Passionate About, Brad Feld doesn't like the word *passion*, but says, "A big part of what I'm looking for . . . is entrepreneurs who are obsessed about what they're doing." By obsessed, he means a team "that will do x, y, and z, and won't stop until they do it."

3. *Learning and Adapting*. In writing this book, one of the experts I interviewed was Randy Komisar, partner at Kleiner Perkins, one of the Silicon Valley VC firms. Randy said that the number one factor he looks for in a team is their *ability to learn on the job*.

Randy continues: "Everybody says they invest in great people . . . Everyone agrees that the founding team has to be smart, they need to be very hardworking, and they have to have integrity—if they don't have those things then it's out of the question to invest in them. But fundamentally, the aspect of being a great entrepreneur that I focus on most after those three table stakes is: will they learn on the job or are they dogmatic and orthodox in their approach?"

How does he figure this out? Randy says that he challenges the team's assumptions and observes their reactions. If they adapt to the questions and objections he brings up, this helps him understand how they will deal with unexpected challenges later in the company's life. If they are able to adapt, he takes this as a sign of being able to take in new information and "learn on the job." On the other hand, if they dismiss his objections out of hand, saying that they will succeed despite that objection, without showing him how or why, he takes this a sign that they won't be able to learn on the job.

***Market Opportunity.*** Second in importance to the team is the market (and for some professional investors, the market is even more important than the team). Now, the important thing here is not just the *size* of the market, but also the current *stage* of the market. If the market is too mature, it may be huge, it may even be growing at a decent clip, but there may already be entrenched players that are difficult to dislodge. Consider a company that wanted to release a new smartphone in 2014, after Samsung, Apple, and others had already dominated this market for several years. While this could be done, it would be a difficult market to enter, requiring hundreds of millions of dollars, since the smartphone market was maturing.

Getting even more specific, let's revisit the mobile smartphone gaming market, which started in 2008 with the release of Apple's iTunes app store on the iPhone. Neil Young, who had experience as a video game industry executive with Electronic Arts, was able to raise VC money for his new company, ngmoco, based primarily on his experience (*team*) coupled with the stage of this new and exciting market (*market opportunity*). The important point about the mobile smartphone gaming market at that point was that it was just moving from the nascent to growing stage, and some forward-thinking VCs started to smell an opportunity.

Over the next few years, many mobile gaming startup teams got funded, many of whom didn't have the experience in the game industry that Young and his team had. They did, however, build great games and they could show some traction, which provided their credibility.

By 2013, the market cycle had run its course, and it was difficult (though not impossible) to get VCs to put money into new mobile gaming. Ngmoco had sold to DeNA for almost $400 million in 2010, and there were many other companies that had done well also.

Now, the market size was still very big (in 2013, mobile gaming had become a multibillion-dollar market) and was still growing; in fact, it was much bigger than it had been in 2010-11, when many of the companies got funded. But, the *market opportunity* had dimmed, as shown in Startup Model #2: The Startup Opportunity Curve. This continued over the next few years until the market matured in 2016, and in 2017 had grown into a $30 billion market and is now the biggest component of the global $100 billion videogame market.

In 2013, I asked one of the initial VC investors in ngmoco whether he was still looking at gaming (since there was still plenty of money to be made by leaders in this field). He said that he was no longer interested in making investments in this market. There were already too many new players in this market, and large public companies, including Japanese giants like DeNA and GREE, were gunning to become leaders, and they had a lot of money at their disposal.

In short, the market opportunity was no longer "green ocean"—the expression that investors use about the stage when it's relatively easy for a small startup to establish a name for itself as a leader in a nascent but growing market.

As we saw with Myth #3: You Have to Be First to Market, VCs aren't always looking for the first company in a market, but they are looking for a company that can dominate a new market. As we look at the Capital Required Curve in Startup Model #2, we see that as the market moves to the later stages, the amount of money that is needed to make an impact on the market is significant (think of phones or cars).

However, betting too early, when the market is nascent, is often not a great bet either, because the market may not yet be developed, and the company will burn through the money too early. Smart VCs are looking to find an early player or leader at the time the market is starting to grow but not yet exploding. The key is for them to get in while a company with a small amount of money can make an impact.

When Mitch Liu and Anu Shukla founded Offerpal, in 2007, the social networking market had many players, including MySpace and Facebook. You might say the market for social networks was maturing at that time. However, as Facebook and MySpace opened up their APIs, a new market opportunity emerged—for social networking apps—the most popular and lucrative of which turned out to be games. This market grew very quickly and spawned many companies, such as Zynga (makers of Farmville) and King.com (makers of Candy Crush), among others. Later, in 2010, when Zynga had become a dominant player in social/Facebook games, it was very difficult to get funding in this market because it had to a certain extent matured, though mobile apps were now becoming big.

***Product.*** If the market and the team are right, then a professional investor will investigate whether the product will be successful and will support building a substantial company, big enough for venture-scale exits.

This means looking carefully at the technology behind the product, the feature sets of this product vis-a-vis its competitors, and the defensibility of the product/market position, not to mention the business model related to the product (i.e., its pricing). The reason this step is considered *after* the other factors is that often a VC-backed company's first product may not be the one that "makes" the company.

The team has to be nimble and knowledgeable enough to create a new product based on evolving market conditions. Even so, the dirty little secret of the VC industry is that many VCs aren't really qualified to tell if the product is better than competitors' products. So they simply look for *evidence* in the marketplace—which can only come in the form of traction.

Randy Komisar complains that when talking about product, most entrepreneurs don't know how to show that their product is really different from others—its defensibility. "Everybody comes in with a product they think is unique," says Randy. "A pink app instead of a green app doesn't really make it unique. Most entrepreneurs don't understand that it's really at its core just an app like the other apps. They need to explain why it's better or different at its core."

Randy explains that when talking about products, entrepreneurs should be talking not just about features, but also about how they will build a company starting with that first product. Randy says, "[Most entrepreneurs today] walk in believing that a feature is a product, that a product is a company, and that a company is a business. They do not understand the difference. They come in with a feature they think is maybe working well in the marketplace and . . . they believe that somehow that's a business."

## The Secret

***For early stage VCs, the market opportunity and the team are usually the most important things.***

If the market opportunity and the team are right, only then will professional investors spend enough time and effort to dig into the specifics of the product and all that entails—including its feature set, pricing, business model, and competitive differentiation.

If these factors are not right, then your company/venture is probably not a good fit for VC funding. Going on and on in your pitch about feature set A vs. feature set B and why your product is so awesome won't necessarily increase your chances of getting financing. It'll just annoy the VCs and make them cut your meeting short.

Remember that most VCs say yes to only a few companies per year. In fact, one prominent VC told me that their partnership was structured such that each partner could join only two new board of directors per year, which meant they could only do roughly two new investments per year. At this pace, by the fifth year of the fund, each partner could be on ten boards, which is a lot of boards to be on actively.

As a result, VCs spend most of their time looking for excuses to say no. While there are superficial reasons to say no ("they were late to the meeting," "they didn't dress well," "there was a typo in their slides," "their slides didn't have enough graphics"), these are not the real reasons why a VC says no.

Usually it comes down to their belief that the market is too far along, or that the market will never materialize, or they have concerns about the team. These last two are related, because it's possible the VC believes in the market but doesn't think that your team is the best team to go after it. In the sidebar after this myth, we look more closely at these reasons.

Understanding why VCs might say no puts you in a better position to move your company along from a first meeting to a second look. This is the goal of the first meeting—it isn't to get an investment. To move to a second meeting, all you really have to do is to convince the VC that the market is in the right stage (and we'll see that VCs pretty much convince themselves about a market's fundability in Myth #6: Talk to as Many Investors as You Can), and that your team is credible. They need to think that you know this market better than just about anyone else.

Of course, this doesn't guarantee an investment, but it does get you much closer to having a follow-on meeting, which will be much more detailed about your product and metrics.

## What About Other Funding Sources?

Of course, VCs aren't the only source of funding for your startup. If you are just starting out, you'll be dealing with individual angel investors and you might be dealing with an accelerator, such as my accelerator, Play Labs @ MIT, or TechStars, or a local accelerator in your university or hometown.

Generally speaking, the criteria that angel investors or accelerators use to admit startups are less restrictive than that of most VCs. This doesn't mean, however, that you should ignore the secret or the lessons incorporated there. Although it's easier to get admitted to an accelerator than it is to get VC funding, you can think of each of them as waypoints on the same road. As you approach an accelerator, you don't have to be as far along in answering the questions that VCs will ask, but you do need to think about similar questions.

Many accelerators (and professional angel investors) consider an additional criterion that's not on this list. They will wonder whether a VC will fund the company after it has left the accelerator. To be confident of this, the partners at the accelerator will want to know whether the company already has elements that VCs find attractive. In this way, you can view pitching accelerators and seed funds as a preliminary step to pitching regular VC funds. Many angel investors, on the other hand, will put money into a startup based on their relationship with the entreprenuer, or if other angel investors they know are putting in money. Or they may just like the product, or know that the market is "big." Their criteria may be much more the criteria expressed in this myth: a good product and a big market.

Many angels have now started to work together in places like Silicon Valley, Boston, and New York. The criteria for these funds is closer to what an accelerator looks for: will this company be able to pitch VCs and raise more money down the road? Which means that any pitch to "professional angels" is also like a preliminary step to pitching to VCs.

Of course, the best way to get VCs to put money in you, is to make some progress on the business. This might allow you to build a profitable company quickly, in which case you won't need VC financing except for expansion. At this point, as we mentioned your metrics and traction in the market become the most important criterion. We'll talk more about these two, metrics and traction, in the next myth, Myth #5: Two Guys and a Business Are Better Than Two Guys and a Plan, since it is such an important part of the reason why any investor wants to get into a startup.

### Sarah Downey on Why VCs Say No: Founder-Related Reasons

Sarah Downey, of Accomplice, a Boston-based venture capital firm, writes in her blog about a number of reasons VCs say no.

Sarah says that sometimes it's hard for a VC to share the real reason they aren't investing. This is usually because their reason to say no is the team itself. They may couch their reason for saying no as "too much competition," when the real reason is that they don't have confidence in the team to execute.

The team is at the top of Sarah's list of funding considerations. For our discussion, let's look more closely into the founder-related reasons why VCs say no:

- **Negative Founder or Team Dynamics.** These range from too many cofounders (more than three), to founders who have job titles that intrude on one another (having both a CEO and a president in the early days of a company is a big red flag).Or this might be revealed in the meeting itself, if the founders aren't gelling, are talking over each other, or one belittles other members of the team.
- **Missing a Key Person.** This one is pretty obvious. For example, the team might not have a CTO or a VP of Marketing or VP of Product.
- **Founders Not Mission-Driven.** If the founders don't seem to care much about what they are building, or are only in it for a really high salary or a quick buck. Sarah gives the example of the recent "blockchain for *x*," where everyone was jumping into the "blockchain" market in 2017 after the price of Bitcoin went from $1,000 to $19,000.
- **Dishonesty or Negative References.** Sometimes entrepreneurs will say something in a VC meeting that the VC later finds out is untrue. Dishonesty is an immediate disqualifier. Almost always, VCs will check random references (by calling people you might know but whom you don't list as references) to try to get honest feedback.
- **CEO or Founder Not Compelling.** This is the hardest one to define, but perhaps the most common. The CEO, says Sarah, will be the public-facing person and must give a compelling presentation. Moreover, the CEO has to inspire confidence in both the investor and the team—and many CEOs just don't because they aren't passionate enough, knowledgeable enough, or just lack that "special something" that is hard to articulate.

Sarah gives the full list of reasons, including market and investor-related reasons, why VCs say no, in her series of blog posts (https://www.forbes.com/sites/forbesfinancecouncil/2018/07/19/why-a-vc-passed-on-your-startup-the-founder-related-reasons/).

# Myth #5

## Two Guys and a Business Are Better Than Two Guys and a Plan

During the dot-com bubble of the late 1990s, a new mythical archetype arose in Silicon Valley and soon spread to other tech hubs: two guys who had quit their corporate jobs and had put together a nice-looking PowerPoint presentation about how they were going to "disrupt" an industry using the internet.

It almost didn't matter what industry it was—whether it was books or pets, etc., as long as it was a "traditional" industry that was going to be upended by the arrival of the internet. These mythical guys walked in and were showered with multiple term sheets from multiple VCs, and they walked away with their choice of investors and millions of dollars in the bank!

This actually *did* happen in the 1990s, sometimes. And not nearly as often as popular culture might have you believe.

And then it became very rare after the dot-com bubble burst in the early 2000s. Since then, venture investors have wanted to see *traction*. Usually this means that you have to build your product (either by bootstrapping it, or with some level of angel funding, or while participating in an incubator/accelerator program), release your product (at least into beta), then show some evidence of how it's doing in the marketplace, before most traditional VCs will consider investing millions into your series A financing.

This then developed into a new conventional wisdom in financing: Two guys and a business (i.e., a product or service that's actually *live*) are better than two guys and a business plan (or a PowerPoint presentation, since very rarely does anyone write a full business plan anymore, at least not in Silicon Valley).

## The Elusive Crystal Ball

This myth really boils down to the importance of *traction* or the lack of it and its impact on your ability to raise financing. The truth of the matter is, though VCs and angel investors don't like to admit this, most of the time they really have *no idea* how well your product or service will do in the marketplace. The idea that VCs have some kind of crystal ball is not really true—their predictive ability most likely isn't any better than yours. If you consider some of the most famous investments that were done on early stage companies (think Apple, Google, Slack, etc.)—did the VCs really know how the business model of the company would evolve or what products would lead to the company's eventual success?

Probably not.

Case in point: Google Glass. In 2013 there was a great picture of many prominent VCs in Silicon Valley all wearing Google Glass. The picture was shown well beyond Silicon Valley—in *Forbes*, the *New York Times*, etc., as Google Glass was hailed as "the next big thing," and two of Startup Land's most prominent VC firms, Andreessen Horowitz and KPBC (Kleiner Perkins Caufield & Byers) led an initiative to invest in Google Glass–related startups. I remembered KPBC setting up the iFund to invest in iPhone-related companies in 2008. This startup market (smartphone applications) produced many successful companies, so this was a "signal" to the market that this new platform, Google Glass, might follow a similar trajectory and create multiple successful startups.

Unfortunately (for anyone who invested in or started a company on this new platform), within a year, Google Glass was considered a dead platform, and Google put it back into development to retool it. While there may still be a market someday for a Google Glass–like platform, clearly this wasn't the right time for it. The augmented reality (AR) market did start to develop several years later, but by then Google Glass had gone back to the drawing board and wasn't considered a major player.

This picture of all these "know-it-all VCs" wearing funny glasses is often cited as an example that VCs don't really know which markets will be successful; they tend to follow the "herd" of other VCs. There are some individual partners at VC firms who have a lot of vision and better track records than most, but what this really shows is that markets are unpredictable and often don't go the way of the "consensus."

Consider Pixar, which was a computer hardware company when Steve Jobs bought it from Lucasfilm and invested a considerable amount of money in it. Although some of the key team members, Ed Catmull and John Lasseter in particular, wanted to make animated movies, that wasn't Steve Jobs's vision, nor was it the product that the company had. Everyone agreed that the company could create revolutionary graphics—but for a long time, Jobs wanted it to be a hardware company selling the Pixar computer, just like his past few startups, Apple and NeXT!

That it would morph into perhaps the most successful film studio of the past fifty years was, at best, unexpected. The journey the company took might be compared to the journey they took on the film *Up*, which was a critical success when it came out, but went through many twists and turns before it got there. As Ed Catmull himself would write in his book, *Creativity, Inc.*, the final product was very different from the original script. Catmull writes, "The path . . . was difficult and unpredictable. . . . There was nothing about where it started that indicated where it ended up."

In fact, you might say the rule of thumb is what William Goldman, a Hollywood screenwriter, wrote at the end of his acclaimed memoir, *Adventures in the Screen Trade*: "No one knows anything."

Actually, it's not a bad analogy (though limited). Sometimes, in the film business, the studio bets on a particular genre being "hot" (such as science fiction, westerns, romance, superhero movies) and finds a team that can execute a reasonable story in that genre. In the case of VCs, many are betting on a new rapidly growing market (PCs, search, animation) and a team that they trust to "execute," more than on the specific product itself. As new markets grow, investors expect that the team will use their knowledge of the market to figure out things like an appropriate business model and additional products, which are almost always necessary to build a real business no matter how successful the first product is (or isn't!).

## External Evidence

Well, if investors don't really know if your product or business model is going to succeed, how do they decide if your company is a good investment?

The short answer is that investors look for *external evidence*. That evidence comes in the form of customer *traction*. During the dot-com days, because many firms with absolutely no traction were being financed, it used to be that you could brief analysts about your product (there is a whole industry of technology analysts like Gartner, Forrester, and many more niche ones focused on specific technology), and that was considered traction enough. Today, that's not considered real evidence—you'll want to show that actual customers or business partners care about your product or service and are (or will be) willing to pay for it.

Of course, if you are making a new mobile enterprise software application and you have ten of the Fortune 500 already *using* your product—that's the best kind of evidence. Short of that, if the product isn't done, but you have ten of the Fortune 500 wanting to be beta testers, that's the next best thing.

Even Facebook, a perfect example of a company that made no money while it grew (and raised ungodly amounts of money along the way), had some level of evidence or traction before it raised its first round of external investment. The site was already adopted and being used heavily by college students—first at Harvard, then at Stanford and other universities. In fact, the usage metrics of Facebook were what convinced investors that this was the "next big thing." This was fictionalized in a scene in the movie, *The Social Network*, where Sean Parker is with a female college student at Stanford who goes to "check the Facebook" as the first thing she does in the morning after their one-night stand. He had never heard of the site. For consumer-oriented sites and apps, usage statistics (how often a site or app is used) are more important than having impressive numbers for the total number of users, etc.

Do you always need traction? I remember telling one entrepreneur that he needed more potential customers (more traction) to get VCs interested (he had already raised money from angels and had some tepid interest from VCs). His response to me was, "This traction thing is bullshit; I don't need traction, I've got patents!"

Now, in a highly technological field, such as pharmaceuticals or network hardware or computer security (which is the field that his product was in), it may be possible that all you need is a patent or set of patents, or simply a product that does something that others find difficult or impossible to do.

Even in that case, if it's a complicated patent or product, acquirers and investors will want to see some evidence that the patent or product actually *works*, by having at least beta customers verify that it does what it says it will do, which gets back to—you got it—*showing traction*. This particular entrepreneur, though he had several unique patents, never got any real traction in the marketplace. Without showing traction, potential venture investors and acquirers were hesitant to plunk down any real money on an unproven technology (despite the patents), and he was unable to raise any significant funds beyond the first small angel rounds. Even though he thought traction was overrated (and was in his words, "bullshit"), traction (or lack thereof) came back to bite him anyway. It turned out to be the one thing he was missing that would have put him over the hump and gotten VC financing.

### Brad Feld on What Comes First—the Traction or the Funding?

In writing this book, I interviewed Brad Feld, partner at Foundry Group in Boulder and a well-known venture investor and author. When I asked him what were the biggest mistakes that entrepreneurs make when fundraising, he said that many entrepreneurs come asking him for funding so that they can go out and build a product, and then they will show traction in the marketplace. It rarely works.

Brad said, "I think a lot of people don't actually understand the importance of not viewing raising money as the driver. In other words, you get financing as a result of what you're doing, not to enable what you're doing, and I think a lot of entrepreneurs get tangled up in this misunderstanding. They view financing as a thing they have to do to be able to go make progress in their business."

Brad added: "In fact, the chance of your getting financing is greatly enhanced by your making progress *before* you get the financing. That's not an argument for bootstrapping. It's just an argument for recognizing that financing is going to follow the work you're doing rather than an idea that you have."

In other words: get traction first and then you will get funding, don't promise investors that you will use their money to get traction.

### When Metrics Can Be Bad

But there is another side to traction that can be deadly when raising money, and it can turn this conventional wisdom on its head. This sounds odd, but sometimes in fundraising, two guys and a business plan can actually be better than having a business up and running. This happens in the case where you have some metrics, but the traction you have is mediocre at best—that can be worse than having no traction at all!

For example, if you have already introduced your product into the marketplace, but no one (or very few users or customers) has adopted it, this can be an even bigger problem than not having introduced it at all!

If you are looking to raise sales and marketing money for this product that doesn't seem to be getting traction, potential investors will be very suspicious. That's because sophisticated investors expect you to have some traction to show not only that the product works but that people want to use it! This can be shown through paid customer adoption, or through a set of metrics that show that customers are using the product (even if it's a free product).

In the world of free-to-play mobile games, where I spent many years, we usually looked at key metrics that told us how well a game was retaining users (one-day, seven-day, or fourteen-day retention), and how well the game was monetizing (we looked at ARPDAU—average revenue per daily active user). If a game was done or mostly done, we'd expect a soft-launch or beta period, during which the game was released to a small but statistically significant number of users, so we could see how well its metrics compared to those of other games.

The flip side of traction is that if the game is done and the metrics are low compared to others in the industry, then you are going to have a very tough time raising sales and marketing funds. In the cutthroat world of mobile games, it can be very expensive to get users, as the market is well beyond the initial stages of the Startup Market Lifecycle. You can easily spend half a million dollars or more *a month* on advertising. If the game's metrics aren't there, you might be throwing that money away because you will pay for ads, get initial users, but those users will basically abandon the game after the first day. This makes investors nervous (rightfully so).

Consequently, raising money for building a new product may actually be easier than raising money for a business that's already running with metrics that are not very good. Once again, this comes down to the stage of the market. This is particularly true in the nascent, growing, and first part of the super-hot stages of the market.

Let's look at two examples of mobile game companies that were started in 2011–12, when the mobile gaming industry was already in the super-hot stage (in mid-2012 and 2013 the market turned to *maturing*).

Bionic Panda had a game called *Aqua Pets*, which had been downloaded several million times on Android. They raised money in January 2012 from Google Ventures and others. Also in 2012, Wormhole games was founded by two members of Funzio, which was a successful game startup that sold to GREE. They released their game, *Tank Nation*, on iPad in 2013, and it got very good reviews.

Both teams were able to raise money based on the background of the founders, without showing a lot of metrics. At this point, investors still were looking for good teams to back in this fast-growing, super-hot market! Those investors that had missed out on the initial phases wanted to get in on the "next big thing"; and many of those that had invested and exited already wanted to repeat that success, which is what drove the transition from growing to super-hot.

Within a few years, in early to mid-2014, I spoke to the founders of both companies—both were unable to sustain the companies based on the revenues of the game. Moreover, they were unable to raise more money from VCs after the initial round, and effectively had to shut down.

Why weren't they able to raise more money? Both teams were credible (entrepreneurs who knew their industries) and had good user reviews on the games. But the market had changed. By mid-2014, we were clearly in the *maturing* stage of the mobile game market, and for a game to be successful, you needed solid metrics and considerably more money than in previous years to make an impact.

That by itself wasn't an issue, but both companies' games were clearly not showing the kind of metrics that would get investors excited at this stage of the market, even if the team's background alone would have gotten funding in an earlier stage of the market.

This was a perfect example of a time it was *easier* to raise money when they didn't have an up-and-running business, just a plan. When they had a business, the numbers weren't great, it became difficult to raise money, and they had to shut the companies down.

## When Two Guys and a Business Plan Is Better

I know this flies in the face of what I just said about *traction*, but bear with me.

Going back to Myth #4: A Great Product and a Big Market Are the Most Important Things, the secret was that the team and the market opportunity were in some ways *more important* than the product itself.

If you are in a new market where there are no experts, and you have a great team with credibility, you may be able to raise money from professional investors without any market traction whatsoever. By showing the beginnings of a product, or even a PowerPoint presentation, if the market is white-hot and investors are looking to get in on it, you can still raise money on a promise.

Of course, this works only if you are in a hot market that people recognize may be the next big thing, and if your team has some background in the area. It could be that you have a strong set of technical folks who were all working in Google Android's core development team, and that you are working on the next set of apps for X (insert some mobile app market here). What VC wouldn't be interested in getting in early if they believe that market X is the next big thing?

So, in some limited scenarios, two guys and a business plan are actually better than two guys and a business in these scenarios!

## Startup Model #3: When Traction Is and Isn't Important (The Inflection Point)

The real secret lies in knowing where you are in the evolution of your startup market, as shown in our Startup Model #1: The Startup Market Lifecycle.

We have delved into different parts of the model; in this expansion of the model, we are dividing the stages into two (more or less equal) parts, as shown in figure 5.1, divided by what I call the *inflection point*.

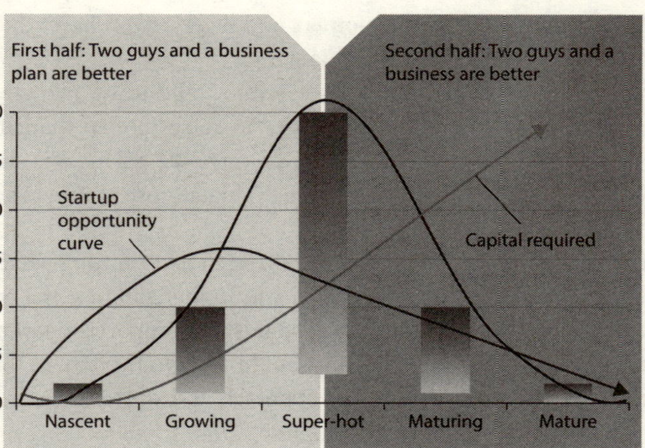


Figure 5.1
Two Halves of the Market and Two Guys and a Business Plan. Created by the author

If you are on the left side of the inflection point (*nascent*, *growing*, first half of *super-hot* stages), then simply having a great plan with some credibility will do it for you. You don't have to show good numbers or traction to get financing—you simply need to show some credibility in the market and a good enough plan (two guys and a business plan). VCs and professional investors will assume you are smart enough to figure it out, since the market is so hot.

If you are on the right side (second half of the Lifecycle: second half of super-hot, maturing, mature), then you must show some traction and it usually has to be more than just raw numbers of users or hits on your website. In the mobile gaming world, as we mentioned, this meant real monetization and retention metrics—and the farther you get to the right of the graph, the more revenue and/or profits you need to be able to show to get professional investors interested, such that in the mature phase of a market, private equity investors (late-stage venture-type investors) care about only one thing: profits.

## The Secret

***Performance can help or hurt you in raising financing; it all depends on the stage of the market and how impressive your traction is.***

Usually this myth is true—what you really need to show to get investors on board is *traction*. The more customers and revenue you have, the more likely you are to be able to raise VC financing.

However, *sometimes* in a hot market, with a solid team, two guys and a business plan may actually find it *easier* to raise money than if their business was up and running. That's because once the business is showing real numbers, it's very easy for investors to evaluate those numbers and say it's not good enough.

Moreover, the stage of the market is critical in determining what kinds of numbers you need to show, which is why understanding the Startup Market Lifecycle and where your market stands is an important part of how you should approach VCs and how you should craft your pitch. In the next myth, we delve into whom you should approach and why.

# Myth #6

## Talk to as Many Investors as You Can

If there's one complaint I've heard from most entrepreneurs in Startup Land, it's that raising money is a full-time job, and most of them would rather be running their startups. Some entrepreneurs who've had unsuccessful startups might complain afterward that they weren't able to raise money to keep the startup going because they didn't talk to enough investors.

Most of the myths in this book represent an underlying belief that may or may not be true. The underlying belief beneath this myth is that the more investors you talk to, the more likely you are to be able to raise your next round of financing (and presumably, at a better valuation). We'll address the valuation part in the next myth.

While the complaint that fundraising can be a full-time job is a reasonable one (I've fallen into this trap myself), it's possible that you are spending time talking to *too many* investors. Moreover, it's possible that after some number of (unsuccessful) investor meetings, you might be better off figuring out the major issue with your pitch/underlying story, particularly with the investor profile you have been targeting. You might be better off talking to fewer investors, focusing on those that are more targeted to your company's strengths or weaknesses. If you don't do this, it's possible you will just be spinning your wheels and burning contacts with potential investors.

## The Sales Funnel Versus the Investor Funnel

In certain industries, salespeople know that as long as their sales pitch is solid, they have to play a numbers game that's called the sales funnel. They have to make sure they have enough leads at the top of the funnel to turn into qualified prospects—some of them will want to see presentations, and some who see the presentation will want to buy the product or service being offered.

But does the same thing apply when you are raising money from venture capitalists or angel investors? While some entrepreneurs would say yes, the real answer is that *it depends*.

I must qualify the statement about the sales funnel by saying that the salesperson needs to know that the sales pitch works and has a reasonable chance of turning into a sale.

The only reason that the sales funnel works is that once you have sold enough of a product, you can start to estimate the percentage of sales leads that will move from one stage of the funnel to the next. You know the product meets a need (or is a desirable product, in the case of luxury goods) and that if you put out the bait, you will hook a certain number of fish. The same is true of consumer startups, which often follow a freemium model these days: if you get enough users to visit your site/app, some reliable percentage of them will turn into paying users, and this drives your monetization. In free-to-play video games, for example, this is what metrics like ARPDAU (average revenue per daily active user) and LTV (Lifetime value) are meant to reflect.

But in a VC fundraising environment, you don't know if your pitch works until you've gone through the entire sales funnel. And if it worked, there is no rule you can deduce about how many VCs will move from one stage to the next—at least not one that you can use, since you won't need to raise money again for another twelve to eighteen months (at which time you will have a different pitch) and the company and market will be at a different point. If it doesn't work, well then, the funnel wasn't really much of a funnel at all. In truth, this myth is really about *quantity vs. quality*.

## How Many Fish in the Sea?

This is best illustrated by a story that a friend told me once about a self-improvement seminar she attended many years ago. There was a young man in the seminar who wanted to get married but wasn't having a lot of success.

The instructor told this young man that he probably wasn't talking to enough young women and wasn't being clear enough up front about what he wanted. The instructor told him he should just get out there and approach as many women as possible and tell them that he was looking for a spouse, and ask if they would go out with him. He got on it right away, and started approaching all the women in his seminar, telling them that he was looking to get married.

We are back to the "pitch" and the "sales funnel" (number of leads, or in this case, number of women the young man was talking to).

Now this might seem like a ridiculous idea (I certainly thought so) in our day and age, but it was based on the same underlying belief as our myth—that finding the right person is basically a "numbers game" (taking the "sales funnel" approach). This approach says that if you talk to enough people at the top of the funnel, some will filter down into the next stage (going out with you), and some will convert (i.e., at least one of those will want to marry the young man).

While a "sales funnel" approach seems logical enough, it's clearly missing some of the magic that comes from meeting the "right" person.

Some (myself included) would recommend a different approach for finding a significant other, or for finding a lead investor, particularly a VC. Sometimes it's not just about the number of dates you've gone on, but the types of people you are approaching and going on dates with.

In fact, when it comes to VCs, the more you narrow down the leads before approaching them, the less time you are likely to waste chasing potential lead investors and the less likely you will complain that "fundraising" is a full time job!

## Finding a Partner

Randy Komisar, partner at Kleiner Perkins Caufield & Byers, makes the point that most entrepreneurs don't take the time to understand the firm and the partner at the firm they are talking to, and I have often found this to be the case.

Randy explained to me when I interviewed him, "I think the first thing is that entrepreneurs don't understand who they're talking to on the other side. . . . They don't understand that the partner is probably as important, if not more important, than the firm they choose.

"They haven't done their due diligence. They walk in blindly and this is where a lot of the unhappiness and dissatisfaction arises. It happens all the time. You're constantly talking to the wrong partner, not understanding that if you get started with the wrong partner, there is a chance you will get a negative answer because venture capital firms don't work that way." (Brad Feld makes the same point in the sidebar at the end of this myth, "Why VCs Are like D&D Characters.")

So how do you find the right partner? I'd say it's not that different from finding the right person for a relationship. Here are some strategies that have worked in both personal and VC relationships:

1. *Get warm intros from people you know (i.e., "setups").* While some people hate being set up for dates by their friends, in the startup world, this is actually the best way to get to a VC. If you spend enough time in Startup Land, you will eventually find advisors and angel investors who know VCs. If they like your idea or business, they will make intros. Some will want something for making intros, of course, and you have to use your judgment here.

Unlike the investment banking world (where a commission is normal), startup VCs generally don't like people who say they will help you to raise money in return for a percentage of what's raised. While a commission on the amount raised is common in other industries, it's looked on pretty negatively in Silicon Valley. Investors generally want all the money raised to go into the company, not to some "middleman." On the other hand, if they are acting as an advisor for your startup and have some equity, then Silicon Valley investors are generally happy with the arrangement, since the advisor's goals are aligned with making the company as valuable as possible.

2. *Common Interests.* Explore activities that you are naturally interested in (practice smart networking). By attending industry or topic-specific events, you are likely to meet individuals who share your interests. This is a better starting place than simply approaching any investor who is a VC on LinkedIn. Common sense in relationships dictates that the more you have in common, the likelier it is that an initial conversation will lead to something more.

This means finding investors who are *already* interested in your market. This used to be more difficult in the days before social media, but today this can be done by following a VC partner online—their tweets, blog posts, or finding companies that they have invested in in the past. If you are starting a Bitcoin startup, there are usually some investors poking around at Bitcoin meetups or tweeting about Bitcoin. Some of those investors may have already invested in a Bitcoin startup, but others are poking around and are favorably disposed to the market, otherwise they wouldn't be wasting their time.

3. *Demo Days and Presentations.* In recent years, another approach has become popular: attending demo days at accelerators. I suppose the analogy here would be speed dating, but the basic idea is that on demo day, potential investors (and potential advisors) will come to see demos from multiple startup companies. If they find one that strikes their fancy, they'll approach them with some kind of interest. Demo days have become popular with the rise of accelerators like Y Combinator, 500 Startups, my own accelerator—Play Labs @ MIT—and many others in Silicon Valley and beyond. If you are not part of an accelerator, there are pitch conferences that serve similar functions in Silicon Valley and in the major startup hubs.

Of course, there is no single "right way" to raise money! There are as many different stories out there of how startups found investors as there are startups that found investors. For all we know, the young man who racked up the numbers of women he approached with his pitch of looking for a wife may have found someone that way.

And sometimes sheer serendipity strikes. Evernote, the popular note-taking app, was almost out of money in October 2008 and was preparing to lay off all its employees. Unexpectedly then-CEO Phil Libin got an email from a customer at 3 A.M. Libin took a Skype call with the customer, who had fallen in love with his product, and two weeks later, Evernote received a $500,000 check, which saved the company. So you have to keep an open mind when it comes to fundraising.

## Quality vs. Quantity: Finding the Right Match

Some entrepreneurs tell me that they expect to pitch thirty to forty investors before finding the one that will fund their next round. In my entrepreneurial career, very rarely have I had to pitch that many investors.

Usually by the fifth pitch, and almost always by the tenth pitch, it's pretty clear whether the pitch is *working* or not. More important, it becomes clear which subset of investors the pitch is working with (for example, Silicon Valley–based VCs vs. L.A–based VCs, strategic investors vs. angel funds, etc.).

If the pitch is working, I'm already on the way to getting at least one term sheet. If not, there's probably something wrong with the pitch—which usually means not the pitch itself (i.e., the slides I'm using to tell the story) but the underlying fundamentals (i.e., the market opportunity we're going after, the team that we've assembled, the product, the business model, or the traction that we're showing).

This last point is important. While most people think the pitch slides are "the pitch," that's not really the case. As we said in Myth #4: A Great Product and a Big Market Are the Most Important Things, when pitching to professional investors, the factors that are most important are the underlying realities: the team, the market opportunity, and, at times, the traction.

While there are many rules of thumb in the fundraising world, in my experience with fundraising efforts over the years, there were two conditions that made it more likely than not that a VC would invest. Usually at least one of these was true. In some cases, both were true.

1. The investor was *already* predisposed to invest in the market that I was in.
2. There was some previous connection to the investor (either I knew them, or one of my advisors or existing investors knew them and made the introduction, or they were connected to my alma mater, etc.).

That's not to say that fundraising success hasn't ever happened by pitching someone completely new, without a warm intro or a common connection. In those cases, the investor usually met condition #1, which is to say that they were already on the lookout to invest in a company in my market, and the team happened to appear at the right time.

The other thing to keep in mind is that there is a process to go through in getting to know someone that you are going to write a million-dollar–plus check to. The more trust there is already (even if the trust is between the VC and an angel investor or advisor already in the company, rather than with the entrepreneur), the more likely it is that your company and pitch will be looked at more seriously and make it through the process quickly. That's why a lot of cold emails to VCs don't work, but warm intros do.

## What's Your Tribe?

Gurinder Sangha was a lawyer with almost no contacts in the VC industry when he founded Intelligize. When I invited him to Play Labs @ MIT to talk about his experience, he gave the indispensable advice that in your first outside fundraising, it's good to figure out what your "tribe" is and then to approach investors who are members of that tribe.

In the United States, says Gurinder, your tribe is typically your undergraduate alma mater. Gurinder went to the University of Pennsylvania, and his first VC and angel investors were . . . guess what? . . . also Penn alumni! In my own case, having graduated from MIT, I was able to leverage the MIT alumni network to get to investors.

You can expand the idea of your "tribe" to be a set of "qualified" individuals or firms who are predisposed to invest in you. That may be because of affiliation, geography, market segment, business model, etc.

Let's look at two examples of companies that thought they were going to raise money in Silicon Valley because that's what everyone does! But they both found out that their market/business models actually meant their tribes were elsewhere.

### Example #1: Raising Money for a Job Site in Latin America

David Reich cofounded Assured Labor in the mid-2000s with friends after graduating from MIT's Sloan School of Management. Their idea was to use mobile phones, which were much more prevalent than desktop computers in developing markets like Latin America and South Asia, to help employers and job candidates find each other. The model was innovative, and their test case was in Nicaragua, with plans to expand to Mexico and then Brazil and perhaps India or other countries in Asia afterward.

After getting his initial product together and completing his test case in Nicaragua, he made the rounds at venture capital firms in Boston and Silicon Valley. While many of them liked the innovation of his idea, many were reluctant to commit to putting in series A financing. While the reasons they gave varied, there was one theme that came through: they were generally uncomfortable investing in companies whose target market was Latin America because they just didn't know enough about the markets.

Dave, who was very much in touch with the pulse of the U.S. tech industry, was constantly frustrated by tales coming out of Silicon Valley and elsewhere of companies raising millions of dollars from well-known VCs with less product and less traction than Assured Labor already had. In order to show even more traction, they moved from Nicaragua to Mexico and struck up partnerships with some of Mexico's biggest cell phone network providers (which they had to work with in order to do the text messaging their platform required). Dave made multiple trips to Silicon Valley to meet with VCs as potential investors.

Dave ended up not getting any Silicon Valley VC investment in his company, and he was quite frustrated. He was, however, eventually able to raise series A financing. He got it from a fund that was established by some wealthy Mexicans who had done well in the U.S. tech industry and the Mexican telecommunications industry, and not from your typical vanilla VC firm.

The lesson here is not that Dave shouldn't have tried to serve developing economies or emerging markets, it's that he could've saved himself a lot of time and frustration by targeting those VCs and investors who were already *predisposed* to invest in Latin America or developing economies. There aren't that many in the United States.

### Example #2: Where Should You Fund a Shopping Company?

In another example, Saurin Shah, the cofounder of Sift Shopping, a mobile shopping app, was looking for funding for his startup. He lived in Silicon Valley and was in touch with the tech funding scene, so he naturally assumed he'd be able to get financing there. He received some initial angel-type funding, but when he started to look for his next round, he found Silicon Valley VCs more resistant than he had expected.

He found that investors in New York were more disposed to invest in consumer "shopping" than Silicon Valley VCs were, even though his startup was based in Silicon Valley! Again, finding investors who are predisposed to what you do is as important as talking to lots and lots of investors.

Saurin told me:

> We were building a product for women. What I noticed is that in Silicon Valley, most investors are men, and they don't really understand products for women, which is why companies like Pinterest, even Instagram, stuff like this, really eluded a lot of Valley investors.
>
> Women shop differently than men. Men shop price comparison. They know their product. Amazon is a search-based experience. You type in what you want. Women browse visually. That alone is very different. Pinterest versus Amazon is a really good example. Pinterest inspires. Amazon is search destination-based. Hence, our shopping was also more browsing-focused.

A lot of the investors couldn't understand that. They wanted to see price comparison. The truth is that yoga pants from LuluLemon are different than yoga pants from Gap. Ask any woman that; they're just not the same. Men shop very differently. You want a fifty-inch Samsung TV, it's easier to price compare across different stores. It's the same product.

Interesting[ly] enough . . . we had a lot more success with investors based out of New York . . . it was different. When I was raising money in the Valley a lot of questions were, "What's your tech platform? What's your viral coefficient?" It was very different. When I went to New York it was like, "Well, of course shopping is going to be big on the phone. What's your experience? What's the UI going to be?" They focused on different things; things that we were better at.

While they were proper VCs, their outlook on the world was different. Silicon Valley is very tech-based. Yeah, they just wanted to know who my engineering team was, and what we were going to do. I'm like, "It's shopping. The tech is important, but . . . it's not what's going to make the difference."

## The Secret

***You are trying to find the right match; it really doesn't matter how many investors you talk to, whether one or fifty. Try to find your tribe and approach qualified investors in that tribe.***

To find the right match, narrow down the possibilities to spend time with the *right* investors. If we take the view that finding a lead investor is a little bit like getting married, you probably don't want to be like the young man indiscriminately approaching every woman in the workshop whether they would want to go on a date to consider marrying him. In other words, *quality* should outweigh *quantity*.

Some amount of research, some warm intros, and finding an investor who is already interested in your market are the keys to keeping your fundraising time down so you can focus on building the company. To do this, you need to research not just firms, but individual partners in VC firms.

You should also ask, "What's My Tribe?"—and whether it's defined by affiliation (college, workplace, etc.) or market segment or business model or geography. Use this knowledge to your advantage to find your first institutional investors.

Also, it may mean that you need to build relationships before you need the money. It also means that you will need to weed out investors that don't seem like a good fit or aren't interested in your market. Investor meetings take time, and as many entrepreneurs complain, fundraising can be a full-time job. The way to have time to run your company and raise money is to make it more about quality and not quantity.

## A Word About Multiple Accelerators

One question that I get asked often is whether a startup should go to more than one accelerator. In fact, at Play Labs, we sometimes got applications from a startup that had been in another accelerator program.

There is no one answer to this question. In some cases, if your startup has been through too many accelerators, VCs and other investors might wonder why you haven't been able to raise significant financing—it could serve as a negative signaling. Accelerators are meant to accelerate a company to get on either a VC track or a strategic investor track, or to get customers and become profitable.

If that hasn't happened, it could mean that there is something wrong with your business model (the negative signaling), or it could be that the market is not in the right stage (too early or too late).

The exception is when the second accelerator is more "specific" than the first, and you are in a specific market that is taking a long time to get going. For example, we had a company called Wonda VR in our accelerator, which was building a development tool that used 360 VR. It turned out that many of their customers were in education, or were corporations who were using it to build training VR applications for their employees. I encouraged Wonda VR to go to an education-specific accelerator after Play Labs (which was focused more on VR). They did, and they continued to grow their revenue in that vertical, so it made sense to go to a second accelerator.

Similarly, earlier I gave the example of Button Wallet, a blockchain company that went to a blockchain accelerator after ours. In this case two accelerators was acceptable.

As an accelerator, we sometimes turned down companies that went through another accelerator and couldn't raise financing afterward, unless their products were specific to video games, which our accelerator specialized in.

### Brad Feld on Why VCs Are Like *D&D* Characters

"VCs," says Brad, "are like *Dungeons and Dragons* characters." This analogy ties in with our themes of mythological journeys and archetypes. He continues:

> "Entrepreneurs talk about this abstraction or singular market type that is a VC—but really when talking about VCs you have to talk about the individual person—whether you are talking about Brad Feld or Fred Wilson. You have to understand that they're different, have different things they like, they approach things differently, they might be collaborating on some stuff but there's plenty of things that one might do that another would never do.
>
> My assertion was: start with the idea that a VC could be an elf, could be a dwarf, could be an orc, or he could be a wizard. They're going to have different skill levels. They're going to have different things in their bag.
>
> They're going to have experience points, different strength and weakness points, whatever the points are, and in fact, a venture capitalist firm is a collection of *D&D* characters rather than a singular thing.
>
> Think about *D&D*, or *Magic the Gathering*, or any other game like that. Each character has a different set of skills, weapons, money, and experience points, and over time develops more. A firm is a combination of different characters—at Foundry Group you might have a mage and a barbarian—and the combination is what you have to pay attention to."

#### *Using This Analogy*

Even if you've never played *D&D* or *Magic*, you can understand three archetypes that are used by most role-playing games: Warrior, Wizard, and Rogue. When approaching a VC partner, you should try to look for signs of the archetype they most resemble. Pay attention to what they say and how they say it.

- Do they talk about overall market growth, or mentoring entrepreneurs, or act like a wizened old man or woman who has insights they can share with you? If so, they may be the Wizard (or Mage or Sorcerer) archetype.
- Do they talk about crushing your opponents and focus on the battle aspect of the market and how you will win and win big? Do they use rough language and talk about "kicking ass?" If so, they may be the Warrior (or Barbarian) archetype.
- Do they talk about being stealthy and leaving others behind through features and strategies? Do they focus on how you can use partnerships and other clever tactics to get beyond the competition? If so, they might be the Rogue (thief) archetype.

# Myth #7

# Take the Highest Valuation You Can Get

Let's say you're successful in raising money from professional investors. In fact, let's suppose you are successful in getting multiple term sheets from multiple VC funds or angel funds. Which one should you go with?

## It's Obvious—Or Is It?

The conventional wisdom is that you should take the highest valuation you can get. After all, that will allow you to retain as much of the company as possible. Let's consider a real-life example.

Suppose investor A offers $2 million at an $8 million pre-money valuation. This means the post-money valuation (valuation of the company after the money is in the bank) would theoretically be $10 million ($8 million pre-money valuation plus $2 million put into the company equals the post-money valuation). In this case, since the investors put in $2 million, they would own one-fifth of the company, or 20 percent (or $2 million out of the post-money valuation of $10 million), while you (founders, employees, and any existing shareholders etc.) would own the remaining 80 percent of the company (or $8 million out of the $10 million post-money valuation).

On the other hand, suppose investor B offers a pre-money valuation of $4 million. This means that the post-money valuation would be $6 million, and investors would own $2 million out of $6 million, so they would own about a third, or 33 percent. In this case, you (founders, employees, etc.) would own only 66 percent of the company (or $4 million out of $6 million).

Obviously, looking at these two scenarios, it would be better to take the first scenario (investor A) because the founders would end up owning more of the company (80 percent vs. 66 percent) and the investors end up owning less (20 percent vs. 33 percent).

Or would it?

The correct answer is *maybe*. There is a lot of complexity that resides under the valuation number. So, the correct answer is really that *it depends*.

Let's add a third scenario to the mix. Suppose there was another investor, C Corp, a strategic investor (a company that wants to invest in you and do business with you—say, a distributor of your product in China). What if this strategic investor wanted to help you grow your business, and could pretty much guarantee you another $1 million in sales in China next year, and wanted to invest $1 million in your business today, but was only willing to do it at the $4 million pre-money valuation, not at the $8 million pre-money valuation?

Suppose also that the strategic investor wanted common stock instead of preferred stock, and didn't care about control provisions like the ability to veto a sale or to have right of first offer or refusal on future financings.

This is where the conventional wisdom gets really murky. While it might still seem obvious to some that the $8 million valuation (investor A) is the way to go, the reality is that the choice is no longer as obvious.

To determine which financing option is best, we will have to delve into the real meaning of a *valuation* (which most first-time entrepreneurs think of in the wrong way). We have to look at how a valuation sets expectations for the company, and how it affects what you can and cannot do down the road.

## What's In a Valuation, Really?

In my twenty-five years in startups, I've learned that entrepreneurs usually have the wrong impression about what a valuation really *means* in a private, early stage company.

In a public company, if you buy stock for $10 and the company has fifty million shares outstanding, then you can reasonably say what the company is worth today on the open market. In this case, it has a valuation of $500 million. If you own one share of stock you can reasonably expect to sell it for $10 (assuming it is liquid enough—that is, that it's not a pink-sheet public company, but a real company listed on a reputable exchange like the NASDAQ or the NYSE).

But let's look at a scenario in which a VC gives your company a $10 million pre-money valuation, and there are ten million shares outstanding. This results in a price per share of $1. Let's suppose that you and two cofounders own three million shares each. Does this mean that you can sell your three million shares for $1 each? Does it really mean that your founder's stock is worth $3 million? I call this public stock analogy #1. And most entrepreneurs think it's roughly true, at least the first time they raise a venture round.

I remember the first time I raised institutional funding—it was at a $5 million pre-money valuation. I remember thinking: Wow, on paper we're millionaires! This was because my cofounder and I owned roughly 40 percent of the company each!

The short answer to public stock analogy #1 is: No, it doesn't mean that you're a millionaire at all, even on paper, let alone *in reality*.

For one thing, investors buy preferred stock, and you and I, as founders, usually have common stock. Preferred stock has preference if the company goes under, so that stock is worth considerably more than common stock. Companies are required to get a 409(a) valuation after a financing event. This is used by the board of directors to set the strike price of options that will be issued to employees. This strike price must be, by law, the same as the "fair market value" of the common stock. If you look at 409(a) valuations of private venture backed startups, you'll see that the "fair market value" of common stock can be as low as one-tenth to one-third of the value of the preferred stock. We'll explore the difference between common and preferred further in "Stage 5: Acquiring the Treasure: Myths About Exiting Your Company."

A second important point to remember is that most startups are illiquid, so you can't really sell your shares—so are they really worth what you think they are worth? As companies mature and march toward an IPO, you can do what's called a secondary sale of your own shares—we'll discuss this further in Stage 5 as well—but this almost never happens after the first venture financing.

There's more. More important than either of the previous considerations is that a valuation set by VCs *is really a set of expectations.*

This is why an experienced team (even with no traction) is likely to get a higher valuation than a new, unproven team, which has only a little bit of traction. The expectation is that the experienced team will do better in the long term, leading to a higher valuation on an exit (sale or IPO) than an inexperienced team, hopefully in a shorter amount of time. Whether or not this expectation is borne out by data is not really known, but certainly this is the expectation.

## Expectations Run Both Ways

I try to make this point to entrepreneurs all the time, and it almost always falls on deaf ears: *A valuation is really a set of expectations.*

An expectation is a bar that you will have to jump over in your next round, and there can be pretty serious consequences if you don't jump over the bar.

What happens to the stock price of shares of a public company if it doesn't meet its earnings expectations? Usually, the price of the stock falls. Let's call this public stock analogy #2.

Let's look at what happens if you have raised money for a private startup (we'll call it Sil.ly), which has yet to finish its product (and thus has no customers), and raises money at a $5 million valuation.

Suppose, a year later, Sil.ly has not only a finished product, but has two customers that are live and paying for the product!

Is Sil.ly worth more now than it was in the previous year?

Almost all entrepreneurs (particularly the founders of Sil.ly) will say: "Yes, we are obviously worth more now. Last year, we had no product and no customers. If we were worth only $5 million last year, I'd say we're worth at least $7 million now, maybe even $10 million!"

That's a typical response, but like much conventional wisdom in Startup Land, it's also wrong. The entrepreneur is still thinking of the valuation as being an absolute number, or even a relative number; in this case, the new valuation is relative to last year's financing.

What's missing from this equation is the question of *expectations.* If the company got a $5 million valuation with no customers and a half-built product, this comes with a set of expectations. Perhaps the expectation is that the company will finish its product and get its first few customers by the end of the year.

But if the startup is in a super-hot space, the expectations might be higher; say, that it gets millions of downloads or millions of dollars in revenue by the next year. A company with these expectations might be valued even higher, say, at $10 million.

But, in our example, if a year later the product still isn't "done" and there are *only* one or two customers, this could end up being a big failure from the point of view of the investors.

In this case, expectations were not met.

In this scenario, it might be reasonable for investors to demand a *lower valuation*, in what's called a *down round*, which can be troublesome because it brings up all kinds of unpleasantness. Once your company is seen as an underperformer, there are questions raised about why the investors should invest in your next round at all, which could lead to your startup shutting down.

There are also all kinds of antidilution provisions that may come into play when you do a down round. A down round is when you get new financing that is at a lower price per share than in the previous round. In Startup Land, a down round can also have a kind of stigma, which is why even existing investors don't like to do down rounds if they can avoid it.

## Startup Model #4: The Pie Versus the High Bar

This brings us to our first "mental model," which is a way to think about an important aspect of your startup journey. This model contrasts two different ways of thinking about valuation, as shown in figure 7.1. The first is the one we are all familiar with:

- *The Pie Model.* In this model, the financing is seen as giving up a piece of the pie to investors, and entrepreneurs are concerned with how much of the pie is left for them and how much of the pie goes to the investors.
- *The High-Bar Model.* In this model, which we'll explore in more detail, a valuation (and associated size of the round) is setting up a bar that the company will have to "jump over" in the next round to be considered a "success."

The pie model is pretty prevalent; but the high bar is not.

Figure 7.1
Two Ways to Think About Valuation—Pie vs. High-Jump Bar. Pie created by the author, high-jump bar used under license from iDraw/Shutterstock.com

If I had a bar that I want you to jump over, and I asked you how high I should set it, what would your answer be? Would it be "higher, higher, higher"? Probably not. If you wanted to be sure to jump over the bar, you'd want it to be as *low* as possible.

Well, in some ways, that's what a valuation is when you raise money. It's an *expectation, or a bar, that you have to jump over in order for your stock price to go up.*

## How High Can You Jump?

When you raise money, you are setting up several bars that you have to jump over:

1. ***Next-round valuation.*** As we said earlier, a valuation comes with an expectation of some revenue or customers or progress you will make. The next-round valuation generally should be at least 50 percent higher (and in some cases 100 percent higher) than your post-money. In one of my companies, we got a $14 million post-money valuation in a seed round! We thought this was a great accomplishment because we gave up very little of the startup in the first round, compared to other startups we had seen. But what we didn't consider was that this meant that the next round would have to be at a $20 million to $30 million valuation. But our company had no revenue. Even if we got to $1 million to $2 million in revenue the next year, it's unlikely we would be able to command that kind of valuation without getting to at least $5 million in revenue or millions of users.

What that means is that you may end up with a down round. A down round is something to avoid at all costs in Startup Land. Let's take my example of $14 million seed financing. If you then raise a VC Series A preferred stock at a $7 million valuation (half of the previous round), this will trigger all kinds of antidilution provisions, and the original investors could end up with a much higher percentage than what they would've gotten at the $14 million valuation. Add to that the new investors getting the lower valuation, and suddenly you may find yourself owning less than 50 percent of the company after one down round.

Moreover, with preferences (see next paragraph), you might find yourself and your cofounders with all kinds of other issues. It's best to have a valuation as a bar that you can safely get over and seek a higher valuation in the next round.

2. ***Preferences on Exit.*** The second bar that is implicit in any standard VC financing is the *preference*. Most preferred stock has a 1× preference, while some have 2× or more preference. (We'll explore this in detail in the Bonus Myths included in the online companion to this book.) But if the investors put in $3 million at a $10 million post-money valuation, then you would think they own 30 percent of the company, right? If you sell the company for $5 million, that would mean that the founders get 70 percent of that and the investors get 30 percent of that, right?

Not quite. Preferences mean that the investors get the first *x* times their money back in a sale. So, if the company sells for $3 million, 100 percent of the proceeds go to the preferred shareholders. If the company sells for $5 million, the investor will still get back $3 million, and the remaining $2 million will be split across the common shareholders. That's assuming a 1× preference. If the investors have a 2× preference, with a $3 million investment, they would get back $6 million first. Since the company is only selling for $5 million, that means there's no money left over for the founders or employees.

Simple 1× preferences are pretty common with series A and beyond in Silicon Valley. Some investors, particularly those in New York and elsewhere on the East Coast who do more private equity (or later stage venture capital investing), might insist on a 2× or higher preference. Sometimes investors will insist on certain preferences if you have negotiated too high a valuation and they really want to get in on the deal, but they are unsure if you will make them enough return when you sell the company.

Preferences can be tricky, but they are another type of "bar" that you have to jump over.

3. ***Valuation on Exit.*** Of course, most series A investors have the right to veto a sale, and this is the highest bar to jump. Why would an investor veto a sale? Obviously, if they bought in at a $10 million valuation and you want to sell the company for $5 million, they might not like that and might veto it. But the bigger issue is when you want to sell the company for some multiple that is appealing to the founders but not to the investors. Suppose you want to sell for $20 million—investors would get a 2× return, right? Most VCs would be unhappy with this outcome, which is baffling to first-time entrepreneurs.

Let's explore why.

## VCs Need Bigger Multiples on Exits

What if you want to sell your company for $10 million? Suppose it's your first company and you and a partner each own 50 percent of it. That would make both of you millionaires, worth $5 million each. However, if you had raised money from investors at $10 million post-money valuation, they would probably be against your selling the company. They would be just breaking even, and VCs in particular don't invest in companies to break even.

In fact, when you and a VC negotiate a valuation, the logic on the investor side goes like this: "Hmm . . . if I invest at $5 million valuation, how confident am I that this team will be able to build this company up to at least $50 million valuation in a few years? How likely is it that the company will be sold for $100 million, or go public for a billion dollars?"

Since most VC-backed companies fail, even a 10× return is not really good enough anymore. For the one or two big winners in a fund, a 10× return is usually only enough to pay back the fund, which really means no return at all for the VC partners themselves. To please their investors, their winners usually have to have 20× or more return.

Remember, a VC fund is in some ways not that different from a startup. They have investors too, and those investors have expectations and, you guessed it, preference. A partner in a VC fund is constantly thinking about his own expectations, where the fund is in its cycle, and how much money it is likely to return to its investors, who are called limited partners.

Randy Komisar says, "When you think about it, I'm in the failure business . . . I think it's 90 percent of all startups that fail. In the venture capital business, probably 50 percent of all the venture-backed businesses fail, and of the other fifty, probably 10 percent, maybe 15 percent, are the real big winners, and the rest are very middling."

This means that VC firms rely entirely on 10 to 15 percent of their investments to make up for their entire fund!

## Valuations Can Limit Your Exit

One of our experts, Jud Valeski, started Gnip in 2008 and had gone through the first two rounds of financing before business really started to take off. From 2010 onward, Gnip was seeing lots of interest from enterprise customers and from social networks.

Given how hot the company was, they had ample opportunity to raise money at very high valuations—$100 million or more. They had raised only $7.5 million to date, and their last round was at significantly less than the $100 million they were being offered. They decided not to take the money.

Jud says:

> A year or so after that is when the business started to fire on all pistons, and growth took off like a rocket. Revenue took off like a rocket.

If you look at the evolution of social networks, this would have been around 2011 or 2012, social network use was exploding around the world. Around that time everything looked like wow, if there's a commercial opportunity in social networking, our company is it!

We had tons of inbound calls from A, B, and C tier venture capital and private equity firms trying to say, 'Hey, we're here if you need us; hey, we'd like to talk to you about doing another round; hey, things are probably going pretty well, how do we get in on this and help you grow more, blah, blah, blah'.

Yeah, the pressure was really there from one of our Silicon Valley–based investors who was caught up, as I would characterize it, in a lot of the Bay Area fervor around our market.

It was clear that what was happening . . . caution was just thrown to the wind with respective valuation. We were advised to do a round at $100 million, $120 million post-money, which we could have done."

Jud concludes by saying that you have to be careful about the fervor that occurs in Startup Land when you're in a hot market and things are going well, because you could end up taking too high a valuation, then limiting your exit options. He added that one of his competitors had raised $75 million, which must have been at a very high valuation, and this limited the ability of other companies to buy them.

Because they hadn't taken too high a valuation in financing, selling Gnip for a good exit was not that difficult, given how quickly they were growing and how their revenue and profits were ramping up.

Jud sold Gnip to Twitter in 2014 for roughly $175 million. But if Gnip had taken money at a valuation higher than $100 million from professional investors, it is possible that the Twitter deal might not have been attractive to the new investors. This was a case where understanding how investors think may have led Gnip *to not raise money at too high a valuation*, which ended up being a good thing!

## Another Example: Think Like a VC

I was involved with a startup that had raised a seed round from a small VC at approximately a $4 million post-money valuation. A year later, the company was growing rapidly, and we had an offer to be bought for a valuation that was around $16 million (I say around, because it included some stock and earnout, so it was hard to say the exact number). Still, this exit would have given the investors a 4× return on their investment in one year, and would have made the founders multimillionaires.

The founders wanted to sell the company. They figured a 4× return in one year would be great for their investors. (A 400 percent return on investment in one year?? Any investor would be happy to have that, right?)

In fact, a 4× return is not a very good return for most venture investors, though it would be fine for most angel investors and even for most corporate/strategic investors. Of course, it also depends a bit on how much money we're talking about. If the investor had put in $1 million in this scenario, he might have gotten back $4 million.

But if his fund had $50 million in it, then getting back $4 million doesn't do much for the VC fund's overall return. For a $50 million fund to return two times its money, it would need to have made $100 million!

This means that the 10 to 15 percent of companies that were the "successes" in the fund would need to return that $50 million to $100 million to make the fund successful. Since this startup was one of the potential "winners" in their fund, the VCs didn't want to sell for "only" 4× return on their initial small investment and make "only $4 million."

The VC would rather have put more money into the company and then shoot for a 10+ to 20+ times return.

The founders, on the other hand, would have been pretty happy with this outcome, because they owned enough of the company to become multimillionaires.

It's important to note there is no right answer here. The right answer, as before, is, *it depends*.

It's possible that the founders and the VC could have made much more money by not selling so early; it's also possible that they may have held on too long, since this was a volatile market that changed every year or two. We'll talk more about whether to sell a company "early" in "Stage 5: Acquiring the Treasure: Myths About Exiting Your Company."

In this particular case, the founders and the VC got into a huge argument—their expectations were mismatched. In the end, a compromise was reached, and the company was sold, but it wasn't a very pleasant experience.

## The Secret

***Think of valuation not as the worth of your stock, but as a bar that you have to jump over. You don't want it too low (because you will give up more of the company) but you don't want it too high either (because you may face a down round or limits on exiting!).***

The real meaning of a pre-money valuation has little to do with the current "worth" of the company. It's really an expectation of how big you can grow the company over time.

While most entrepreneurs think only in terms of how much of the company they're giving up, it's useful to think like an investor and see how high you want to set the bar. You also have to think in terms of a stock price—it can be sky high or it can be low—and each has its benefits and pitfalls. It's possible that you won't be able to meet sky-high expectations. It is my experience that startups rarely meet expectations. Sometimes, things go better than expected in a shorter period of time (the "rocket ship"), but more often, things (customers, revenue, traction) take much longer than expected.

There are many ways in which a higher valuation isn't always better than a lower valuation—it can limit your options on an exit, it can create a bar that is too high for you to jump over, it can lead to a down round, and perhaps even stigmatize you as a company that has "failed" just as it's finding its way.

The most important thing is to find investors whose expectations are aligned with your own in terms of running the company and raising more money, as well as the type and scale of exit you are looking for!

### It's Not Just About the Money

While this myth was about valuation, there are other noneconomic factors that you need to consider when deciding which investors to move forward with. Here are just a few of these factors:

1. the reputation of the investors
2. day to day control
3. composition of the board
4. helping with the business

This is why it's important to understand your investor's nonfinancial expectations. In the same way that you would be wise to know your cofounders' motivations, it's also important to understand your investor's motivations, and to go with investors whose motivations are more closely aligned with your own.

Alex Haro, cofounder of Life360, a super successful mobile app for families to keep track of each other, says that entrepreneurs tend to look for high valuations because they are too afraid of dilution. Alex emphasizes that the most important goal when evaluating investors is whether you want them on your board of directors or not. Echoing what some of our VC experts emphasize, make sure that the partner who's going to be on your board is someone who will add value. Not only is every VC firm different, but as we saw in the last myth's sidebar, individual partners inside the VC firm are very different.

This value may come from a strategic investor (a corporate investor) who wants to do a deal with your company. Life360 did many such deals, with companies ranging from BMW to ADT (the security company), which helped them grow.

Alex concludes, "All of our board members are awesome; really building a strong board is important. If you can get that out of a strategic [partnership] like we've been able to, that's super awesome, but I think first and foremost, a lot of the value that an investor brings should be at the board level. If you're not excited to work with them, if you're not excited for them to be a partner . . . I think it's a huge mistake to pick them just because they gave you the right valuation or because you assume that you're just going throw them to the side and use their money."

# Bonus Myth #B-2

## Raise as Little (as Much) Money as Possible

---

*"Entrepreneurs are way too obsessed about dilution, or their slice of the pie. They should be focused more on growing the size of the pie."*

—ALEX HARO, COFOUNDER OF LIFE360

---

This myth gets into the issue of how much (if any) external financing you should raise, and when. It also reflects on who *controls* the company, an issue near and dear to the hearts of many entrepreneurs.

This myth exists in many variations, all centering on two of the themes of this chapter: control and dilution. The first version of the myth might be stated in different ways, with the same underlying belief:

- If you do raise money, you should raise as little money as possible, because you'll give up less of the company now (the *dilution argument)*.
- You should minimize the amount of outside financing you raise because the investors will take control and will kick out the founders, bringing in outside management (the *control argument*).
- Rather than taking more money now, the valuation of the company will grow in the future, so you can raise more money later and give up less of the company now (the *delayed dilution argument*).

This myth is part of our first set of dueling myths. The opposite myth is that you should always raise *as much* money as possible, rather than the least amount possible. Why? The underlying beliefs represented in this version of the myth are all about *risk* (and as a result, *dilution* and *control* in the future).

▶ To read the full text of this **Bonus Myth**, including the idea of not raising any money or raising as much money as possible, and the sidebar, Gandalf vs. Saruman, please download the Supplement to *Startup Myths and Models* from www.zenentrepreneur.com ◀

# Stage 3

## Travel Companions

## *Myths About Hiring and Management*

---

During the hero's trials, he may find help in the form of allies. It can be one of the hero's tests to find out who can be trusted in this new world.

JUSTUS R. STONE

---

### Introduction to Stage 3

In mythological journeys, the choice of companions is usually a key factor which determines whether the adventure is successful or not. These companions are not just those who start on the journey but also those who join along the way.

In *The Lord of the Rings*, for example, the plan was for Frodo and Sam to leave the Shire and meet Gandalf. But in a series of events, both Merry and Pippin join Frodo and Sam (while Gandalf is nowhere to be found). This choice of companions has great implications for the adventure down the road. The group is hesitant to take on Strider (Aragorn), but his joining the adventure ends up being among the most important choices the company makes. In Rivendell, they pick up additional companions, some of whom are meant to be with them for only part of the journey, while others join the adventure to the end.

## *Overview of the Myths*

A startup journey, while different from mythological journeys, brings with it similar challenges. Sometimes, the people we start the journey with (our cofounders) aren't the ones who end up being the most valuable down the road. The choice of how to build the management team, particularly in the early days of the company, is critical. Moreover, the MVPs of the startup journey may end up being companions who arrive later on.

This stage is about the hiring and firing of startup employees, including management team members. The myths presented here kick in once you have to hire more than one or two people. For most entrepreneurs, hiring is an area where mistakes are made early and often, though not necessarily by choice. Moreover, successfully building a company is not just about hiring and firing, but about how to manage employees who may have different strengths and weaknesses. Finally, several of our experts point out that the types of people that make successful employees and managers needs to change as the company grows.

In the Hero's Journey, Joseph Campbell lays out eight different archetypes that appear in many different mythological adventures. While some of these archetypes best represent investors and advisors ("threshold guardian" and "mentor" archetypes), a number of the most important archetypes manifest as employees during the entrepreneurial journey. The "ally" is the archetype that is most often associated with cofounders, but could easily be someone that is brought on as a very early trustworthy employee who becomes the CEO's confidant. For example, Steve Ballmer at Microsoft or Sheryl Sandberg at Facebook are early employees who were technically not founders but played an outsized role in the journey of the startup itself. On the other hand, the "trickster" archetype is one that provides humor and unexpected stops along the journey, and sometimes our employees serve this role. Perhaps one of the most difficult and common archetypes is the "shapeshifter," someone who seems like they are there to help the founders on the journey but end up having their own agenda. In a typical adventure they might end up being servants of the enemy, but in a startup journey, they are most often someone who the founders start to trust, but whose own agenda ends up causing incredible turmoil for the startup. The mapping between an archetype and a management team member or employee is not necessarily a one-for-one mapping—any companion may have elements of multiple archetypes.

Any hero or heroine learns very quickly that the companions on the journey, mythological or entrepreneurial, often end up having a direct impact on whether the journey is successful or not. By the end of the startup adventure, most first-time entrepreneurs are usually much wiser about hiring and firing based on mistakes and actual experience with people. By understanding the secrets behind the myths in this chapter, you don't have to make those same mistakes on your entrepreneurial journey.

# Myth #8

## Hire the Most Experienced People You Can Find

*"Let's have no more argument. I have chosen Mr. Baggins . . . If I say he is a Burglar, a Burglar he is . . . or will be when the time comes!"*

—GANDALF

In *The Hobbit*, the prequel to *The Lord of the Rings*, the dwarves need an extra traveling companion, and they turn to a wise old mentor (as many entrepreneurs do), in the form of the wizard Gandalf. When Gandalf first chooses Mr. Bilbo Baggins as their burglar, it appears to the rest of the team that the old wizard has made a big mistake—Bilbo has never burgled anything in his life!

But Gandalf saw something in the inexperienced hobbit that no one else saw—by the time the party reached the Lonely Mountain and had to face the dragon, Bilbo had not only become very good at his appointed task, but had gained the trust and respect of his fellow adventurers, having saved them time and again from danger.

In the early days of a startup, when there isn't much money available, this kind of thing almost always happens: you hire someone who doesn't have any experience, but who is smart, eager, and quick to learn. This person ends up being one of your most valued employees in the early days, someone I would call an MVP (most valuable player).

As the company grows, there is usually more of an emphasis on hiring both the "most experienced" and the "best" people you can find, which is the common wisdom that leads to this myth.

In a startup, hiring the wrong person for a key position can be disastrous. In a place like Silicon Valley, where talent is hard to come by, you could lose not only the months it takes to find out that the employee is not the right person, but also the many months to find a replacement. Moreover, it is possible that hiring the wrong person and not realizing it soon enough can lead to disaster—for the product or the customer base of a startup.

## The Area of Natural Weakness

This is particularly true in what I call the area of "natural weakness" of the company.

Most startup teams have a natural weakness—an area of the startup where the founders aren't very comfortable, because they have limited experience. As a result, they end up hiring the wrong person, sometimes repeatedly, resulting in a "revolving door" position. In fact, the existence of a revolving door position is a pretty good indication that this is the area of natural weakness for the founders.

If the founders come from a technical/engineering background, the area of natural weakness is usually in sales and marketing. If the founders come from a sales and/or marketing background, then the area of natural weakness tends to be the engineering side. Sometimes the area of weakness is in product management, which can be an area of weakness for either engineering or sales/marketing-oriented founders.

The lead position in the area of weakness is often the hardest to fill in a startup—and it's usually either the lead technical person (CTO or VP of engineering) or the lead sales/marketing person (VP of sales, VP of marketing), or the lead product person (VP of product). Filling this position with the right person can make the startup. Filling it with the wrong person (repeatedly) can break the startup.

## When Too Much Experience Gets in the Way

Conventional wisdom is that you should hire the most experienced person you can find (and afford) for a position. But as we've seen with the Startup Myths, conventional wisdom can often get you into a lot of trouble!

First time (and even second and third time) startup teams are often impressed by people who have *big* names on their resume. This could be a candidate who has worked for a big, well-known company (like Google or Oracle or Microsoft), or who may even have worked for a well-publicized startup that grew really fast.

The founders, impressed by these credentials, hire the person as their VP of sales or VP of engineering, and expect it all to work out. But, taking a key leadership role in an early stage startup, especially when it's in the area of natural weakness for the founders, is like agreeing to do a tightwire act between two skyscrapers without a safety net. And people who work for big companies are used to having plenty of safety net (although they may not admit it).

Sometimes it becomes clear very quickly that the new hire, armed with tons of experience at a big company, isn't the right person for a dynamic, rapidly moving startup. This could be because the candidate is used to having more support at a bigger company, or isn't flexible enough to adapt their tactics or strategy to what's needed at the startup in its current stage.

When this happens, it often takes first-time entrepreneurs some time before they let the person go. Logically speaking, the person they hired has the resume that *should allow them to be successful* at that position. Because the employee has so much experience, the founders hesitate to let them go right away, until things reach a head and then the founders end up firing the employee on the spot after many months of frustration on both sides. This then leads them to hire the next sales lead (or tech lead or product lead), and the revolving door has started.

Alex Haro of Life360 told me during our interview, "I think people put off firing for far too long. Every time I've fired someone, I've told myself, 'I need to do this even sooner next time.' Every single time!"

Alex isn't alone—almost every entrepreneur I interviewed regrets not firing some people sooner. They almost always admit they had an intuition that this person wasn't working out, but they didn't act on that feeling early enough for so-called logical reasons. At the top of these reasons is "experience."

## Startup Model #5: The Four Quadrants of Hiring

One way to avoid these conventional mistakes is to think about hiring and firing using the "Four Quadrants of Hiring."

I was first exposed to this model by one of my mentors early in my startup career. The more hiring and firing I did, the more I realized how important the principle behind these four quadrants was.

Now I make sure that the founders of every startup I work with really understand these quadrants and make a conscious effort to evaluate where new hires (and even existing employees) fit in to this model.

As with many such models, we have two axes, which intersect to form four quadrants. The two axes in this case are:

1. ***Experience/Competence.*** This axis is a straightforward assessment of how well the person's experience (for new hires) or competence (for an existing hire) matches the job. For a programmer, it might mean that they have programmed in similar languages in the past, or have built similar types of applications. For a product manager, it might mean the size, scale, or nature of products they have managed before. Usually a person's *experience* will come through on a resume, but *competence* can be tougher to measure during the hiring process—the only way to reliably measure it is by looking at the work they have done for you after you have hired them. So think of this axis as "experience" for a new hire and "competence" for an existing employee.

For a new hire, a "low" experience level would mean that they haven't done the work before, and "high" experience level means they have had the exact same job at some well-known company before.

For existing employees, a "high" technical competence means they know how to do their specific job very well (for example, they know how to build stuff in the current programming language well). A "low" competence means they are not doing the job very well, as assessed by an expert that you trust. In an area of natural strength, the founders are usually good enough to assess competence. When I was CEO of my first startup, my cofounder and I wrote much of the original code—so it was easy for us to assess whether a new developer was a good coder or not. For sales and marketing, we weren't as experienced and it was a bit harder for us, though with sales there is a clear metric that is quantifiable (how much they sold during a period of time).

2. ***Cultural Fit.*** The second axis is a little more subjective, but has to do with how well a person matches the culture of your startup. Every startup has a culture, whether the founding team is conscious of it or not. This cultural fit includes (but is not limited to), working style, communications style, work schedule, and more important, how success is measured on a task or a project.

For example, in terms of working hours, some startups consist of people with families, who like to start early and go home early. Some startups consist of a lot of people who are online at midnight on Skype talking to each other while working from home. Some startups like to go to dinner together at 7 P.M. (or order pizza in). Some startups have no problems with people working at home one or two days a week, while others have a big problem with it.

However, more important than these "soft" cultural factors is "working style." Some people need to spend time planning a solution before they jump in. Others like to jump right in and then come up with a plan after they have gotten their hands dirty. Some like structure and schedules, others are comfortable working with fuzzy specifications and changing priorities from week to week (or day to day). You may hire someone who's great at following a particular methodology, but your startup may not be using that methodology. This leads to low cultural fit as they insist that this particular methodology should be used. Another sign that someone may not be a good cultural fit is that if you need them to jump on a new problem, but they are hesitant to do so because they want to work on the same thing they've been doing all along. Adaptability is, in my experience, one of the major ways to assess cultural fit. The other major one is often communications style. Sometimes in a startup, the cultural fit is to cc: everyone so that everyone is aware of the status and challenges of a particular task. In other startups, it's exactly the opposite—you want to only communicate with your immediate superior. In a startup, reporting structure is also often fuzzy in the beginning. Though technically a VP of Sales might report to the CEO, if there are two founders, it's very likely that the VP of Sales has to answer to both of them, because they are both on the board of directors.

Now that we have the two axes, you'll see that they make four quadrants, which I have numbered clockwise from the lower left as #1 and ending with #4 on the lower right.

As a general rule, I have found that entrepreneurs (especially first-timers) place much more emphasis on axis #1 (experience/competence) than on axis #2 (cultural fit). The context of the Four Quadrants will show why this may be a mistake.

As with all Four Quadrant models, two of the quadrants are simple and two are, well, more complicated. Let's start with the two easy ones:

- *Quadrant #1:* **Low Cultural Fit/ Low Experience or Competence.** This is one of the easiest quadrants to base decisions on. If a person fits into

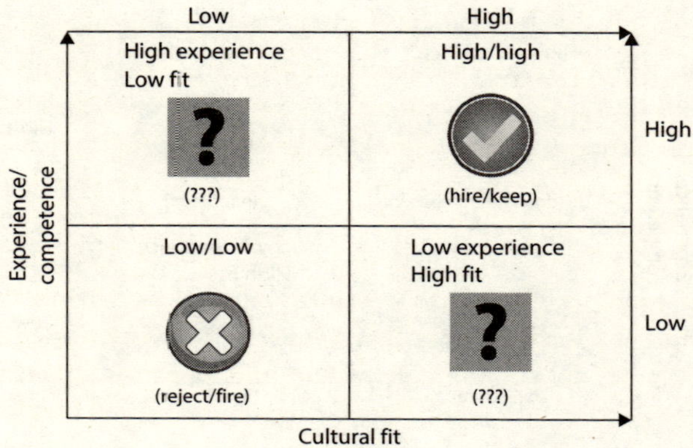


Figure 8.1
The Four Quadrants of Hiring. Created by the author

this quadrant, they aren't a good fit for the job and they aren't a good fit for your startup. It's pretty obvious what you need to do: don't hire them. You will see many candidates during the hiring process who fit into this quadrant. You may also find many people who fit into this quadrant after you have hired them and watched them work. It's pretty obvious what to do here too—you probably have to let them go—and you can't wait too long or your startup will run into problems!

• *Quadrant #3*: **High Cultural Fit/ High Experience or Competence.** It is easy to decide to hire someone who fits in this quadrant, but that someone is hard to find. If you do find someone that matches the culture of your company and has a high degree of experience in the job/tasks required, then definitely hire them! And if an existing employee is fitting into this quadrant and has shown they are competent and a good cultural fit, it'll also be pretty obvious what to do—try to keep them and make them happy!

The real trick is to recognize people who fit into the last two quadrants (#2 and #4) and to make the right decisions quickly. These last two quadrants include people who cause turmoil in startups, and conversely, these quadrants are where you might find the "hidden gems."

Most of the bad hiring (and firing) decisions come from not identifying which quadrant a candidate or employee fits into quickly enough.

Let's look at the two quadrants that usually lead to trouble.

• *Quadrant #2:* **High Experience/ Low Cultural Fit**. Unfortunately, I find that many new startup hires fit into this quadrant, and this is the source of this

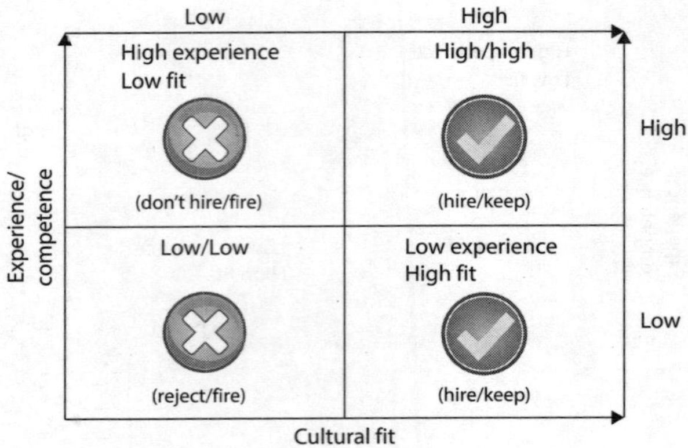


Figure 8.2
Conclusions for employees in the Four Quadrants of Hiring. Created by the author

myth. Among existing employees, this may be someone with high technical competency, but whose working style causes problems for the rest of the team. Again, cultural fit can be defined in many different ways. The tendency is to hire someone with a big resume, whether or not they "fit in" to the way you want to build your startup. Why? Because they have the experience and *should know* how to get the job done.

- *Quadrant #4:* **Low Experience/ High Cultural Fit.** This quadrant includes people who fit well into your company, but who may not be the most experienced programmer/salesperson on the team. "Fitting well" isn't just about getting along with everyone and liking to go to lunch. Rather, this kind of employee jumps in enthusiastically to learn new job responsibilities; they solve problems for customers; and they stay late to figure out the solution to a pressing problem rather than passing responsibility onto the next guy. Their main drawback in the early days is that they don't seem to have the many years of experience doing X that another candidate might have.

So, what do you do with individuals in these two quadrants?

The action to take depends on whether you are hiring a new employee or are evaluating an existing employee. The bottom line is that you should try to let go quickly (or not hire) employees who may have high experience but low cultural fit, and you should hang on to (or give a chance to) employees who may not have exactly the experience you need, but who fit your startup's culture well.

### Too Much Experience Can Lead to Inflexibility

I once hired a guy from a big game company to be our lead programmer. He was very experienced (and presumably) competent. He said that he was fed up with big companies and wanted to be in a smaller, more creative, less structured environment (which, by the way, they all say when interviewing for a startup!).

After a few months of working for us and seeing just how "unstructured" our environment was, he decided that he wanted to go back to his former employer—they had given him "some structure" around the tasks he was working on and how he would be measured. We had no such structure in our company—we just expected him to take charge and "get whatever shit done that was needed" in our product. He wanted to spend all his time building tools that made the development process easier (rather than actually writing code for our games). In a bigger game company, this can be an option, but in a small game company, you can't have developers who aren't writing a big chunk of code for your games.

Sometimes, an employee who is really competent or has a lot of experience becomes inflexible in what they know and how they do things. One startup founder told me that he wanted his tech lead to work on a new project but she refused, saying she was going to work only on the first project which she was hired for, or she would quit. This was an employee with high experience but low cultural fit.

He felt stuck between a rock and a hard place. This can be disastrous for a startup, not just because of the impact on the individual employee. It can end up degrading the overall culture of the startup, poisoning it in ways that are not healthy.

### When the Mix Isn't Right

Another aspect to think about when hiring is not just the cultural fit or experience/competency of a single employee. You are building a team, and simply hiring people who are good at *x* and *y* but who won't work together well can be just as problematic.

Jud Valeski, reflecting on his early years at Gnip, says

Early on it was "we're only hiring the best, most experienced people, period." After a year and a half of doing that, it was a mess.

"Too many head chefs in the kitchen is a problem. You need sous chefs, you need prep, that's true. I learned that the hard way. We let nearly half the company go after about a year and a half, and that was in large part due to a lot of the dynamics that showed up there."

## The Secret

***Getting people who are a good "cultural fit" is more important than getting the "most experienced" or "best" people in a startup.***

Startups move at a different pace than big companies. Sometimes, they even need to turn on a dime, and people need to be able to pick up completely new skills or enter into a new market.

Some of the best employees I've had in startups didn't have much experience when we hired them, but they constantly applied themselves, took initiative, and often expanded into areas that were not originally part of their job responsibilities. Some of the worst employees I've had in startups had a lot of experience, but only wanted to deal with their particular "area of responsibility" and rarely worked well with the rest of the team.

By using the Four Quadrants of Hiring as a mental model to think about hiring and firing, you can make decisions much more quickly and find the right "mix" for your company.

### Alex Haro on Startup Employees, from Generalist to Specialist

Another factor to consider when hiring is that just as startups evolve and grow, so do the tasks that the individual positions encompass. So, you may have started with one person doing both QA and support, but over time you have to hire dedicated reps for each.

Alex Haro describes it well. He grew Life360 from a small company to one with hundreds of millions of downloads:

> Up to twenty-five people, you're just hacking at it and trying to get product market fit, and everyone can do everything because there's so much to do it doesn't matter. It's easy enough to keep all the trains moving in the same direction.

Once you pass twenty-five and you get closer to fifty, people have to become a lot more specialized. You've got much more acute problems, and you can start trending way away from the jack-of-all-trades to the people that are experts at what they do, and can help you fix the problems that you need to fix, and can scale predictably to hundreds of employees. The problem is, the jack-of-all-trades and the people that can help you scale from fifty to a hundred or to a thousand, even, are usually not the same people.

This can lead to awkward situations, where people that were instrumental in the early stage of the startup don't work so well as the startup grows. It can seem like disloyalty to let them go. I have seen this phenomenon in almost every single one of my startups as they grew. Usually, as founders, you try to find places for these early employees, the "jack-of-all-trades" to fit in. Sometimes it works great. Other times, it doesn't and you have to let the early employee go—which might be a mutual decision or might be a very difficult one that you have to make.

Each time I did that it was heart-wrenching, it sucked, I lost sleep, I still feel bad about it, but it was the best thing for the company and I was instantly relieved. And two weeks later things were much, much better because it was the right decision for the company.

# Myth #9

## Get Out of the Way and Let People Do Their Jobs, *or* I Can Do It Faster Myself!

This myth concerns the natural progression of entrepreneurs from individual doers (programmers, salespersons) into managers, and then, as the company grows, to managers of managers.

These two dueling myths, "Get out of the way and let people do their jobs," and its opposite, "I can do it faster myself," represent two extreme ways of managing with direct reports. Not only are these bits of common wisdom often tossed around in Startup Land, they reveal very different ways of thinking about management on the part of the founders/entrepreneurs.

Suppose you started the company by writing the code and you consider yourself a very good coder. How well will you do as a manager of other programmers? Or, if you're a founder who sold the initial product to the company's first few customers, how well will you manage the transition to managing salespeople—or managing regional managers of salespeople?

Before Randy Komisar became a venture capitalist, he was a "virtual CEO," and one of his specialties was mentoring entrepreneurs to become better managers.

Randy says, "Once you have a team, the biggest challenges are 1) how you hold your team accountable once you put them into place; 2) how you judge them; 3) how you communicate expectations; 4) how you regularly communicate your vision to them; and 5) how you assess their performance at those things."

In essence, this is the day-to-day task of management in any company, whether it's a startup or not. Randy also points out that most people, not just entrepreneurs, struggle as managers, particularly in setting expectations and then holding their direct reports accountable. On the other hand, I have found that entrepreneurs often are inexperienced managers, and they expect their direct reports to understand their expectations, often getting angry or frustrated when those expectations aren't met.

## A Myth Eating Its Own Tail

It turns out that these two dueling myths represent a continuum. Most founders end up falling too far on one end or the other—and become either micromanagers, or, in the other extreme, absent managers. A micromanager is a boss who is around too much and constantly asking for status updates, rather than letting you do your job. An absent manager is someone who is around too little—who doesn't check up on your work enough, and is generally out of touch with what's really going on.

I have found that entrepreneurs tend to become one of these. Why? It turns out that each of these management styles is usually the result of ingrained beliefs about ourselves and our attitudes toward the work of management.

- *Myth #1: I can do it faster myself.* This myth, which in the short term has a kernel of truth, is one that many entrepreneurs believe when they hire people to take over a specific job that they are growing out of. The entrepreneur gets frustrated at how long it's taking someone to finish a task, and the entrepreneur thinks it would be quicker to do it himself or herself, rather than waiting for the employee to get it done. This occurs in the area of "natural strength" for a founder. I have to admit I've been prone to do this in early stages of startups—I will just jump in and write some code rather than letting my employees do it. The problem here is not that the entrepreneurs can't do it faster—usually we can—but it ends up being less effective for the company in the long run because the founder doesn't have time to be a full-time programmer.
- *Myth #2: Get out of the way and let your employees do their jobs.* This opposing myth, which also has a kernel of truth, comes up in many engineering circles. I often heard it among my colleagues at MIT, and it's born

of a usually deep-seated belief that the "real work" is done by engineers and "doers," and that managers are guys who do no real work and then take credit for the work that others do. (A memorable depiction of this belief is in the movie *Office Space*, where the manager just walked up with a coffee cup offering platitudes.)

Let's delve into both of these in more detail and see if we can learn something about being a good manager in a startup environment.

## Why Entrepreneurs Become Micromanagers

There's a story (presumably true, though possibly mythical) about Bill Gates a few years after he started Microsoft. He had instructed his engineers to build a text editor using only 4k of memory. Well, that's a tall task, and when they couldn't do it, he threw up his hands in frustration. No one saw him for the next two days; then he emerged, having written a text editor that used only 4k of memory! This not only showed his engineers "how it's done," but also affirmed his belief that he could get things done "faster" and "better" than the engineers. This happened back in the early 1980s, but the same thing happens today. I have to confess I've done the same thing myself a few times, when a developer wasn't able to get something done that I felt could be done with a little bit of cleverness and effort.

This situation is frustrating for an entrepreneur. On the other hand, the emotional result of "doing it yourself" is that you get to be the "hero"! After all, isn't that what the hero's journey is all about?

But let's look at this story from the employees' point of view. How would you feel if your boss did this? On the one hand, it's great to have a boss who knows what he is doing. This kind of boss can help you. On the other hand, having him dip into your code, or having your boss "showing you up" can be very frustrating.

I'm not saying that there aren't employees who need to be shown now and then *how it's done*. There are. But on the other hand, this isn't exactly a scalable strategy—there is no way Bill Gates could have written all of Microsoft Office or Microsoft Windows by himself while he was CEO of Microsoft, which was a public company at the time! And if he had tried, you'd have thought he was nuts.

So, what's the next best thing to doing it yourself? It's to have it all done "my way." This is what leads to micromanaging every part of the process. The hallmark of a micromanager is wanting it done their way and dictating every aspect of how an employee works.

Now, there are many examples of micromanagers who've accomplished great things, like Steve Jobs, when he created the first Macintosh. He got great things done, but a lot of people who worked for him have revealed that it came at great personal cost to them in their out-of-work life. James Cameron, the director of *Titanic* and *Avatar*, is known for being an unapologetic (and almost neurotic) micromanager during the filming of his movies.

But I would argue that for each example of a micromanager who gets great things done, there are probably tens if not hundreds of examples of micromanagers who haven't accomplished great things; they are just difficult people to work for, and any star employees end up quitting as soon as they can find a better, more healthy environment.

## Undercutting Your Managers is an Example of Micromanaging

For many entrepreneurs, the problem is compounded when they have managers reporting to them who are also managing direct reports. The entrepreneur's sudden disconnection from his workforce can feel strange, and he may resort to micromanaging his managers.

Alex Haro, of Life360, says, "As an individual manager I'm actually not bad. Managing ten direct reports, I was pretty good."

"Then going from ten to even fifty," continues Alex, "I started to have to hire managers to manage the people that were initially my direct reports. The problem that I really messed up is not that I didn't trust my managers, but when they did something that I didn't like, it was too easy for me to step in and try to fix it . . . versus letting them settle it. I really undermined some of my managers because I wasn't trusting them to either succeed or fail on their own."

Alex concludes, "I was stepping in and trying to manage for them. I think the individual engineers appreciated that about me, but the problem was that the manager could never actually successfully set themselves up to be a proper manager and help the company scale and grow."

## The Consequences of Being a Bad Micromanager

The obsessive micromanager is like the rider of the horse in an old Buddhist story. In this story, the rider tries to tell the horse every step it should take to get to a destination. For anyone who's ever ridden a horse (and even if you haven't), it's pretty obvious that this is the wrong way to manage the horse.

Rather, you need to point it in the right direction and give it an indication of the speed you want it to go. If it tries to get off course, you can correct it by pointing it in the direction of the destination again.

Sometimes an entrepreneur becomes a micromanager who also constantly denigrates the work of their employees, again reflecting the myth of "I could do it better myself." This constant criticism and theoretical one-upmanship can lead to real morale problems with employees.

I invested in a company once where the entrepreneur was constantly micromanaging his employees and contractors. Some of them joked about his "abuse"—i.e., harsh statements he would make about their work or their place in the company. He even did this with contractors, some of whom were working for stock and had agreed not to get paid until the company had more funds. There's nothing more frustrating than doing someone a favor, and having them treat you with disrespect.

When I noticed this entrepreneur denigrating his employee the first time, I took the entrepreneur's word that the employee was "incompetent." When it happened again (with a different employee), I started to suspect that something else might be going on. When it happened yet again with a third employee, I knew it was the pattern of a terrible manager with an overbearing, insecure personality who felt the need to belittle his employees. The company failed several years later.

## When It's OK to be a Micromanager

Being a micromanager is associated with trust issues—namely, that you don't trust your employees to do the right thing. Actually, there are scenarios when it's not only OK, but may be *necessary* for you as an entrepreneur to be a micromanager. These situations usually involve a level of uncertainty about an employee.

When you first start working with an employee, you may not know how good they are or even if they are competent at all. You may need to check in much more often with a new employee than you would with someone who's worked for you for a while. However, with new employees, this micromanaging phase shouldn't last more than a few weeks or a few months maximum—if it does, there is clearly a problem with either the employee or the manager (or both!).

It's also OK to be a micromanager if you suspect that an employee is bullshitting or really doesn't know what they are doing. In my experience, this happens more often than you might think. Some employees just interview well and talk a good game. When I lived in Boston, I found that this often happened in the non-technical world; these were people who had worked in IT departments of big companies. They were well paid but usually weren't that efficient at getting things done. Sometimes they talked a very good game, but turned out to be overly political.

When I moved to Silicon Valley, it became much harder to spot the "bullshitters" because the big companies were all tech companies—including companies like Apple, Oracle, and Google. Because they spoke the language of startups and innovation, it was much harder to spot a "talker" who wasn't a very good "doer," as they tended to take credit for other people's work as well.

Micromanaging a bullshitter is a pretty good way to find out what kind of work they are doing versus what they say they are doing. For example, if they say it's going to take two weeks to do a task, and you sit with them every day, the task should be getting done proportionately over the two-week period. Sometimes they'll say they overhauled someone else's code, when they did very little. You won't know unless you look at the code instead of just taking their word for it. The micromanaging phase should last just long enough for you to evaluate whether it makes sense to let this employee go (remember the Four Quadrants of Hiring and Firing).

On the other hand, if you have to spend all of your time micromanaging someone, then something is wrong. Either they are not being a valuable employee, or you are not being a good manager.

## Why Entrepreneurs Become Absent Managers

Let's look at the other extreme: the absent manager. If a micromanager is like a waiter who butts into your conversation too often, an absent manager is like the waiter who's not there when you need them. This can be equally frustrating for the restaurant patron and the startup employee.

Now, the absent manager might literally "not be there," for example: *my boss is traveling all the time and is not around to answer questions*. Or, it could be a metaphorical "not there"—that is, my boss is in his office coding all the time, but he's so busy I'd rather not bother him with my questions, but as a result, decisions that should have been made last week still haven't been made.

There is really only one very good reason for an entrepreneur to become an "absent boss"—and that is that they are in the process of moving from being "doers" to "player coaches" and they still have a lot of work to do themselves. If it's because the entrepreneur is traveling all the time, then it's time to get a manager who is local and can give the time and attention that employees deserve.

However, even in those cases, there is a point in the startup journey when you realize that you will continue to have too much work to do into the foreseeable future—right up until the company becomes a profitable enterprise, or to the point of exit (selling the company), or until it goes out of business.

In the late 1990s, I had started and was running a small consulting company called Inner Vision Technologies. We were helping corporations deploy solutions around Lotus Notes. I was the sole owner and had several employees, but I found that I had critical roles on more than one project. I was billing on these projects, so if I didn't do my portion of the work, our billings suffered.

I also found that on days when I was coding, I wasn't spending time managing the employees or the clients on other projects, and the quality of work on those projects suffered.

Eventually I came up with a rule that helped significantly: I would spend the mornings managing others, and only when I had done enough managing would I start to code. Although this sometimes led to longer coding sessions in the evening after my employees had gone home, it worked much better than doing it the other way around. Coding is a task that can take many, many hours, and if I jumped right in when I got to the office, I suddenly became an "absent" boss—I would never get around to doing proper management because the coding *still* lasted well into the evening!

## Underlying Beliefs: Trust and Insecurity

There are underlying beliefs, held by many founders of startups, that lead to one of these management issues. These beliefs start with our two myths ("Get Out of the Way and Let Employees Do Their Jobs" and "I Could Do It Faster Myself!"). Let's delve deeper into the emotional makeup of the entrepreneur.

In the case of micromanagement, it's instructive to look inside to see what's driving this behavior. Not only do you feel like you can do it faster (which might be true in the short term), but that you feel like you have to do it yourself because everyone else is "incompetent" (which reveals underlying issues of trust and how secure you feel in your work and with the people around you).

Feelings of superiority, even if they are sometimes justified, are also a form of insecurity. It's one thing to be confident about your skills; it's another to be constantly calling out your employees to prove to them how much "better" you are than they are! If you want to constantly step in, like Bill Gates with his text editor, and always be the "hero"—rather than letting others learn from their mistakes—then you are in danger of being a bit of a showboat, and this can lead to many more problems if a startup is to grow.

One approach is to learn to take a deep breath and ask yourself why you feel the need to act this way. If you do this, you can course correct more easily than if you simply "react" to a situation. Because entrepreneurs are under a lot of stress, they can be wound up pretty tight. Sometimes this leads to insecurities that can easily be justified (or disguised) as "just trying to make sure it's done right!"

## Management Isn't Really Work, Is it?

Just as with micromanaging, there is an underlying belief system that usually drives absent managers—and that is that management itself is not "real" work. Engineers in particular tend to be absent managers, because they are at heart "doers" who do not see the real value in managing (often incorrectly, as I was forced to admit to myself).

There's an unspoken belief, particularly within the tech world (though I assume there is something similar in other realms) that managers suck. Okay, maybe it's not so unspoken, but as an engineer, I have felt that way myself. It was a pretty common view among my peers at MIT. Cartoons like *Dilbert* and shows like *The Office* promote and reinforce this idea.

The problem with managers, the thinking goes, is that they end up taking all the credit for the work, which is really done by the doers (in this case the engineers). Meanwhile, every time they check in with you, they are taking valuable time away from your getting work done. If they would just stay away, that would be so much better for the engineer, the manager, and the company!

Do you suffer or subscribe to this point of view? I certainly did. As a result, among engineers, there's this second "unspoken" belief that "when I become a manager, I'm going to do a better job than my managers did with me! I'm going to give the engineers a lot of freedom to get their work done without bothering them all the time."

Then, when an engineer becomes a manager, the tendency is to give engineers a wide berth—and that can lead to absenteeism.

This can be as problematic as becoming a micromanager. Contrary to what my former engineering colleagues think, *management is real work*, and it takes a certain amount of time to be done right. Managers not only need to understand what their direct reports are doing, they need to plan for risks and contingencies, and they need to see how that fits into the overall objective they are trying to achieve for the company.

### Two More Examples: Engaging More Versus Backing Off

One reason that entrepreneurs become absent managers is that they tend to relinquish responsibility for areas that are not their natural strength. For example, a technical CEO might cede all responsibility for sales and marketing, while a nontechnical CEO might cede all responsibility for building the product. But as a CEO, you are responsible for *the results* in all of these areas, whether they are your area of expertise or not, so you can't just step away.

I remember one game company at Play Labs in which the CEO lacked technical expertise, and his cofounder, who was the CTO, was in charge of building the products. This is a pretty typical distribution of work for founders. However, in this case, the product features were taking much longer than the estimates the CTO had originally given to the CEO, and the CTO was taking lots of time working on features the CEO didn't think were the most important. The CEO came to me, frustrated, because he felt that he wasn't equipped to evaluate whether his CTO was doing a good job or not; so in a way he had stopped "managing" the CTO and had become an absent manager. But he was basically blaming his cofounder for the company's problems to his investors.

I told him that he had gone to the extreme and he needed to spend time understanding some of the issues that his cofounder (and the developers his cofounder was managing) was facing. This didn't mean micromanaging, but at least touching base with the CTO, asking intelligent questions, and then engaging the CTO in making tradeoffs with features they might have thought they needed but were turning out to be more difficult to implement than originally thought. They finally got their differences resolved and were able to ship their first product in a reasonable amount of time.

On the other hand, founders often become overbearing micromanagers in areas of their natural strength, or areas they feel they should know. Another example occurred in our accelerator with a very young team. The CEO and his cofounders had very little experience with business (they were still in school), but they were all excellent coders, including the CEO. They were lodging together in an apartment in Boston for our summer accelerator and the CEO came to me frustrated with his cofounders because they were lethargic and spending too much time just playing video games and not pushing according to his priorities. When I dug deeper by asking more questions, I discovered that part of the "lack of motivation" he was seeing was caused by his pushing them to work on his schedule—making them get up early and work late, without a break. He had done the best he could at emulating what he thought a CEO should do (having never been one before), and was pushing his team to finish tasks at his deadlines. The team, who were young and on naturally different schedules, felt they needed a break, which they got from playing video games during the day since they had no other time away from work. We discussed having him back off a little on the micromanaging, and involving his team in decisions about work hours, priorities, scheduling, etc., and giving them personal time away from him, since he had become so intense. The environment became more productive after he made these changes.

## Management Includes Managing Risk

One way that management is "real work" is that managers need to be able to manage risks and evaluate estimates. Simply taking estimates from underlings and then adding them up into a project plan isn't really doing management. It's just being an adding machine.

Software projects, in particular, are notorious for going over budget and taking longer than expected. A good manager will assess whether the plan is realistic, and look at alternatives if the current plan (which may have been based on employee estimates) isn't realistic.

A good manager needs to assess whether particular employees are up to a certain task, and if not, he must mobilize resources to help them out, or consider letting them go. The only way to do this is to check in with employees often enough to make sure they haven't gone too far down the wrong path.

On the other hand, a manager who puts together estimates of how long things should take, without involving his employees in the process, might run into the opposite problem! He has become a micromanager, and delay may come in the form of rebellion to being micromanaged. Or maybe the manager is just too optimistic about how quickly the job can be done. Digging deeper into the motivation of the manager and the employees (or cofounders, as the case often is with early stage startups) is almost always required. Sometimes pushing too hard can have the opposite effect of what you are trying to achieve.

## The Secret

***Find the middle way. Don't be a micromanager or an absentee manager!***

So how do you avoid falling into either of these traps?

Despite what my Stanford Graduate School of Business degree says (that I have an M.S. in management, i.e., *Management Science*), I would argue that management is as much an art as a science. Of course, you can follow the rules, but to be an effective manager, you have to use a combination of logic (the rules), intuition (what is your gut telling you?), and experience (how does this compare to other situations you've seen in the past?).

The key is to find a middle way between being a micromanager and an absent manager.

To do this, you have to spend some time doing some introspection and looking for patterns. Have you had to fire more than one employee? Has more than one of your employees left? If so, why?

Key questions to reflect on:

- Do you think you are better at *x* than your employees? Do you feel the need to let them know this often?
- Do you trust your employees to do a good job, or are they likely to screw up if you give them too much room?
- Do you know what your direct reports' strengths and weaknesses are?
- Do you trust their estimates of how long it will take them to complete a task, or do you find yourself constantly revising?
- Do you like to spend more of your time "doing" and less time "managing"?

By digging into these issues, you can avoid becoming the "creepy, mean" boss who hovers over your employees and micromanages them, or the "absent" boss, who's never around. Then there's the worst of all possible worlds—a combination of the two! You can find your own management style that leverages your strengths and recognizes your weaknesses.

### Remembering the Middle Way

There's a scene in the film *Little Buddha*, starring Keanu Reeves, that always helps me remember to find the middle way (though Keanu's fake Indian accent as Siddhartha is a little distracting). This scene is based on an old Buddhist story.

After spending the first part of his life as a prince, Siddhartha became an ascetic with some companions in the forest. He denied himself all comforts and luxuries, even surviving on as little as a grain of rice a day. The story goes that one day, he decided to get up from his meditation because his hunger was bothering him.

He decided to walk along the river, and there he overheard a teacher instructing his student on stringing and playing the sitar (an Indian musical instrument), so that it would play well.

"If you tighten the string too much," said the teacher, "it will snap, and if you leave it too slack, it won't play . . . "

As soon as he heard that phrase, the starving Siddhartha realized what he had been doing wrong. He had been holding the string too tight as an ascetic, eating almost nothing. Similarly, those who indulged themselves in the opposite way were living a life that was "too loose." He realized that there was a middle way, which would allow the instrument—his body and consciousness—"to play music."

As entrepreneurs-turned-managers, we have to find a middle way, between the micromanager who is frustrating to work for, and the absent manager, who is never around and just as bad to work for. To do this, we have to have a little bit of self-awareness. By taking a deep breath and examining our beliefs about ourselves, the value of our employees, and our beliefs about "doing work vs. managing," we can find that Middle Way.

# Myth #10

## Better Management Causes Faster Growth

In my first startup, Brainstorm Technologies, we grew quickly during each of our first three years, with a relatively inexperienced management team. OK, not just *relatively* inexperienced—we were *very* inexperienced. My cofounder Mitch and I had just graduated from MIT, and I became the CEO just before my twenty-third birthday, having had only about six months of work experience total. My older brother, at the ripe-old age of twenty-five, joined us shortly thereafter, and the three of us served as our management team for the first few years of the company's life.

While I have some nostalgia for those early days, probably the best adjective I can use to describe our management style was "erratic." I would come up with an idea, and we would scramble around trying to make it happen, rearranging our organization and goals to match our latest "brainstorm." Yet, during this time, despite our relative inexperience and erratic management style, the company grew like crazy. Perhaps the company was called "Brainstorm" for good reason.

### Bringing in "Better" Management

A few years later, our investors, who were both VCs and strategic investors, decided it was time to bring in a "professional" manager, and they brought in a CEO who had been at a very large consulting organization. Our startup had grown both a product arm and a consulting arm by then, and it was difficult to manage both under the same roof.

As the more experienced manager came on board, processes began to improve, accountability began to improve, and both roles and goals were better defined. Our focus began to improve, as the new CEO decided to sell off our products business and focus on the services business.

The management and the investors seemed to have a better handle on how well we were doing with our key accounts, and where our key challenges lay. There was also better strategic planning and actual budgets being put in place.

All of these are hallmarks of a "well-run" organization. In short, after hiring a professional manager as CEO (and effectively kicking out the founding CEO—that would be me), it seemed that the company was better managed.

Unfortunately, within a year with the new CEO, the company's performance began to falter, as we lost the differentiation and marketing exposure our products brought us (by selling them off), and then we lost some large clients on the consulting side. Within two years, the company was out of business.

So, while we became "better run," we also went out of business.

In another well-known example, Zynga grew very quickly and erratically under its founding CEO Mark Pincus, and even went public at a $7 billion-plus valuation. However, Pincus's management style, like many entrepreneurs', was very erratic, and the board decided to bring in a more experienced CEO, Don Matricks, who had previously grown Microsoft's Xbox business. There was no doubt that Matricks was a better and more experienced manager. Zynga started to be better managed; unfortunately, despite being "better managed," losses grew while revenue and users fell like a rock. Within two years, Pincus and the board decided it was time to bring the founder/CEO back so that Zynga could grow its mobile business. Even though it was a public company, it needed a startup-type manager to get out of its funk, at least for a little while. It wouldn't be long before Pincus left again and another better "manager" was brought in. We've seen this many times, including Steve Jobs's much ballyhooed return to Apple in 1997 after he had been kicked out in 1985 in favor of experienced "manager" John Sculley. We also saw it with Jack Dorsey at Twitter, Michael Dell at Dell computers, and on and on.

## Wait, Wait, Don't Tell Me

What's going on here? Traditional business school teaches us that these things—the day to day science of management of the company—should influence how well the company is run. In turn, how well the company is run—its processes for managing HR, finance, sales pipeline, and product development—should impact the company by giving it better financials.

The problem is that "better management" at best helps you control costs, increase accountability, and results in more structure and less chaos. This in turn should lead to better profitability.

Development processes (whether they are agile, RAD, waterfall, or otherwise) tend to lead to better coordination among the product team, and higher quality releases of products. Better budgeting tends to lead to fewer unexpected expenses. Better management of salespersons tends to lead to a more predictable pipeline and revenue forecast.

But none of these things by themselves lead to rapid revenue growth, and this is the crux of the problem. At best, they can help you to manage growth (if there is good growth), or to increase profitability (if there is any profitability, which for most startups is nonexistent).

As I said earlier, most of what we learned in business school worked well for profitable, mature companies in a mature market. Most of these models, unfortunately, just don't work for most startups. A better managed company should lead to better profitability—but since most startups are *not* profitable to begin with, their survival often has more to do with momentum (growth) than it does with efficiency for the first few years of its life.

## The Gray-Haired Polo Shirt–Wearing Guys

I remember meeting a friend of mine who worked for a very "hot" startup in Cambridge in the mid-2000s—ThingMagic, which was founded in a garage by five MIT alumni to bring RFID (radio frequency ID) technology to major retailers like Walmart.

I had heard the buzz about the company, as it was seen as a potential IPO candidate, and I was delighted when I realized I knew someone who worked there. When I asked her how things were going at the company from her perspective (she was in finance), she answered in much less enthusiastic tones than I had expected. She said things were "so-so."

When I asked her why, she said that the investors, who had put over $20 million into the company, had just brought in the traditional "gray-haired, polo shirt–wearing guys," and things were changing. The startup phase that she liked (and which was why she joined in the first place) was pretty much over as processes and bureaucracy were put in place. My friend left the company shortly thereafter, and as she expected the company fell well short of its sky-high expectations.

In the years since, I have often thought about this exchange with my friend. How had the startup, which literally had the word "magic" in its name, lost its magic? And why was she *so confident* that the new management wouldn't work out? Why did she think the party was over once the "gray-haired polo shirt–wearing guys" were taking over?

After all, many hot startups need better management as they grow, and it wasn't unusual to bring in an outside CEO to help with that growth. As we saw in Myth #8: Hire the Most Experienced People You Can Find, and Myth #9: Get Out of the Way and Let People Do Their Jobs, *or* I Can Do It Faster Myself!, entrepreneurs don't always make the best managers, so it's only natural that the investors and/or board of directors might want to bring in more experienced managers, isn't it?

## Are Experienced Managers Better at Managing than Entrepreneurs Are?

In the old days (and by old, I'm talking about the 1990s and earlier)—VCs had a playbook for tech startups. The companies were (almost always) founded by technical types who had built a product, made a discovery, or patented some new process or technology. The playbook was to fund the development of the product, then bring in an outside CEO to help manage the process of bringing the product to market, as we saw in Myth #4: A Great Product and a Big Market are the Most Important Things. The experienced CEO would bring in other "experienced" managers, including a VP of Sales, VP of Marketing, etc.

The very first term sheet I ever got from a VC explicitly stated that within 120 days of their investment, they would bring on a new CEO. This wasn't a question; it was just how things were done.

This still happens, because many technical founders are eccentric. But a few years ago, a study done in Silicon Valley showed that startups that grew and were still run by their founder generally outperformed startups that brought in outside CEOs.

Truth be told, I'm not a big one for scientific studies done via "surveys" of startups—I think there are so many factors in the success or failure of a startup that most of these survey studies may find some correlation but completely miss the point of *why* a particular startup was a success or a failure.

But this one actually made some sense to me. If you look at some of the great companies, going way back to Ford, IBM, Microsoft, and Apple, the founders ran the company for a long time.

For more recent examples, you can look at companies like Dell, Facebook, Salesforce, and many others. Even Google, which was famous for having brought in Eric Schmidt as CEO, was in many ways very closely influenced by its founders, one of whom eventually took over from Schmidt as CEO—ensuring a continuity of culture.

I've already said that founders tend to make bad managers. Talk to anyone who has worked for a well-known billionaire founder like Marc Benioff (founder of Salesforce.com) or Larry Ellison (founder of Oracle) in the days of wild growth. You'll hear stories that would make a business school professor blush. Ask early employees of Facebook what it was like to work under Mark Zuckerberg as compared to a more experienced manager—they'll show you weird facial expressions as they talk about his management style. But you can't argue with the results achieved by these founder-CEOs over a number of years of growing their startups into market leaders and industry powerhouses.

The real secret here is that process and management make a company run more efficiently and with less drama; they help a company *manage* growth. Rarely do they *cause* growth. In fact, they may even *inhibit* growth.

That's why whenever I hear about a recently hot startup bringing in a new CEO as a "savior," and investors get excited, I roll my eyes. Not always, mind you, just usually.

Let's take another example, Twitter, which was run by its founders for a long time. At some time before the IPO, they brought in a more experienced manager, Dick Costolo, to help take the company public. He was supposed to manage the transition from a high-growth company to a profitable, public, high-growth company. A few years later, as Twitter's growth slowed down and the stock price, which had initially shot up because of the sky-high expectations placed on it, also came down. Suddenly, Costolo was out and the board brought back one of its founders, Jack Dorsey, as CEO so that the company could start innovating and growing again. Whether Dorsey was the right guy to take over Twitter at this point is being debated even as I write this.

But many boards tend to swing between one of two modes after their companies experience a spurt of initial growth. They tend to think that either:

1. The company has grown too fast or is doing too many things. (We need a CEO who is less erratic and a better manager. Thus, the answer is to bring in an outside CEO.)
2. The company isn't growing enough. (We need to bring in a founder type who will shake things up and make the company grow again. Can we bring the founders back?)

You can look at almost any hot startup that has gone through an initial growth phase only to falter later, and you can literally draw a sine curve that shows where the company was over time between growing and faltering. Lucky is the company that finds an outside CEO or professional manager who can improve processes, build accountability, and also have the foresight to invest heavily in projects that end up *causing* real growth for the company. These guys or gals are like "diamonds in the rough," and often end up being trusted by both founders and investors.

## It's the Product/Market Fit, Stupid (Not the Expected Value)

Bringing in outside managers may lead to a better-run company, but it doesn't always lead to more innovation or more growth. Bringing back founders doesn't always lead to better management, but is more likely to lead to more innovation, which in turn at least has the chance to lead to more growth (though not necessarily more profitability, which often depends on processes and procedures).

Paul Graham, founder of Y Combinator, was famous for saying that the most important goal for any startup is to create a product that customers want. Everything else, Graham concludes, is a distraction.

I would add that you also need to find the easiest and most efficient way for those customers to hear about and get your product—i.e., the marketing/distribution strategy, which is often the key difference between startups that succeed or fail.

In my experience, entrepreneurs are usually much better at this than professional managers. Usually, an entrepreneur is someone who sees an opportunity and goes after it, regardless of how hard it looks or how "crazy" it seems.

They also tend to find the cheapest, most direct way to go after it. More experienced managers tend to "weigh the risks" and calculate the expected value based on the likelihood of different outcomes, usually based on the historical data presented to them by their direct reports.

This isn't always a bad thing. When a company has grown and is sitting on a lot of money, it's worth considering whether going down a certain path will be a blind alley, or whether there are better uses for the money. This is why it's best to measure the "expected value" and ROI of each decision in a dispassionate, logical way.

The problem with the "expected value" approach is that the future, particularly in startups, is unpredictable. To paraphrase former Israeli Prime Minister Ehud Barak (who may have been paraphrasing the famous New York Yankee Yogi Berra): "I rarely make predictions . . . especially about the future."

In business school, you learn to compute expected values of different options based on percentages. Where do the percentages come from? Based on historical values and the best "predictions" possible. The problem is that in startups you have to throw out all historical data because if there's one thing that predictable *it's that you can't predict what will happen next*. This means that any expected value calculation based on percentages of likelihood is entirely suspect in Startup Land.

I remember being in a spreadsheet class at Stanford with a professor who had quite literally written our textbook on spreadsheet modeling. I asked, What if the percentage likelihood of different scenarios (the *inputs* to the model) were wrong?

"Then all the outcomes will be wrong," he answered.

"But where are you to get those values?" I asked.

"That's where you, the manager, have to trust your gut as a manager, based on your experience to date."

In startup markets, which have not been around long enough to provide meaningful data or historical reference points, you have to trust your instincts. The vision of the entrepreneur is more reliable than spreadsheets or predictions. This is precisely because startup markets are unpredictable!

Therefore, expected value calculations are complete bullshit when it comes to startups. Startups that are successful usually get there by pursuing an opportunity that a big company decided not to pursue because the "expected value" wasn't big enough! If and when the startup proves or creates a brand new market, suddenly big-company thinking comes in and the big players will look at expected value, and decide whether to build their own product to compete with the startup, or to simply buy one of the leading players in the newly emerged market.

## The Secret

***Growth isn't caused by good management; it's caused by an increasing number of customers wanting your product and getting it.***

Since I meet a lot of entrepreneurs in Silicon Valley, I often find that startups have hired more people than they need, or have overinvested in technology infrastructure. Usually they are startups that have raised a lot of money to do so (startups that haven't raised much money don't usually have this option).

When I ask why they do this, they usually reply, that's how companies *scale*. These aren't, as you might expect, entrepreneurs fresh out of school with no experience; some of them have been part of very successful startups or big organizations like Google or Facebook or Oracle.

"You can't do it all by yourself," they will say, as if lecturing me. "You need to delegate these things to competent people, who will cause your organization to grow." Yet many of these people end up laying off all those extra people or the company ends up running out of cash. Why?

Because they were assuming that scaling means infrastructure and process. Infrastructure and processes *can support scaling*, but it *doesn't cause scaling*. This is as much true for a well-known, growing public company as it is for a small startup. The only thing that causes scaling is more customers or users of your product or service!

## When Infrastructure Goes Wrong

Back in the late 1990s, I was part of the founding team of Service Metrics, which sold to Exodus, a member of the NASDAQ 100, for $280 million in Exodus stock. (Unfortunately, with the dot-com crash soon to follow, the stock quickly became worthless.) Exodus, which was the #1 web hosting company in the world at the time, made the mistake of overinvesting in "infrastructure," taking on large amounts of debt to finance large data centers around the world in anticipation of growth of the internet.

Exodus wasn't managed poorly; most people would agree that the CEO, Ellen Hancock, wasn't a bad manager. After all, she had had senior roles at IBM and Apple, and before taking over at Exodus, she had proceeded to set a NASDAQ record of 19 consecutive quarters of 40 percent quarter-over-quarter revenue growth. In 2000, the $29 billion market cap exceeded even that of her ex-employer, Apple Computer.[1]

Yet in 2001, Exodus stock fell and it filed for bankruptcy. It had simply spent too much on infrastructure, borrowing too much money to be an ongoing profitable concern, and our stock quickly became worthless.

I tell this not as a dot-com war story (since many people involved with the venture did quite well by selling their Exodus stock), but rather to explore *where* growth comes from and how it should (or *shouldn't*) be managed.

Managers are good at managing anticipated growth—they aren't always good at predicting where (or when, or how) it'll slow down or what the next big product might be when the first one's growth slows down. Remember, any experienced manager who has spent time in a big company (and business school before that) will be doing expected value calculations in their heads, using the past (either their own past at a big company or the startups' recent past). Unfortunately, as I said earlier, expected value calculations don't work in startups because if there is one truth in startups, it is that the past does not equal the future. In other words, things will change. They may change for the better or the worse, but the reality will almost certainly be different from what's predicted.

On the flip side, while entrepreneurs are usually good at finding a new growth opportunity, they aren't always great at managing, as we saw in the last two myths, and if the company is growing it can feel like employees have to hold on for dear life.

Even more important than managing your growth is to understand what factors in your product and your market are *causing* the growth in the first place. It's usually some combination of product/market fit and distribution strategy, combined with the growth of the overall market.

Once you identify the factors causing growth, be sure not to lose focus on these factors. Unless you are constantly on top of finding those opportunities for growth, all the best management won't be able to save the ship when it hits an iceberg.

---

1. Wikipedia, "Ellen Hancock," accessed December 18, 2019, https://en.wikipedia.org/wiki/Ellen_Hancock.

### Randy Komisar on Why Leadership Isn't About Making Speeches

When I did my first startup, I used to make lots of speeches to our employees. Having just come out of school, this was my impression of what a good leader does to motivate his team.

Randy Komisar, who has experience mentoring many types of CEOs, was quick to point out that this thinking is faulty:

> First of all, a lot of people believe that leadership is a style, and not a skill. They think they either they have it or they don't.
>
> They don't understand that everybody can take their (own personal) style and become effective leaders if they understand their strengths and weaknesses, and understand what a leader needs to do.
>
> They think being a leader is about either making big speeches or giving a direction, but they don't understand the human side of it. Being a leader is also about how to connect with people, how to motivate people, how to show people you're interested in them, and how to get people to believe in a bigger cause, a bigger vision. So, by and large, if we talk about good managers being rare, then good leaders are *rarer*.

Randy coaches entrepreneurs to really understand the motivation of their employees:

> People want to work for a purpose beyond the bottom line. You can build sort of a mercenary culture but by and large that's not what motivates the best people. You need to reward people but you need to motivate people.
>
> Motivation is not about money, it's about having some bigger vision than the success of the founders or the success of the investors or even the success of your own stock options. It's about achieving some values and so making clear what those values are . . . you know, being able to paint the picture clearly to people how to get there. And where they are on the path.

Randy concludes that you can have effective leaders with any kind of personality style: "I mean these are all the aspects of leadership that are important, and as I said, style doesn't matter. You can have people who can do that with great oratory, or you can have people do that quietly and shyly, sort of like Larry [Page] at Google—but it needs to be clear, it needs to be sincere and authentic, and it needs to be communicated."

# Bonus Myth #B-3

## If I own X%, Then My Stock Is worth $x!

Not long ago, I was speaking with the founder of a very successful gaming company about some misconceptions he had encountered when the company was sold. He brought up a myth that caused him some amount of heartache with some of his key employees.

Let's say that his company was sold for $100 million. Here is the myth his employees believed: If, as an employee, my options represented 2 percent of the company, then I should receive roughly $2 million, right?

Wrong. Like most myths, it's not entirely wrong, but there are complexities that make it not entirely right.

As I began to think about it, most employees have this misconception. Even investors, advisors, and other stakeholders often have the same misconception.

After all, 1 percent of $100 million should be worth $1 million. But the actual distribution of funds in the sale of a company, while based on the cap table at the time of an acquisition, may vary significantly.

▶ To read the full text of this **Bonus Myth**, including the various issues with common vs. preferred stock, options, and the waterfall model of acquisition consideration, please download the Supplement to *Startup Myths and Models* from www.zenentrepreneur.com ◀

# Stage 4

## The Road of Trials

## *Myths About Going to Market*

> The original departure into the land of trials represented only the beginning of the long and really perilous path of initiatory conquests and moments of illumination. Dragons have now to be slain and surprising barriers passed—again, again, and again. Meanwhile there will be a multitude of preliminary victories, unsustainable ecstasies and momentary glimpses of the wonderful land.
>
> JOSEPH CAMPBELL

### Introduction to Stage 4

Napoleon once said that no battle plan survives contact with the enemy. The same is true of most mythological adventures, and unfortunately for those who would like to get prescriptions for startup success, it's also true for most startup adventures.

In the first part of *The Lord of the Rings*, for example, Frodo and Gandalf's plans to meet up and leave the Shire together go completely awry. Frodo and Sam (joined by Pippin and Merry, who weren't even part of the original plan) are pursued relentlessly by Black Riders, and Gandalf is, well, nowhere to be found. If it weren't for the help of an unexpected companion, Strider the Ranger, the Hobbits may never have made it to their first resting point at Rivendell.

Later, when the Fellowship sets out in earnest from Rivendell, their plan is to go over the mountain through the pass of Caradharas, but a combination of bad winter weather and Saruman's meddling makes it impossible to cross, and they are forced to take the more "dark, dangerous route" through the Mines of Moria!

### *When Things Go Wrong on the Startup Journey*

It might seem strange to be referencing scenes from *The Lord of the Rings* to describe what might happen on a startup adventure. But sometimes the best way to illustrate a point is to use common references that vividly display the point; these two aspects of the journey of Frodo are prime examples of two of the ways things can go wrong: we lose the people we expected to be with us on our journey, and the path that seemed so clear at the beginning starts to look murky, dangerous, and perhaps even impassable. Like Frodo and his team of adventurers, we are forced to find another (perhaps darker and more dangerous) path, filled with a different set of twists and turns than we originally anticipated.

In almost every startup I've been in, the best-laid plans *usually* go wrong, prompting a need to improvise if the journey is to be successfully concluded. Usually the time when the startup plan goes horribly awry is when you introduce your product, which you've been working on diligently for many months. Sometimes (a minority of times) the product is received better than expected. In a majority of cases, the first version of the product isn't received nearly as well as the rosy projections that the founding team put forth to the investors. This could be because of the product itself, but more likely it's about the adoption rate. Suddenly, the number of customers you projected in month three after your product release seems unreachable.

For many entrepreneurs, this is the first time it seems like the outcome of the startup adventure is out of their control. Until then, it may have been easy to find some seed funding or to build the product. In some ways, releasing your product is akin to encountering your adversaries for the first time on the road, like the Black Riders in *Lord of the Rings*, or the Imperial stormtroopers in *Star Wars*. Suddenly the startup adventure gets much more dangerous and the possibility that your startup won't make it becomes a very real possibility!

### *Overview of the Myths*

For this stage, I've adopted Campbell's stage, the "Road of Trials," to delve into the challenges of taking a product to market successfully and navigating these treacherous waters. Just as importantly, it's about recognizing when a product is not doing very well, and when it's time to change your strategy.

This happens often enough that we can list some common complaints from entrepreneurs about why the product isn't taking off. One is that the product is fine, but that their sales guy isn't doing his job selling it! Another is that all the team has to do is to add feature x (or feature y), and the adoption curve will change. Still others blame it on the amount of money being spent (or not being spent) on getting the product out to the marketplace! (If only we had more money, then we could spend it on marketing, and this would drive many more users to our product or website.)

But the underlying issues the startup team is facing are often more complicated than these simplistic myths. Sometimes the startup needs a whole new business model. You might have a health or wellness related product you want to sell to end users, but you find that FDA approval or insurance payments make your product better for doctors. At other times, a change is needed in the product itself, which involves contracting, expanding, or refocusing it. Sometimes the change comes when you take something you've learned from customers in market A and apply it to a completely different market!

More often than not, successful startups recognize something in the market from their first product and then pivot toward or away from that something to get a product that ends up taking off. Just as Bilbo would never have found the Ring in *The Hobbit* if he hadn't lost the dwarves and the wizard in the dark tunnels of the Misty Mountains, you may never find the thing that can change your adventure and propel your startup to success if you don't have challenges on this Road of Trials!

# Myth #11

## Focus, Focus, Focus

This is one of my favorite myths, and it helps to explain one of the most interesting secrets revealed in this book.

Let me explain.

At the heart of this myth lies an important truth: founders of startups need laserlike focus to get things done. Look at the founding of any startup and you will probably find a period of time when the founders had to put in almost superhuman effort to get the company off the ground.

Anyone who has been on a startup journey will notice that the advice "focus, focus, focus" is given throughout the journey—by advisors, cofounders, investors, board members, consultants, well-wishers and yes, even distant relations.

I've given the advice myself to many entrepreneurs, particularly when they were trying to do too many things. The important question and the controversy arise when you dig deeper and ask—just *what* should you focus on? And for *how long*? And when should you *stop focusing*?

This myth is built on the idea that as a startup founder you shouldn't get distracted. The implication is that if you encounter an obstacle or another opportunity, you should be careful to not get distracted from what you are "supposed" to be doing—i.e., focusing on the "vision" of the company.

The problem is that many successful startups end up in places that are different from where they started. They may end up with a different product for the same market or an adjacent market. Sometimes, the really big opportunity is "lurking" nearby and the only obstacle to pursuing it is this notion of "you have to be focused."

In my opinion, many people in the startup world pay too much attention to vision and not enough to the role of serendipity and unexpected opportunities that present themselves during the journey itself. True gold is often discovered with exploration of the landscape, not with tunnel vision. Yet you often need tunnel vision to get anything done. Unlike big companies that have the funds to pursue several projects at the same time, startups are built on the sweat equity of their founders, and there's only so much time and attention you have as a founding team. Therein lies the underlying tension which forms the basis of this myth.

## A Famous Example

Let's start with a very famous example from the startup world. When Bill Gates and Paul Allen started Microsoft, their first product was a version of the BASIC programming language for the emerging personal computers, starting with the ALTAIR computer. They were successful in this, and even companies like Apple came to them to get the BASIC programming language. When I was a kid I used the Applesoft BASIC language—I didn't realize it was just Microsoft BASIC under a different name.

A few years into the Microsoft journey, IBM came to town and asked the Microsoft founders if they had an operating system for their soon to be released personal computer, the IBM PC. This was a bit of a departure from what Microsoft was doing—in fact they were working *with* the developers of operating systems, not *competing against* them.

Moreover, Microsoft didn't have an operating system. They didn't even have the beginnings of an operating system. Yet they recognized that if they could provide it to IBM, there was an unparalleled opportunity near the arena they had been playing in.

This is an example of serendipity on the startup journey. The Microsoft founders turned around and bought QDOS from another developer for $50,000 and turned it into MS-DOS, which they presented as the base of their operating system for IBM. The rest is, as they say, history. Microsoft went on to be a multibillion-dollar software company.

Although many decisions played into Microsoft's success, the choice to follow a new path was a monumental one and the one that is most associated with Microsoft becoming the largest and most valuable software company in the world (at the time).

I have worked with lots of venture capitalists and advisors, and I know many of them would have told Microsoft to "focus" on its core competency—building programming languages for computers, not building operating systems. Operating systems would have taken a lot of work and resources away from their core competency. You might say that the founders of Microsoft decided to ignore the conventional wisdom of *focus, focus, focus*. And perhaps it's a good thing they did!

Now I'm not saying that most venture capitalists would admit to giving this advice *after* the fact. If they had given Bill Gates and Paul Allen and Steve Ballmer this advice, and the team had ignored it to go on to great success, those same VCs would take credit for investing in a team with such business acumen and foresight!

The truth of the matter is that entrepreneurs need to act on intuition as well as logic. The reason you have a startup in the first place is probably because you had a hunch, and ignoring conventional wisdom about how most startups are risky and fail, you decided to follow it. Sometimes, during the journey, an entrepreneur will have a hunch, based on an unexpected meeting or unexpected market event; and it's worth following up on that hunch, even if it could be considered "off focus."

## My Own Example: Virtual Currency in Facebook Games

Let's look at my own experience. I was helping out Offerpal Media, which was a company started during the social networking apps craze in 2007. Facebook games were relatively new at the time and free to play was a fairly new business model. No one knew whether end users would actually pay real money in these games for virtual goods or currency.

Offerpal had originally started with a social widget that would use lead generation (what we called offers, such as signing up for Netflix, or buying a subscription for a magazine, or asking for an insurance quote) as a way for users to get rewards. These rewards would be paid for by the advertisers whose offers were being fulfilled.

Originally, we thought these rewards would be physical items that users could get by convincing their friends to fill out offers on their behalf. For each offer that was filled out, the user would get points toward their real-life reward. That's why the company was called MyOfferPal initially, and this was the main vision that the investors bought into, using the social widget on social networks like Facebook and MySpace.

However, the founding team of Offerpal, led by cofounder Mitch Liu, had an idea that instead of physical rewards, we could give users virtual currency as a reward in the newly created world of social gaming.

We weren't sure it would work. We didn't know if users were willing to do things like sign up for offers like Netflix or fill out surveys in exchange for virtual currency in games. And in fact, our technology wasn't really oriented toward working with games, which would be a b2b2c (business to business to consumer) model rather than a d2c (direct to consumer) model.

Finally, we weren't sure if the investors would buy into going in another direction (being a monetization provider for social games rather than building a consumer widget, which were the hot things at the time), or if they would give us the same advice that they always give entrepreneurs: focus, focus, focus. ("You said you were going to do *x*, so why not focus on *x*? If that doesn't work," they might say, "then you can explore something else.")

We decided to do a little skunkworks project, and we approached a few emerging Facebook game makers. One, called *Fluff Friends*, had been started by a Stanford alum, Mike Sego, whom I messaged on Facebook to see if he would be open to discussing the idea of "offers for virtual currency."

Since the d2c (direct to consumer) technology platform the company was building was complicated (built in Java for industrial strength and scalability), we decided to use an earlier, simpler, prototype that had been quickly built in PHP. We quickly hacked together a new proof-of-concept to show how this new idea would work to reward virtual currency, and we showed it to the *Fluff Friends* founder. Mike said he was willing to try it out, to give users virtual currency in the games for free (in exchange for filling out offers). We ended up calling what we built in this prototype an "offerwall," a new term that the industry went on to adopt.

To make a long story short, we implemented the full offerwall the following week as quickly as possible and without distracting any resources from the "main product" that the company was building. It worked.

It worked very well. Revenue shot up from nothing to thousands of dollars per day. Soon the company signed on other early adopters in the Facebook gaming space, including Presidio Media, which was started by experienced Silicon Valley entrepreneur Mark Pincus, who had built a social poker game. Since it wasn't clear at this point in the market that end users were going to pay real money for virtual chips and virtual goods in free-to-play games, our offerwall became the standard form of "alternate payment"—a way for users to get currency without directly paying for it. That second client grew very fast and later became known as Zynga, which had a hit game called *Farmville* that drove many millions of dollars through the offer wall per month.

This virtual currency idea was a side path from the main road. We took the departure, and Offerpal's revenues grew very quickly from zero to the neighborhood of many tens of millions of dollars in a few years—one of the fastest ramps I've personally seen in startups. Although the company later had some issues (and had to transition out of Facebook games to mobile games, renaming itself Tapjoy), there is no denying that the founding team unearthed an opportunity that was not obvious from the start, and they rode it to great success.

## Startup Model #6: Where and How Deep to Drill? Focus Versus Explore

And this is where the traditional wisdom of "focus, focus, focus" breaks down.

Let's use an (admittedly dated) analogy: suppose you are looking for oil and the landscape looks a little like figure 11.1. And suppose you convince some investors to back you and you start looking for oil at point A, because it seems like the best bet—you suspect there's oil somewhere in this patch of land and the most reasonable and best guess is that you should start digging (or drilling) at point A.

Suppose you are drilling at point A and you find some oil, but you find that it dries up pretty quickly.

What should you do? If you *focus, focus, focus*, you will keep drilling at point A. But the bigger oil reserve might be at point B or C! You get an opportunity to check out point B—should you go? Or should you focus your resources on point A, where you have already found a little pocket of oil? How about point C, which is even farther away? Do you have resources to drill that far away?

Too often, by taking the advice to "focus," we close our eyes to other possibilities that might exist. While this analogy is a little simplistic,

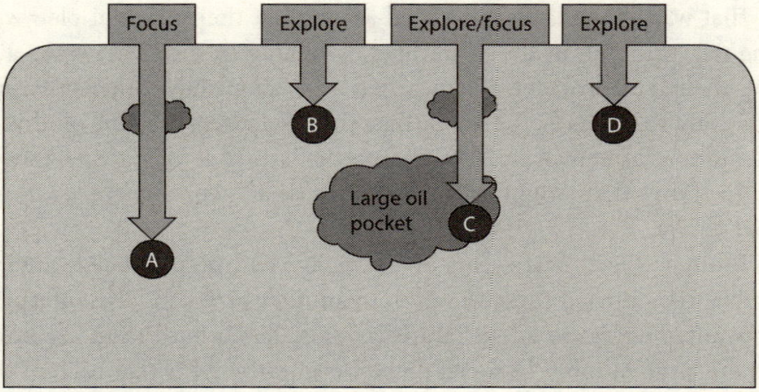


Figure 11.1
Focusing vs. Exploring. Created by the author

I believe it gets the point across. If you don't drill around at other places in the vicinity, and do it before you run out of money, then you may never find the big pocket of oil at point C.

This isn't an exact analogy when it comes to startup—going to an adjacent product or market isn't quite the same as just doing the same thing on another plot of land nearby. Perhaps a better analogy might be: what if the pocket at C is actually gold, or natural gas, or platinum, rather than oil? Now you start to see the possibilities you have to stay open to in the startup adventure!

## Example: Searching Social Networks for Gold

As another example, when Jud Valeski and his cofounder started Gnip in 2008, they knew they wanted to focus on the emerging world of social networks and APIs for programmatic access to the public data that was being created in these emerging networks. Their first idea, which was funded by VC Brad Feld, was to talk to the social networks (whose expertise was not in building APIs for programmatic access) and get them to let Gnip run their servers and provide public APIs to the world.

They met with many social networks during the first year. After twelve months and many discussions, they weren't able to get a single social network to say yes to allow them to run their APIs (and willing to pay them for doing so).

That was about as clear a signal as any that their original plan wasn't going to work. But, in the meantime, by talking to social networks about being their API provider, they learned a lot about how other enterprises might want to access all the public data that users were creating on this new medium, social networks. This was particularly true of disaster-recovery organizations that might want to know what people were posting to social media.

Though their first year of focusing hadn't produced anything tangible, they turned their attention to another problem. The enterprises, who wanted access to all social media data, had a hard time keeping up with the large number of social networks and the APIs that each of them provided (which were constantly changing). This was in the days when MySpace and Facebook were emerging leaders, and LinkedIn; Twitter, Pinterest and others were just starting to appear.

So they decided that the real gold was "nearby," and by turning their attention to these enterprises, they could create a single API that all of these companies could use to get access to all the different social network data, without having the hassle of learning and maintaining each social network's API.

They discovered that not only did companies need this, but they were willing to pay for it! That's of course the sign that you might have discovered some startup gold. I always tell entrepreneurs to pay attention if or when a customer/prospect says, "What you have is nice, but what I really need, and am willing to pay you for right now, is *x*. Can you provide that?" You then need to figure out if there are other customers who need the same thing.

In this example, the Gnip team then began a period of almost extreme focus again and built a product that became the leader in providing social network APIs, eventually selling to Twitter for $175 million in 2014.

## The Other Extreme: Jack-of-All-Trades

OK, let's now look at the other point of view. It's possible, as shown in figure 11.1, that you drill lots of holes in points A, B, C, and D and never get to the oil (or gold or natural gas), because you never drilled deep enough.

This is the danger of becoming too "unfocused," where you never explore an opportunity to enough depth to find the gold because you are doing too many things at once—what is sometimes called the "jack-of-all-trades" effect (i.e., master-of-none).

This has happened to me and many others in the startup world too, which shows why Startup Myths always mask underlying complexity. For example, in my first company, Brainstorm Technologies, we found ourselves with a suite of products that were add-ons to Lotus Notes, and a consulting business that was based on that technology, and a consulting business that was doing large fixed price government projects that had nothing to do with that technology. These were each very different businesses, and a result perhaps of *too much exploration* on our part.

When a startup is doing too many things, it's hard to do all of them at the same level of quality. And quality/depth is in fact one of the most important characteristics of a startup that distinguishes it from a big company. A small team of excellent minds that are laser focused can accomplish much more than a large team of mediocre minds working nine to five for some giant behemoth in the same time frame.

## Focusing on a Specific Market

Sometimes focusing is a matter of digging deeper into a specific vertical market. At Play Labs, we had one startup that was selling a general platform for building VR 360 video experiences. They were selling to "everyone" who might want to build 360 video, and they had a product already in the market with several hundred customers. I encouraged them to look for a pattern "use case" that might be the "killer app" for their technology, which could be used in many different ways. They had been quite successful in selling to various educational institutions and corporations using the product for a variety of use cases, including educational/training experiences, interactive marketing brochures, and other markets.

In this case, it turned out that they needed to focus on the use case that showed the best product/market fit, which was in fact building educational/training experiences. So they decided to focus on educational/training experiences, which was by itself still a significant market. By doing this, they were able to focus on building features for this market that may not have been as important to other user cases. Although this market isn't for everyone, they were able to focus on investors who were also interested in this market.

The decision of whether to go horizontal with a product or to focus on one or more use cases is not an easy one, but it can be the key factor in the success or failure of a startup. As with the other myths, there is no easy answer, and it must be taken on a case by case basis.

## The Secret

***Focus, Explore, Focus***

The real secret here is that a startup team needs to alternate between periods of exploration and periods of extreme focus, keeping an eye open for nearby opportunities.

The periods of exploration are used to find the best place to focus. Focus usually means that you have the right strategic plan, that you have found a pocket of oil (or gold), and need to focus to get it out of the ground. When success is simply a matter of execution, and how well you execute, then it's the right time to focus.

But even this is more simplistic than the reality. You can't just say, "OK, our first product didn't work, now we need to find something to pivot to." In fact, even during the initial time of focus, you need to pay attention to signals and clues that are coming in from the market, from customers, and from partners. By the time you make a decision to focus, you should already have gathered the data on the adjacent market opportunities through your interaction with the market.

The truth of the matter is that while many will give you advice on how and when to pivot, this mysterious process is still more of an art than a science. Sometimes pivoting is all about focusing, while other times it's about exploring. We'll talk more about the ways to pivot and make sure you cover the right terrain in Myth #14: Fail Fast, Pivot Quickly.

Many, many startups begin with a plan or product that will never be very successful. Of course, you don't know this at the beginning, but it's important to be able to see clearly how well your current product/market focus is progressing.

This is unique to startups and may not apply to other types of small businesses, because of how quickly startup markets evolve. Knowing when to focus and when to explore is, of course, more of an art than a science, but is often the key factor that can drive an otherwise mediocre startup into one that has rapid success and growth.

### Jeff Bussgang on Stages of Product/Market Fit: From Jungle to Highway

Jeff Bussgang, general partner and cofounder of Flybridge Capital Partners, and a professor at Harvard Business School, gives the following metaphors for the stages of a startup as it finds product/market fit.

In his book, *Entering StartUpLand*, Jeff provides a road-building metaphor to describe how a company goes from its initial search for product/market fit to a well-defined company with a plethora of customers that is trying to scale:

*Jungle*. In the jungle stage, which Jeff describes as "pre-product/market fit," the founders are hacking away at some raw jungle. Early stage startups often feel this way—there is raw opportunity in the jungle, but it takes lots of hacks to open up some throughway in the midst of a heavy jungle. The profile of people who join startups at this stage need to be "risk-takers and explorers," according to Jeff, and the motto of the startup is still "build it!"

*Dirt Road*. In the dirt-road stage, there is some semblance of product/market fit. This usually means that you've got your first few customers and there is at least a path toward repeatedly selling the product to more customers and defining yourself as the leader in this market segment. The opportunity is still pretty raw but you are starting to find a repeatable business model. In this stage, the motto of the startup is "sell it!"

*Highway*. At the highway stage, you have already identified and proven a repeatable business model. It's the same with cities—they build highways where there is proven traffic and a need for smooth flow and infrastructure to keep things going. The people who join at this stage, according to Jeff, tend to be people who can "optimize" and enhance. The motto of the startup at this stage is "scale it."

Many startups lose their way in the jungle phase or the dirt-road stage. Those that make it to the highway stage are recognized as successful startups and are typically on their way to becoming public companies. Startups we know that have been very successful, like Google, Facebook, and Airbnb, are no longer startups; they have passed beyond the highway stage and are now multibillion-dollar companies.

# Myth #12

## My Product Failed Because My Sales Guy Sucks

This myth gets into the causes of a scenario I've seen again and again in tech startups: the "no traction" scenario.

Well, maybe not "no traction" exactly; most startups are able to get one or two beta customers to try their product, usually by pressuring friends of the founders to use the product. Sometimes, one of these friends turns into a paying customer, although at a reduced rate. But scaling beyond the initial customer(s) doesn't happen—so it's a case of "minimal traction."

This myth applies to startups that have a sales force—typically b2b (business to business) types of companies. For direct to consumer companies, where the product is downloaded as an app, or is simply a website, see the corresponding Myth #13: If Only We Could Spend More on Marketing!

With b2b companies, the scenario usually goes like this: the company has built a product, has been through a beta cycle, has even hired an "experienced sales guy" to sell it, but the company isn't able to get many sales. It may have gotten one or two customers, but the new sales guy isn't able to close much more business, falling far short of the optimistic expectations of the founders.

At this point, the founder (often a technical or "product" guy) says it is the fault of the sales guy. The salesperson usually says that it is the fault of the product—if the tech team would/could only add "feature *x*" then "account *y*" is destined to close.

So, whose fault is it, really? The founder's? The product team's? The sales leader's?

The answer is that it's probably some combination of factors that's keeping the product from getting traction. It's very possible that the salesperson isn't very good at selling; it's also possible that the product isn't quite ready for prime time yet. However, it's more likely that the product is not quite meeting the needs of the market, so the underlying issue is one of product/market fit.

## Who's Responsible for Getting Customers?

This discussion begs the question of who's really responsible for getting customers. Is it the VP of sales? Is it the founder/CEO? The product manager? The first sales rep?

Most founders of b2b startups have enough contacts to get one or two customers in a target market (otherwise they probably shouldn't be starting a b2b startup in that market). What that means is that a founder shouldn't complain about a salesperson not being able to close any customers if the founders haven't been able to close the first few customers by themselves.

If an entrepreneur—someone who knows enough about a product/market to quit his job and start a company to build a new product—can't convince at least the first two customers to buy the product, how can we expect a sales guy (who knows much less about the product and market) possibly be able to do it?

I'm not saying that sales guys can't sell new products. I'm saying that they don't understand the product as well as the founders, who are usually responsible for identifying the problem/pain/need/trend that the product solves.

If the company hasn't gotten its first few customers, then it's most likely the founders' fault and not the salesperson's (at least not initially).

When Gurinder Sangha started Intelligize, a startup that made a successful SaaS (software as a service) application for securities lawyers, he understood the problem that the lawyers were facing very well. He had worked as a securities lawyer himself. As a result, he was able to meet with lawyers in this field, and was able to show them how well the product would serve them. In fact, he sold to many of the first customers himself, and then later brought in sales reps and a sales leader, and Intelligize kept growing.

As the founder, he remained the company's best resource for selling into a law firm because he spoke their language.

Once a startup has gotten its first few (legitimate) customers, then at least there is a record of success showing that the market is receptive to the product. If nothing else, a good salesperson should be able to leverage that success to get a few more clients to try it.

## Two Ways to Tell If Your Sales Guy Really Sucks

After a product has sold a few times (to real, arms-length customers—i.e., those beyond the founder's friends), then it's on the first salesperson (whether the title is VP of sales, VP of business development, or simply sales rep) to figure out how to scale the sales.

A good salesperson is usually able to take some saleable product or service and get it in front of the right people at target customers, and shepherd that through the sales process. That process includes understanding the fit between the product and the customer and not promising things that the product can't do. A good salesperson is not a magician.

A bad salesperson is usually good at presenting a pipeline, and may even be well spoken, but usually doesn't hustle enough, or doesn't cover all the bases with a customer to consistently get sales.

If your product is not selling enough, there are two symptoms that can reveal whether your salesperson actually sucks, and it's all about the pipeline they present to you. This also applies if you are an investor/board member and the person showing you their pipeline is the entrepreneur (the CEO, rather than, say, the VP of sales).

The symptoms are: *The Never-Changing Pipeline* and *The Ever-Changing Pipeline*. Both are equally disastrous for a startup that is trying to meet a set of expectations, and both can only be discerned by looking at the sales pipeline and comparing it to those from previous months/quarters.

## The Never-Changing Pipeline

This one is easy to spot. One month, the pipeline has a healthy set of impressive prospects, some of which are "almost there" but haven't quite signed on the dotted line. The next month (or quarter, depending on your sales cycle), the pipeline looks exactly the same, with the same customers "about to close"! Perhaps there are a few new ones added at the bottom of the pipeline. This gets disastrous because the company is always waiting for that "big customer" to close—and they never actually sign on the dotted line!

The one caveat here is that if you have a long sales cycle, it may take you three months or more to figure out that the salesperson isn't really moving things correctly in the pipeline. It's harder to tell on a month-to-month basis in those sales cycles—perhaps the salesperson is doing the job right, but the nature of the long cycle means that's not readily apparent. However, even for those with long sales cycles, if after three months the pipeline hasn't changed at all, something may be wrong, or the salesperson may not be getting accurate information from the prospects.

### The Ever-Changing Pipeline

At first glance, this pipeline looks healthy: each deal is at a different stage of closing—some early, some late, and perhaps one or two near "verbal" and "about to close." You look at the pipeline the next month (or quarter) and it also looks healthy, with one or two customers about to close. The only problem is that they are completely different customers from the last month's. When you ask what happened to *x* or *y* from the previous month, the salesperson explains some logical reason why they have dropped out of the pipeline. Then, the next month (or quarter) you see the pipeline again, and it has a completely different set of companies about to close, and once again your "hot prospects" from the previous month have dropped off completely without any explanation. Of course, you will have some prospects drop off for valid reasons (budget, lack of a champion or sponsor at the prospect, etc.), but when it happens to every prospect that is "about to close" then something is definitely wrong.

### Product/Market Fit: Beware the "Sales/Product Death Match"!

What do you do when you are in a "minimal traction" state? You need to diagnose quickly whether it's the sales guy's fault, the founder's fault, or the product's fault.

How do you know when a product is not meeting the needs of the marketplace? This seems like a question with an obvious answer, but it usually is only clear after what I call the "sales/product death match." Usually this is a symptom of the underlying problem—a lack of product/market fit.

Sometimes, the first (and in many cases the only) salesperson will declare after talking to a few potential customers, that if only the product had feature *x*, then he/she could close the sale.

The product guys then go about implementing feature *x*; by that time, the potential customers are no longer in the pipeline. The delinquent sales guy then comes up with another set of technical issues or features that aren't present that make it hard to sell, and on and on.

While the initial requirements may reveal a deficiency in the product, this is clearly an example of a salesperson who isn't doing the job well and a product organization that is not pushing back. There is a natural tension between sales and product development that is healthy, but it can become unhealthy very quickly.

If sales is presenting a feature that a customer really needs before they can use the product, a good salesperson should be able to establish enough rapport with the potential client(s) to get them a) involved in the development of that feature as early beta testers, and b) to commit to buying the product if that feature is added.

If they can't do that, or if your startup goes through this cycle more than once—i.e., the salesperson promises sales if a feature is added, the feature is added, then the salesperson requests a different feature, all the while making no sales—then there is either a serious deficiency in the salesperson, or the product/market fit is not there.

## Scaling Beyond the First Few Customers

Paul Graham, of Y Combinator fame, says that he believes that startup founders have to do things that don't scale. In particular, he's talking about the first few customers—the founders have to figure out a way to not only get those customers themselves, but to make sure they are happy, rather than relying on a sales organization/VP of sales or a service organization/VP of customer service to do that.

Once that is done, then it's time to build the right sales (and marketing, though we'll talk about that in the next myth) organization to scale the product sales. That's what salespeople are for—taking a saleable product that has some fit in the market and scaling that to many customers.

At Offerpal, we scaled revenue very quickly in a few years. Before the scaling, the founders had to figure out the "pitch" to social game developers and make sure it worked. Once that was done, we handed over the pitch to salespersons who then gave the pitch to many more game developers, and this led to rapid scaling. It was only because we knew the pitch worked on some number of game developers that we could hand it over to "salespersons."

Later, the market for Facebook game advertising changed and Offerpal was no longer able to sell that specific product to Facebook game developers. At that point, it was time to find a different product, and the company pivoted to advertising for mobile app developers by buying Tapjoy. The reason Tapjoy was so attractive was that the founders of that company had already figured out the product/market fit for mobile game developers, and their product was scaling. After the acquisition, Offerpal (which later changed its name to Tapjoy) could then take the new mobile product and use its existing sales/marketing organization to scale that business even more quickly than the Tapjoy team was able to do on its own.

That's what a good sales organization can do: scale a product that has been shown to meet the needs of a market segment on a small scale.

## The Secret

***It's the founder's job to make sure there is product/market fit and the product is "saleable"; the salesperson's job is to scale sales by building a pipeline that moves.***

This secret behind the myth is really about understanding why a product is not selling. Although the goal is not necessarily to assign blame, a diagnosis is critical if you are going to get out of the "minimal traction" scenario. The reasons are usually some combination of product (usually one of the founders) and sales organization (or in the case of many startups, the single "sales guy") combined with the needs of the market.

Unlike in established organizations, where you can easily tell an effective salesperson from an ineffective one by looking at sales numbers, in a startup, especially in the early days, you have to look deeper than those.

Even a bad sales guy can sell an excellent product that fits the market's needs. A good sales guy can't sell a product that doesn't meet the needs of its customers, but perhaps they can identify some potential items the product is missing and get customers to commit to a sale on that basis.

If you are a founder, you have to sell the first few customers yourself. If you can't sell the product, how do you expect a salesperson, who knows the market and product less well than you do, to be successful?

And yet, blaming the salesperson, without first selling a few products themselves, is what many entrepreneurs end up doing; thus, this common refrain: "My sales guy sucks!"

Once you've sold to a few customers, hopefully these will become viable reference customers; then it should be much easier for a salesperson to sell the product to new prospects in the same market. If they can't, or if you start seeing the "ever-changing" and/or "never-changing" pipeline traps, then it's possible it's time for you to make a change in your sales organization.

# Myth #13

## If Only We Could Spend More on Marketing!

The corollary to Myth #12: My Product Failed Because My Sales Guy Sucks in the world of direct to consumer startups is when a founder throws up his or her hands and declares (to employees, investors, board members) that they simply don't have enough money to market the product.

Almost every failed consumer startup founder I've ever met will tell you that if they'd had more money to spend on marketing, their product/site/app would have been more successful.

Is this true? On one level, yes. If any startup spends more money on user acquisition, then it's likely the startup's site/product/app will get more users. More users mean more sales, and the chances of success go up. But, as with most of the myths in this book, if you hear this excuse, you really have to dig deeper to understand the true reasons why a consumer-oriented product or service doesn't catch on. Just spending more money doesn't ensure success. In fact, it often masks underlying problems with a product, particularly as a market starts to evolve to the later stages of the Startup Market Lifecycle.

## The Expensive World of Mobile Games

I saw this often in the mobile game industry as it started to mature. While many of the entrepreneurs who got into the game industry in 2009 and 2010 (and even 2011) found that they could get their games noticed by spending a modest amount of money, by the time 2012 came around, marketing mobile games had become an expensive proposition.

In the years from 2013 onward, you needed to spend two to five dollars *per new user* if you were buying installs via the leading mobile ad networks, and even the best games lost half of their users by the second day. This meant that the cost per user who played your game for more than one day was easily double the CPI price (four to ten dollars per returning user on the second day using the).

Since the most successful games had millions of players, this meant that to get these users strictly through paid marketing promotion (which was the most popular way to get users) would require $2 million to $10 million or more!

Needless to say, most of the tens of thousands of startups that were now producing mobile games did not have that kind of money. Even if you consider a one-to-one viral/organic ratio (i.e., each paid user who plays your game tells one friend), and cut the numbers in half—$1 million to $5 million— these amounts would still be prohibitive for all but VC-backed startups (and many of those also failed).

As you might expect, many small mobile game developers started to fold in late 2013, and this trend continued across the next few years. I started to hear, "if only we had more money, my game would have succeeded" from many mobile game developers. This was similar to what a lot of consumer-facing startups during the dot-com days said as well—we ran out of money to get visitors to our website.

Referring back to the Startup Market Lifecycle, the market was starting to move from the "super-hot" phase to the "maturing" phase. While some of the biggest hits in mobile gaming (measured by total revenue) were still to come, the market was no longer easy to penetrate and the market opportunity for new startups was severely restricted compared to what it had been.

As I said earlier, there is some truth in this myth. If the game company had spent more marketing dollars, they would certainly have gotten more users—no one can argue that. But whether those users would have stuck around for very long, or would have converted into profitable users for the company, is a whole different discussion. And those are the real factors that determine whether more money would have helped the startup succeed, or just postponed its inevitable failure.

To understand these factors, you have to get inside the numbers.

## What Startups Can Learn from Big Enterprises: ROI, LTV, and CAC

Most startup founders have the impression that big companies are wasteful, ineffectual, and lack vision, initiative, and risk-taking. One of the ways that this manifests in big companies is that they are always looking for a return on investment (ROI) before they spend on anything. That's why working for a bigger organization can be frustrating for entrepreneurs, who tend to operate on insight and gut feeling.

Startups rarely if ever worry about ROI. This is usually for one of the following reasons: 1) they have little funding, so they have no money to invest in projects, or 2) they have quite a big budget (usually raised from VCs), but they are focused on getting "users" and "scale" rather than "profits," so they think ROI is a meaningless calculation.

In fact, the refrain I often heard in business school is, "the more customers we get, the more network effects there will be, and we will be in a dominant position from which we can make outsize returns. . . ." The examples, of course, are companies like Amazon, Facebook, Twitter, and eBay, which didn't make any profits for many, many years while they built up a significant user base.

While there is some logic to this, it was by watching mobile gaming startups that I found out that big companies weren't really as dumb as I and most startup founders thought. If you delve into the numbers of most mobile gaming startups that failed during this time, you find that most of those games would not make back the money that they spent on user acquisition. The ROI was essentially negative. The easiest way to calculate this is to use two metrics—lifetime value (LTV) of a customer and customer acquisition cost (CAC). If LTV is less than CAC, then the ROI on spending marketing money is essentially negative. If the LTV is more than the CAC, then it is worth investing in marketing because eventually, the users will become profitable customers (even if they aren't on day 1 or even day 30).

Now, that's not to take anything away from the games that were created or released at that time—many of them were great games. They were fun. Some had great graphics. Others had addictive game play. But they didn't make more money than they would need to spend in order to get users at this time of the market. This of course had as much to do with the Startup Market Lifecycle as anything else, as the market had become crowded and expensive, whereas many of these same companies might have become profitable and sold for many tens (or hundreds of millions) of dollars only a year or two earlier.

Some games were viral and were able to get lots of users for free, which brought down their effective cost per install (eCPI), which for mobile games was the same as the CAC. Those games were more likely to spend marketing dollars, because for each user they paid to get, there was a certain number of free users they would also get, which brought down the effective CAC. The more viral a product becomes, the less it costs to get a customer, and the more likely it is that LTV > CAC.

This wasn't just true for games, but all kinds of mobile apps. I remember a lunch I had with Jason Citron, founder of Discord, whose first game, Fates of Fury, wasn't producing the kind of metrics that showed they could build a big, profitable business (we'll discuss Discord more in the next myth). However, they had decided to release a chat app for gamers, which was getting hundreds of thousands of new users per month. When I asked how much they were spending on those users, the answer was nothing. The users were virally coming on, encouraged by the initial user base who would introduce the product to their friends. Although Discord was not profitable (and would not be for many years), the CAC was essentially zero—which meant that any investor could look at it and realize that it could one day become a profitable business.

Traditional physical product businesses solve this problem by changing the price. If it costs two dollars to build a doohickey, and it costs one dollar to get a customer for that doohickey, then the price needs to be at least three dollars, right? You can use that same logic to determine the pricing of a car, with its component parts, shipping, administration costs, right down to the percentage that dealers earn when reselling the car.

Unfortunately, when your product is free to use—which is the case for many free-to-play games—this is not a meaningful calculation. You can make things in the game (usually acquired by users using virtual currency and in-app purchases) more expensive, but then it's possible that you will have even fewer paying customers than before.

## Before Network Effects Can Be Achieved, What Metrics Do You Need?

That said, there are many examples where network effects really do matter. eBay is one of them—the number of buyers and sellers that signed onto the system mattered. If you want to sell your product on eBay, you can be sure that there will be somebody out there to buy it. Similarly, on a social network like Facebook, the number of people who are on the network affects the number of people who will find the network useful. In some cases, with messengers and chat apps, users will drag their friends and family onto the app.

By finding investors who are happy with a "maximize market share" strategy, a company like Facebook could be unprofitable for years and then at some point they could roll out ads to their millions of users and eventually start making billions of dollars from that.

Unfortunately, in Startup Land, though every startup now claims to be like Facebook, every company isn't Facebook. The problem is that for each of those examples, there are many more that made the same argument but never got there. One of the most important things to understand about network effects is that it's not just about how large the number of users is, it's the density of users that matters.

To be clear, if a product is not making money, that doesn't preclude it from being successful, but as we have shown, *unit economics do matter at some point*, particularly when the market enters the maturing phase. In particular, the cost of getting new customers is critical—if your product is getting tons of new customers for free (through word of mouth, etc.), then it's a good sign that you have the kind of metrics that will eventually make your startup financially successful as well!

Most of the mobile game makers who ran out of money and didn't have enough to market their game, weren't able to convince someone (investors, publishers, etc.) that their game's metrics were good enough that they would eventually be profitable.

That's why initial metrics are so critical. I had one game company founder tell me that his LTV (lifetime value) was equal to one dollar, and he could get users for slightly less than a dollar. Ignoring the fact that there are costs other than marketing, this might be a situation where you could acquire users at least pseudoprofitably. Then I asked him what level of scale he was dealing with, and he told me the number of users he was buying was small—hundreds per day.

I told him that if he got what he was looking for—more marketing dollars—he wouldn't be able to stick with buying hundreds per day. He'd be buying thousands, if not tens of thousands, of users per day. The problem was that the metrics changed as he started to drive more volume.

The LTV (lifetime value) went down and the CAC (customer acquisition cost) went up. This wasn't that uncommon with mobile games. So now his LTV was really something like seventy cents (after Apple's 30 percent cut), and the costs of acquiring a user was well over a dollar and a half and rising.

## Network Effects and Density

If network effects are truly there, you should be able to demonstrate them in some small way and show metrics that indicate that having more money will let them scale. Facebook did it with incredible density of users—on college campuses where it was introduced, it spread like wildfire (cost of user acquisitions was virtually zero in those days as it spread through word of mouth), and most people signed up because their friends were signed up. As they graduated and became young professionals in the real world, they were still signing up their friends, which eventually allowed Facebook to spread across many more sectors of the population.

If you look at LinkedIn, even when the number of users was small (say, less than fifty thousand), it had incredible density. I was one of the first fifty thousand users, and its density was in one industry: high tech. I joined because other computer programmers I knew were joining.

Density is a kind of metric that can show how network effects are really achieved. There are some legitimate businesses where network effects matter. Also, when you have density, your cost of user acquisition goes down. Why? Because people talk to each other in the "dense" market, and you get additional customers for free. If you paid four dollars for one customer, but that customer got three friends to sign up for your product/service for free, then your effective CAC is actually a dollar per user, not four dollars. It's much easier to have a lifetime value of one dollar than four dollars in a freemium product.

In the earlier example of Discord, the density came from gamers, who wanted a reliable voice chat app that they could use while playing other games (and that was better than Skype, which had all kinds of issues at the time). If you have some level of density within a user group, your CAC should go down, as Discord's did, to very little because existing users will bring new users onto the product.

## Growing a Family Network: Life360

One of the examples we keep coming back to in this book is Life360, which was a smartphone app that helped families communicate. The company went for a few years without significantly scaling, focusing on building the right user experience. But Life360 wasn't your typical startup. Investors stuck with them because there really was an inherent block to scaling, but it was temporary—most families in the beginning had only one smartphone and everyone else in the family had either a feature phone or no cell phone at all. By late 2010 and after, when multiple family members began to have smartphones—particularly the cheaper Android devices—the company really started to take off and could begin demonstrating its network effects across families.

The difference is that Life360 was able to convince its investors to put money behind its vision because they were able to show some results along the way. Eventually, Life360 became one of the most downloaded apps of all time, with hundreds of millions of downloads. The vision paid off because there were logical reasons why scaling would take time, and tangible network effects when all family members had smartphones.

## Calling All Shoppers

Let's look at another mobile app company: Sift Shopping, like Life360, spent the first year growing modestly.

Saurin Shah, the founder, says that he had approximately sixty- or seventy-thousand registered users, whereas one of their competitors had two- or three-million users—a definite difference of scale.

Saurin says, "they probably had a better word-of-mouth coefficient than we had, but it was not word of mouth only. It was also quite a bit of marketing spend."

Like many mobile startup founders, Saurin wasn't able to convince his investors to put in the kind of money that was necessary to scale the shopping app to the same scale as some of his competitors. Both Saurin and his investors were counting on organic growth, which never happened.

But which came first, the organic growth numbers or the investment? Refer back to Myth #5: Two Guys and a Business Are Better Than Two Guys and a Plan: most likely, the metrics weren't there to convince investors to put more money in.

The investors wanted to see better organic growth compared to their competitors', otherwise it might be too expensive to spend the kind of money that would be necessary to catch up to his competitors.

Eventually, Saurin and his board decided to pivot the company away from the consumer app, because they didn't have the metrics needed to convince either his existing or new investors to put in the large marketing budget that might be needed.

## How Much Should You Spend?

I remember when we sold our mobile game company to Japanese gaming giant DeNA, I asked how much marketing budget we could have to spend on our games. My new boss's answer was: "Unlimited."

I thought this was ridiculous—how could we have an unlimited marketing budget?

His caveat was that as long as LTV > CAC (the customer lifetime value was greater than the customer acquisition cost), we could keep spending. As soon as LTV < CAC, we would have to stop spending.

As an early stage startup, we weren't used to tracking these things so closely, so we had no idea how much we should spend. This is something that startups can learn from bigger companies—how to measure unit economics and how to spend money profitably on user acquisition.

In the mobile game world, this particular public company measured LTV as the amount a group of users spent in the sixty days after installation. So, if there were ten thousand users on day one, they would add up all the spending of those users for the first 60 days, then divide the number by ten thousand. If they spent ten thousand dollars, then the LTV would be a dollar. Your own business may be use a different period of time, but most freemium models will have a similar model of dividing the total revenue generated by a group of users by the total number of users (which includes users who don't pay anything and some subset of users who do pay).

For SaaS and b2b businesses, the LTV is different—you would have to pick a time period that makes sense—say, twelve months or twenty-four months, and add up the customer revenue. Your cost of customer acquisition would be different too—consisting of the salaries of salepeople, etc.

## Startup Tool #3: Calculating LTV and CAC

This worksheet can help you calculate your cost of user acquisition and lifetime value. You have to pick two time periods—periods of your marketing campaign (in number of days), and then measure the revenue generated by all users you acquired during that campaign. This is particularly useful for freemium sites, where some of your users are not paying and some are. You can also use it if your site or app has a freemium or paid user model.

| Some Basic Date Information | | |
|---|---|---|
| Campaign Start Date: | _________ (a) | The date your marketing spend started.<br>Example: April 1 |
| Campaign End Date: | _________ (b) | The date your marketing spend ended (for this measurement).<br>Example: April 5 |
| # of Days in Campaign: | _________ (c) | If you want to measure per day, you can calculate this as (b)–(a)<br>Example: 4 days |
| Total Lifetime Period: | _________ (c) | The time period you are measuring revenue for.<br>Example: 60 days, 90 days, or 1 year. |

| Customer Calculation Worksheet | | |
|---|---|---|
| Total Amount Spent: | _________ (1) | Total amount spent during that period.<br>Example: $10,000 |
| Total Paid Users: | _________ (2) | Users that were acquired directly by marketing spend.<br>Example: 2,000 |
| Total New Users: | _________ (3) | The total number of new users you got during the campaign period.<br>Example: 5,000 |
| Total Organic Users: | _________ (4) | Calculate by (3) – (2)<br>Example: 5,000–2,000 = 3,000 |
| CAC (paid): | _________ (5) | This is the cost of customer acquisition for a paid user.<br>Divide (1) by (2).<br>Example: $10,000/2,000 = $5 per user |

| Customer Calculation Worksheet | | |
|---|---|---|
| CAC (effective): | ________ (6) | This is your real CAC, or effective CAC. Divide (1) by (3).<br>Example: $10,000/5000 = $2 per user |
| Total Revenue for Cohort: | ________ (7) | This is the total revenue generated over your target period by the users in (3).<br>Example: 3,000 users generated $15,000 in revenue |
| LTV: Lifetime Value for a Customer: | ________ (8) | This is how much money per customer. Divide (7) by (3).<br>Example: $15,000 / 5,000 users = $3 LTV per customer |

Finally, your LTV (8) should be greater than your CAC (6) for you to profitably acquire users. How much more it needs to be depends on factors beyond marketing spend.

| Profitability Calculator: | ________ (9) | Take (8) – (6)<br>Example: $3 – $2 = $1 profit per user |
|---|---|---|

## The Secret

***It's not just about how much money you spend on marketing. Look under the hood at LTV and CAC. If you can't convince investors to give you more money for marketing spend, your metrics are probably off.***

The underlying kernel of truth behind this myth is that your product didn't get as many users as you would like because you didn't spend enough money on marketing it.

The reason for that is most likely that you *didn't have* enough money for marketing. That means you either need to find a cheaper way to market your product, or you need to convince someone to give you enough money to market it the way you want until you can prove the network effects, if any.

But the fact that didn't happen reveals the real reason a product may not be working—inability to show the metrics (the ROI) that would convince someone to put money into marketing the product. There are many reasons why that might have happened, but in the end, they usually come down to a failure to show promising metrics, or to show metrics that can scale, or simply bad unit economics.

While there are some companies that have true network effects, and investors are willing to fund them until the network gets big enough to have real defensibility, the network effect should show up in a reduced cost of user acquisition (because people in the network will pull in other users). Also, most investors would ask you to figure out the ROI, and often are only willing to give you the money you need if you can defend the investment.

This isn't all bad—it can force you to find a different way to get customers than by simply spending on marketing. The most successful and dominant products had a CAC of zero in the early days because of density in a particular population. But products that are inherently viral or which have great word of mouth are few and far between; if you can show that your product is one of them, then you are in good shape. The underlying secret behind this myth can force the startup to become more creative in its approach to taking its product to the market.

# Myth #14

## Fail Fast, Pivot Quickly

As a complement to the traditional advice to "focus, focus, focus," we come to another piece of advice that is thrown around regularly in Startup Land: "Fail fast, pivot quickly."

The term "pivot," taken from sports or dancing, has become extremely popular in the startup world. And in the last few myths, we saw how pivots were often *necessary* when initial products failed to meet expectations. In this myth, we'll explore how you should pivot, and sometimes when you shouldn't pivot at all!

The conventional wisdom in Silicon Valley and beyond has become that you should "fail fast" so that you can move on to something that may have more potential to build the "next big thing." Should you really abandon a product when it isn't doing well, and do something else? Or should you hold on to your initial vision until you can find traction with your current product?

Underneath this myth and talk of pivoting is *opportunity cost*—that is, what if I could be more successful if I spent this amount of time doing something else? This applies to a product in a startup. It also applies to your own time in being founder of a startup: if you feel that your startup isn't doing as well as it could, should you leave to do another startup? How will this impact your cofounders, your investors, etc.? How will it impact your mental and financial health (though we'll talk more about stress in Stage 6: The Underworld and Return: Myths About Life and Death in a Startup).

## Startup Model #7: The Four Quadrants of Pivoting

Let's talk a little bit about how and where (figuratively speaking) companies might pivot.

To explore how startups pivot, let's look at a theoretical model, bringing back the useful construct of the Four Quadrants. In this case, let's look at the Four Quadrants of Pivoting, formed, like all such models, by the intersection of two very different axes: market and product.

- **Axis 1: Market.** This axis is simply showing markets that you are currently in. If you look to the right, this shows expansion into an adjacent market. Of course, as in most axes in Four Quadrants models, the market axis can be defined in many different ways, so this is more of a "theoretical" or "subjective" axis than a real one. For example, if you were in the mobile gaming market, an adjacent market might be the social (Facebook) gaming market, or the console gaming market. If you were building document management solutions for law firms, an adjacent market might be corporate law departments or government agencies. If you were selling to financial services companies, an adjacent market might be a subset of the very vast financial services segment (brokers, for example) or insurance companies. You might even consider consumers who are logging into financial websites as a "different" market, a little farther down this axis.
- **Axis 2: Product/Technology.** The second axis is your particular offering. It consists of your product and its underlying technology and parts. For example, if you were building a document management system for large insurance companies, the subcomponents might be a document database, a version control system, a user interface for managing workflow, etc. When you travel adjacently along this line, it might be another product built on similar technology or a subset for companies like yours. Suppose you are a mobile gaming company and have built a kick-ass analytics engine. You might pull this product out and offer it to other mobile app developers. The more "generic" analytics engine might have slightly different requirements, but uses much of the same technology as your initial game analytics did. So, this axis means starting with your exact product, and moving farther on this axis means finding a "completely different" product.

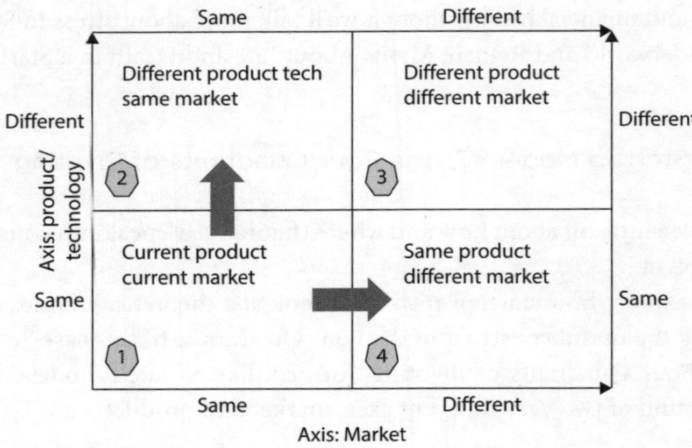


Figure 14.1
The Four Quadrants of Pivoting. Created by the author

Although direction along both of these axes are relative and subjective, they provide a pretty good mental model to think about pivoting, as is illustrated in figure 14.1: The Four Quadrants of Pivoting.

Looking at figure 14.1, let's start with Quadrant 1 (starting from the lower left and counting clockwise). This is the product and/or market that your startup is currently going after. It might be enterprise software for the financial industry. It might be analytics for mobile games. It might be a consumer social networking site or app.

If you ever play old strategy board games like Risk, or study military strategy, you know that it's usually easier to win and hold on to a territory that is adjacent to one that you are already in or control. While I personally believe that the military analogy for business has been overdone, in this case there is some truth for startups. It is (usually) much easier to move from Quadrant 1 to one of the adjacent quadrants (2 and 4, Same Product, or Same Market) than it is to shift to Quadrant 3 (Different Product and Different Market). Let's look at each of these quadrants in more detail:

- ***Quadrant 2: Same Product, Different Market.*** A more accurate description of this might be "similar product, different market." The main idea of this quadrant is that it is an area that you can move to without modifying your product a whole lot. The "movement" from your current quadrant is primarily a sales and marketing movement, though it may also require some product work.

One way to think of movement from a market perspective is to move to an adjacent market. Another way to define a movement of market is to think of being more specific or more general. You would be moving to a smaller market if you had created a product for "everyone" but found that you were getting traction in a particular segment and so decided to focus on that segment. A bigger market would be the opposite—making the product more generic to be used by everyone in the market and not just your initial target segment. Here are two very famous examples:

- Facebook started out catering to a specific market: college students. That was part of its original mission, if it had one. Then, at some point, the company broadened the market to "everyone" and it became a social network for the masses. The fact that its core user base was graduating and entering the real world made this an easier transition than it might have been otherwise.
- Looking at the traditional SQL database world, Sybase was a general database and a competitor to Oracle, the first and largest relational database company. However, Sybase found that they had particular success in a specific segment, the financial services industry. This was partly because of their architecture, so although Sybase continued to be a general-purpose database, they found ways to focus on certain markets. This is a very common movement and is based on the strengths of a particular product/technology offering.

  In both of these cases, neither company's product failed; they either narrowed or expanded the product line to achieve bigger success.

- ***Quadrant 4: Same Market, Different Product***. In a move to this quadrant, your startup finds some need that exists in your current customers (or prospects) that you didn't know about before, and you end up building a product for this market. As two examples show:

  - Intelligize made a SaaS product for SEC and securities lawyers, which made it easy for them to check precedents by pulling up other SEC filings that were similar (their first product was called "Precedent Checker"). While this was a need, they found that these lawyers also needed help in responding to SEC queries. In fact, this turned out to be a bigger need than the first one, and so they created a product around that ("SEC Comment Checker"). This was a different product, but for the same market. Although the product was different, they were able to leverage their existing technology and experience to build the new product quickly. As they expanded their set of products/features within this single market (securities lawyers), they became the leader in that space and eventually sold to LexisNexis.

- In my first startup, Brainstorm Technologies, we made tools to help companies connect their Lotus Notes groupware applications/databases to apps developed by Microsoft Visual Basic. While doing this, we were asked to implement solutions for our clients, many of whom wanted to use the product to pull data out of Notes and put it into a SQL database (like Oracle or Sybase) or vice versa. We then created a product that did this, called DataLink for Lotus Notes, which became our best-selling product. This was a different product that we sold to the same companies we had been selling our first product to!

In each of these cases, the resulting opportunity was bigger and more lucrative than the first opportunity. When this happens, it's a cause to celebrate—don't berate yourself for choosing the wrong need/product in this market in the first place! In fact, if these two startups hadn't created their first product and gotten in the door, they wouldn't have learned about the bigger opportunities looming in the same market.

- ***Quadrant 3: Different Market, Different Product.*** This quadrant is, of course, the most difficult to pivot to. It usually requires a complete restart of the company, since you're in another business with a different product. How does this happen? Sometimes it can happen if you identify a new opportunity in another market and your company acquires another company:

    - As an example, Offerpal was one of the leading ad networks in the Facebook gaming space. It decided at some point to acquire Tapjoy, which was in an adjacent market—ads for mobile games. Afterward, as Offerpal's Facebook business declined, it changed its name to Tapjoy and became a leading mobile ad network, moving completely out of its initial market and product.
    - In another well-known example, BEA Systems (founded in 1995 to do a type of middleware) acquired WebLogic (which made a new thing called a web application server) in 1998 as the web was booming. As the web app server became its main business, BEA changed its branding and became known for its web application server much more than for its previous middleware.

- Slack, which went on to become a billion-dollar–plus platform for enterprise collaboration, originally started as a game company. They ended up pivoting into a totally different space and different market, even though they used some of the underlying technology they had built originally to do it. Contrast this with Discord, which built an app (different product) for the same market (gamers) in its highly successful pivot.

## Fail Fast? Pivot Quickly?

This phrase, "fail fast and pivot quickly," is tossed around a lot in Silicon Valley, and has gained popularity through the recent "Lean Startup" movement.

For many companies that successfully pivot, however, it isn't a wholesale shift from product A to product B all at once.

Usually the company has some success with product A, and it is this mild success that positions them to see the opportunity for product B (or from market A to market B). If the company had simply shifted or pivoted before they had given product A enough of a chance, they may never have gotten to product B.

As in the examples in this myth and Myth #11: Focus, Focus, Focus, for example, Microsoft moved from a development tools company to an OS company; BEA became a web app server company; Offerpal became Tapjoy, a mobile ad network. The pivots happened *years into* the life of the company, and in each of these cases they had some success with their first products. The real pivot was more like an add-on initially. They didn't just shut down the old business on day one of the pivot. What happened was that this "new thing" grew so big that it took over the company itself.

## A Cautionary Tale: Pivoting for Investors

It's become common for startups that are joining accelerators to pivot based on feedback they get from the accelerator or their mentors. However, there is a danger in pivoting to a different market simply to accommodate a particular investor (who may be an accelerator, a VC, or a strategic investor).

As an example, we had one company that pitched us an idea at Play Labs to build an augmented reality (AR) application for books. We weren't that excited about this application, but liked the team. We told them to try to pivot to some other market we might be more excited about if they wanted to be in our accelerator. They ended up going to a market that appeared more lucrative, the escape room market. We were more excited about this market and invested in them and let them into the accelerator.

The thing that we didn't really take into account was that neither of the two cofounders was superpassionate about this market. They were pivoting just to get into the accelerator. This is almost always a bad idea. Startups are hard, as we'll see in the final stage of the entrepreneur's journey, Stage 6: The Underworld and the Return: Myths About Life and Death in a Startup.

It's important that the entrepreneurs understand the market they are going after better than the investors do. If you are pivoting just to get money from an investor, it's possible the investors understand the market better than you do, or that neither you nor the investors really understand the market. You should pivot only when you have had ample time to explore a market and have decided that there is a product/market and personal fit between your team's strengths and weaknesses and the market you are going after.

## The Secret

### *Fail Slowly, Pivot Carefully*

You might say the *real* secret to many pivots is to survive long enough on an initial product so that you are in a position, a year or two down the road, to recognize a much bigger opportunity.

The conventional wisdom in Silicon Valley has become to abandon products quickly, not giving them enough time to prove themselves, and often not giving the entrepreneurs enough time in a market to really, truly understand the needs in that market. Pivoting should be done using validation that you have gotten while you were trying to sell your first product into the first target market.

Sometimes the pivot is really a skunkworks project that one of the founders has a hunch about. Think Myth #11: Focus, Focus, Focus. This "small project" quickly grows so big that it eventually becomes clear that is where the real opportunity is.

So, should you pivot or shouldn't you? As with many myths in this book, the answer is: it depends,

In the sidebar, let's look at two successful companies we have been following throughout this book—one that did a pivot and one that didn't: Gnip (the social network API) and Life360 (the mobile family social networking app) to look once again at the complexities of the decision "*to pivot or not to pivot*."

### A Tale of Two Startups: One Pivoted and One Didn't

*Gnip and pivoting in the social network marketplace*

In Myth #11: Focus, Focus, Focus, we told the story of Gnip, which successfully pivoted to Quadrant #4 (similar product, different market). After a year of trying to sell their product to social networks, they used this knowledge to sell the APIs to enterprise developers who wanted to access this public data. The enterprise market proved more lucrative.

Jud Valeski, reflecting on this experience, says: "We went and knocked on all the doors of the social networks (which we called publishers) . . . No one bought it . . . After a year of being told no, one thing we did pretty well is we diligently said if we were told no for twelve months we were going to stop doing whatever it was we were doing. In hindsight, I think that was pretty smart . . . We had a time frame. We had a definition for what success or failure meant in that time frame. We didn't necessarily know what we were going to do if we had to say no, but we knew we were not going to continue beating our head against the wall."

*Life360 and the decision not to pivot*

Sometimes, though, you want to stick to your guns because you have the right product. When Alex Haro and his cofounder started Life360 in the wake of the Hurricane Katrina disaster, they knew they wanted to start a company that would help families communicate and coordinate using mobile devices. When they introduced their app in 2008, they got very few users.

Using the conventional wisdom, they might have "failed fast and pivoted," but they believed in their vision to help families, and they persisted. In 2010, suddenly, every member of the family had a smartphone, and the network effects that Life360 was waiting for started coming into play. By 2019, Life360 was one of the most downloaded apps of all time, and the company went public.

Alex says, "Yeah, and I think we get credit now for being way ahead of our time on our vision, but we're only now proving the stuff we were talking about six years ago. Even though it took us two and half years before we really started to get any users . . . we were constantly testing and validating. We knew for a fact that families wanted something along what we wanted to build, and we knew that the mobile market wasn't ready to support it, but we knew once the market was there, we'd be able to put the pieces in place."

Alex adds: "A lot of the successes out there, people sometimes think, 'Oh my god. This popped out of nowhere.' But the reality is that the founders have been trying for much longer than is immediately obvious."

# Bonus Myth #B-4

## There Is No Such Thing as Bad Publicity

This is one of those myths that is tossed around frequently, particularly after a company has had some bad publicity.

At the very least, the argument goes, any kind of publicity should let many more customers know about your company and your product, right?

Well, not always. I can attest that some publicity is bad and you should avoid it—but I didn't always believe that was the case. In fact, I'd say that I subscribed to this myth, which was why I agreed to go on *The Daily Show with Jon Stewart* in 2011, which ended up being a PR disaster.

Like all myths, this one has a kernel of truth to it. If you can get past some bad publicity, the company can emerge stronger, but that doesn't mean you won't lose some customers or some luster.

▶ To read the full text of this **Bonus Myth**, including the various ways to understand publicity for startups, please download the Supplement to *Startup Myths and Models* from www.zenentrepreneur.com ◀

# Stage 5

## Acquiring the Treasure
## *Myths About Exiting Your Company*

---

After defeating the enemy, surviving death and finally overcoming his greatest personal challenge, the Hero is ultimately transformed into a new state, emerging from battle as a stronger person and often with a prize.

The Reward may come in many forms: an object of great importance or power, a secret, greater knowledge or insight, or even reconciliation with a loved one or ally. Whatever the treasure, which may well facilitate his return to the Ordinary World, the Hero must quickly put celebrations aside and prepare for the last leg of his journey.

DAN BRONZITE, "THE HERO'S JOURNEY"

---

### Introduction to Stage 5

We've now reached the stage that everyone who joins a startup looks forward to—finding the treasure! Of course, in Startup Land, this is *usually* a very lucrative exit (a sale of your company for more than $*x*) or an IPO.

What is the $*x*? It depends on whether you went down the VC path or were a bootstrapped startup. Another type of exit, the initial public offering (IPO), is popular when the stock markets are doing well. Technically, an IPO is not an exit, but a financing event, but if you are lucky and still own some meaningful percentage of the company, it means your stock will be worth some millions of dollars (for real, this time).

If you didn't raise any money from outside investors, then $*x* can be a much smaller number causing a celebration. It could be a few million dollars or more. If you did go down the VC route and have raised a series

A round of financing and/or follow-on roads, chances are your VCs won't be happy if you don't sell the company for *at least* $100 million.

It's at this stage of the journey that our heroes and their allies usually learn that exits are not as simple as they might appear at first glance. Valuation on an exit is different from valuations in financing rounds (which were based on expectations, as you'll recall from the myths in Stage 2). In an exit, the valuation should be the real valuation, correct?

Again, it depends, and that's what these myths are all about.

In mythological adventures, the treasure is usually known. In *The Hobbit*, there was a literal treasure (guarded by the dragon Smaug), which the adventurers hoped to get. In other cases, the treasure might be rescuing a princess (as in *Star Wars*), defeating an evil, dark lord, or simply getting home (as in the case of Odysseus in the *Odyssey*). Joseph Campbell said that sometimes the treasure was a magic elixir that gave special powers and insight to heroes after they completed their adventure. In this sense, even if your first startup fails, like my first startup did, you still get the magic elixir, the powers and insights that come from having completed the startup journey.

### *Overview of the Myths*

On a practical note, this chapter goes over some of the burning questions and assumptions you might have as a first time (or perhaps even second or third time) entrepreneur about finding the treasure. For one thing, when is it the right time to sell the company?

This is a complicated question—and anyone who says the opposite is shining you on. I know founders who were offered $100 million or more for their companies during the dot-com boom, only to turn down those offers because they thought they were going to go public and be worth well over $1 billion (in most cases, unfortunately and possibly predictably, that didn't happen!).

On the flip side, I've met many entrepreneurs who sold their companies for $10 million, $20 million, even $50 million or less than a $100 million, who later realized that they could've sold for a lot more if they had held on for a few years. Mark Zuckerberg famously turned down a $1 billion offer for Facebook. In hindsight, it seems like he made a good move, but it's rarely that simple. The key is a combination of factors, including fully understanding the Startup Market Lifecycle, which we'll revisit in this chapter.

Negotiating a sale of a company can be complicated. We'll also look at the different ways to exit, including secondaries and IPOs, as opposed to outright sales. Once upon a time, selling to a public company was considered as good as getting cash. Then, after the dot-com crash of the early twenty first century, it wasn't. This is because many public companies were doing acquisitions with overvalued stock, which later crashed, resulting in valuations that were significantly less. Weren't the founders of the acquired companies able to sell the public stock? In many cases, the stock they received was restricted stock, which means it couldn't be sold for six months or more, which was just enough time for the stock market to crash.

Structuring an acquisition for the best possible outcome is also very difficult to do. It would seem from the the discussion about public stock that it's better to get all cash, isn't it? It turns out the answer is: not necessarily. We'll delve into the complexities of structuring acquisitions with the myths in this chapter. How much should you expect to get up front, and how much should you allow for an earnout? Again this seems like a simple answer (it would be best to get it all up front, wouldn't it?) but the real answer is more complicated as earn-outs are used to get the valuations up to levels that acquirer wouldn't be comfortable paying if the transaction is structured with 100 percent up front payment.

Of course, no set of myths in this book would be complete without delving into the psychological factors that come into play in any startup journey—and this stage is no different. We'll look at the reasons why you *think* the acquirer is interested in your company, and then look again at what might be the *real* reason. This is important when you are deciding whether to sell and for negotiating a sale.

# Myth #15

## At This Rate, My Startup Will Be Worth Twice as Much Tomorrow!

Many first-time entrepreneurs are flattered when they get their first acquisition offer. Even a relatively small acquisition offer—for, say, a million or two, seems like amazing progress (small only by Silicon Valley standards, since a million dollars or two is nothing to sneeze at in most parts of the world!).

This myth, like many of the myths about valuation in Stage 2, arises from entrepreneurs not understanding how and when the company's valuation increases (or decreases) with the overall market.

The heart of the logic behind this myth goes something like this: If the company is two years old, and was worth almost nothing (let's say, one dollar) when it started, and if someone is willing to pay $2 million today, then the company is currently on a very fast track upward. If that current trend continues, the company should be worth $4 million in another year, and $8 million after that!

Or, if the revenue is at $3 million per year today, and someone is willing to pay $10 million for the company, then if the company does $6 million next year (i.e., double the revenue), then the company should be worth $20 million next year (double the valuation), right?

In fact, if the startup is growing, and this logic were correct, then all you have to do is hold on—just wait until the revenue grows, and the valuation will grow, right?

Wrong. Like many of the secrets underlying the myths in this book, the truth is more complicated than that!

The problem is that neither linear nor exponential growth patterns really work in startup valuations in a predictable way. Nor do profit multiples. Revenue multiples are often used, but even those aren't reliable—in fact, they vary greatly through the lifecycle of the company, and most important, through the stages of the market (as defined in the Startup Market Lifecycle).

## What's in a Valuation, Part 2

In Stage 2: Fuel for the Journey: Myths About Raising Money, we explored the disconnect between what entrepreneurs *think* a valuation means in raising financing, and what it *really* means.

A valuation for startups is really *a set of expectations* about the future performance of the company, which is almost always tied to the expectations of the market they are in. *Thus, the way the valuation of a startup changes is based on changes in expectations as much as any actual changes in revenue or customers.*

To truly understand how valuations of startups grow (and fall), you have to understand several factors (not necessarily in this order):

- Why do acquirers want to buy your company? We'll deal with this in more detail in Myth #16: They're Buying Us Because Our Product is Awesome! The upshot is that it's usually possible to figure out *why* someone wants to buy you, and this ties to how much they will pay for your startup.
- What stage in the Startup Market Lifecycle is your market in? Another way to ask this is: How hot is the market? A subsequent question to this one is, what kind of position does your company have in this (hot or not-so-hot) market? If you are the best-known company in a super hot market, you can get a significant premium over one of the many "me-too" players in a market. Even if the market is no longer super hot, but you are the best known company, that gives you a premium while valuations for others in the market are falling.

## Startup Model #8: Valuation Evolution by Stage

Companies' valuations tend to follow the overall market. This is true for public companies, whose valuations skyrocket during a bull market. However, it turns out that for startups, this (the market) is by far the most important factor in determining how much that startup is worth! And to arrive at a valuation, you have to figure out what stage of the Startup Market Lifecycle your particular startup market is in.

Let's revisit the stages of Startup Model #1: The Startup Market Lifecycle. In this model, you'll recall, the stages are *nascent*, *growing*, *super-hot*, *maturing*, and *mature*.

### Valuations Evolve with the Stage of Market

So what's a company worth in each of these stages? For software startups, you can usually value a company based on a multiple of revenues. The multiple of revenue seen by startups during these stages is graphed roughly in figure 15.1: Multiples of Revenues on Exit for Startups.

Note that this multiple is often used to *justify* a valuation rather than to set it, since in Startup Land every negotiation is exactly that—a negotiation. Since startups are considered an inefficient market in general, there will of course be exceptions, but these rough estimates give you a sense of how valuation multiples evolve with the stage of the market. By quoting these ranges in the appropriate stage of the market, you can usually get an acquirer to agree to a valuation in this range.

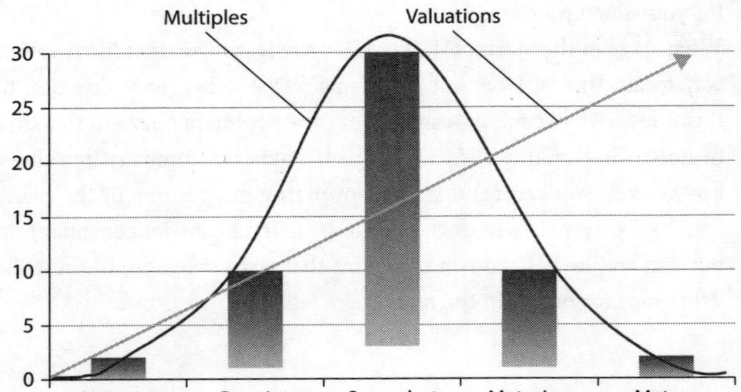


Figure 15.1
Multiples of Revenues on Exit for Startups. Created by the author

- *Nascent:* If the market is in this stage, valuations are hard to pin down because most acquirers don't really understand the market or why they need to spend money to acquire anyone in the market. Since companies at this stage of the market don't have a ton of revenue, most acquisitions in this market can be seen as "acqui-hires"—acquiring for talent, not product.
- *Growing.* In this stage of the market, valuation multiples start to grow. Because the market is relatively new, it's hard to quantify, but usually multiples are between 3× and 5× revenues for startups, and even acqui-hire prices start to rise. For example, in the social gaming market, early leaders like Zynga and SGN were able to buy other Facebook game companies for a few million dollars each, and these games usually had less than a million dollars in revenue—typically on the order of hundreds of thousands of dollars in annual revenue, but growing fast.
- *Super-hot.* When a market becomes *super-hot*, it's easy to get more than the 3× to 5× revenues. There are many examples of 10, 30, or even 100+ multiples of revenues in *super-hot* markets (though the very high end of these numbers is usually for companies with little or no revenue). Even acqui-hires during this market are inflated—and if you have a team of people who have experience in a *super-hot* market, you can usually sell your company for a decent amount, even if you don't have a product that's working or generating any revenue. In a super-hot market, recruiting talent into existing companies can be tough, so acquirers are willing to pay a premium to get a team that has worked together before and has experience in the market. As an example, when mobile gaming became hot, GREE, a public Japanese gaming company, bought OpenFeint, a leading network for mobile games, for over $100 million in late 2010. The total revenue of OpenFeint in the previous twelve months was less than $1 million—a revenue multiple of over 100! The reasons were twofold: GREE felt that it had missed the mobile gaming market in the West, and OpenFeint was a leading mobile gaming network—with over 70 million users.
- *Maturing.* As a market enters the maturing stage, valuations come back down to earth. You may still be able to still get a 3× to 5× revenue multiple, but consolidation has already begun, and there are usually more players than will survive in the market. As the market finishes maturing, there will be great money made by the emerging leaders (those who can still get 3× to 4× revenues), but many companies either

shut down or are sold for some nominal amount. As an example, in the mobile gaming space, the same acquirer, GREE, bought Funzio for $200 million in 2012. While that seems like a bigger amount, Funzio's revenues were already in the $50 million per year run rate, so the multiple of 4× revenue was much less than what it would have gotten with the same revenue a year or two earlier, when the market was super-hot. Also, Funzio had become the mobile leader in its type of games, which added a premium that other companies in this space were no longer getting. As an example, in 2012, Zynga, which had been valued in the public markets at 10× revenues, saw its stock fall back to earth, and was back at the 3× to 5× level, which was in fact the precipitating event for the transition from the *super-hot* stage to the *maturing* stage.

- *Mature*. When a market is mature, there are public companies in the market, and valuations are now based on multiples of earnings rather than of revenue. This is the traditional world of business that business schools like Stanford and Harvard and Columbia have a lot to say about. This stage doesn't mean that there isn't a lot of money to be made by the players that have established themselves. There is—it's just that it's hard for new startups to get in, and established players aren't interested in paying any kind of premium over cash flow to buy a company during this phase. P/E ratios in the stock market are an example of valuations being based on a multiple of earnings.

Within each stage, of course, if you are perceived as a leader, then the multiples tend to be in the higher end of the spectrum.

Also, while the "valuation multiple" curve goes up and down as the market matures, the "actual valuations" curve goes up and to the right. This means that if you add up all the actual valuations of companies funded or sold at each stage of the market, the numbers will be significantly higher in later stages of the market. This is because as markets mature, startup companies that become winners in the market have significant revenue—eventually in the billions—so even though their revenue multiple is lower, the absolute numbers are much bigger.

In 2016, mobile gaming companies like Kabam, King.com, Outfit7, Niantic, and others valued at a billion dollars or more went public or sold. If you added up all their valuations, they were higher than all the game companies sold in, say, 2010 or 2011 or 2012. By 2016, the mobile gaming market was a $30 billion market—much larger than it was when valuation multiples were sky-high. By the end of the decade, revenues were approaching a $70 billion market.

### Secret #1

***What your company is worth depends on the stage of the market and your position in it. Don't get confused about this.***

This secret brings us back to the reason why this myth exists. Entrepreneurs assume that if their company is doing $*x* in sales, and someone is willing to pay 5× to buy the company today, then they should just hang on until they double their sales. They will now have $2*x* in sales, and using the same *multiple*, they will now be worth 10×, right?

Wrong.

The real secret underlying this myth is that the *multiples* vary based on the stage, and you should keep this in mind when you decide whether you should sell your company.

If you can get 5× during a *super-hot* market, you might only be able to get a 2× or 1.5× multiple on revenues in a maturing market. So, if you double your revenues, your company may *actually be worth less than it is now*! This seems counterintuitive to pretty much every entrepreneur and investor I've ever met when they are involved in a valuation discussion. They simply can't imagine that the market is going to be in a different stage next year than it is this year!

In traditional business schools, we are taught that the best approximation for the future is the past. Unfortunately, in the reality of Startup Land, this can be considered a myth and the only reliable rule seems to be: the future will not equal the past.

What if your company has no revenue? This happens to consumer companies that are valued based on its number of users. Twitch, for example, had minimal revenue when it was acquired by Amazon for $970 million. Many traditional business schools graduates were at a loss to explain why. But the market for esports and streaming games was just getting started! Twitch did have 55 million monthly users, so this translated to a multiple of $17 per user. Moreover, if you are a company that is being valued highly in a *super-hot* space because of your number of users (and not your revenue), again you may assume that if you double your number of users, your company will be worth at least twice as much!

This may or may not be true—in fact, as the startup market matures, there is no guarantee that you will continue to be valued based on "users"—you will need to start showing revenue and how you will monetize those users.

This is a concept that seems straightforward in theory, but entrepreneurs can never seem to get their heads around it in practice. Thinking like an entrepreneur, it's hard to imagine how your company could be worth *less* if the company is making more progress (more customers, more users, more revenue)

The future is always bright, since entrepreneurs tend to be optimistic in nature and are always "selling the future." In fact, it's one of the traits of successful entrepreneurs that they are always selling a brighter future to employees, investors, and customers.

A great example is the consumer virtual reality (VR) market in games and entertainment—companies were getting significant funding and being valued pretty highly in 2015 and 2016. By 2017, the enthusiasm from investors had cooled significantly for consumer VR startups—and many VR startups were finding it hard to raise the next round of financing at *any* valuation, let alone at a higher valuation than they were getting in 2015 or 2016!

How is it possible that your company could be worth less a year from now even if you have more (customers, revenue, etc.)? It's simple math—if your revenues go up by two but your multiple goes down by more than two, the total valuation will be less!

### *How to Use This Secret in Timing Your Sale*

Ideally, if you understand this myth and this secret, you want to *not sell* the company during the nascent/growing phases. Instead, just wait until a market is in the super-hot stage, time your sale to the top of the market, just before or at the peak, and you'll walk away fat, smart, and happy!

Unfortunately, this is usually a pipe dream. It's very difficult to predict the *exact* top of a market. It is usually not that difficult to tell what stage you are in, if you have been through several startup markets, but predicting how long each stage will last and whether you are at the beginning or end of a stage is the real trick, and it can be very difficult to determine.

The only reliable way to know exactly when a particular market stage ends is through hindsight. However, looking at valuations can give you a pretty good sense of which stage you are in.

This brings us to the second secret underlying this myth.

### Secret #2

***Because it's difficult to predict the exact top of a market, this means you are selling your company either on the way up, or on the way down. Which would you rather do?***

It's good to sell at the top of a market. It's generally much better to sell on the way up than on the way down, because when valuations are falling, acquirers often put acquisitions on hold. If valuations in a market are falling, then all they have to do is wait, and your company will be worth less tomorrow than it is today!

On the other hand, when valuations are going up, acquirers are motivated to move quickly to buy companies, for the same reason that leads to this myth among entrepreneurs—because the price may be going up tomorrow! Get it today!

I've known many entrepreneurs who turned down great acquisition offers, particularly during the dot-com boom. One entrepreneur turned down a $120 million offer. Many years later, during the mobile gaming boom, another entrepreneur turned down a $400 million offer (with the support of his VCs) because they wanted to build a billion-dollar company. In both cases, the company ended up being worth much less a few years later.

Remember that in startups, the past does not equal the future!

### *To Sell or Not to Sell?*

The decision of whether to sell now or to wait is never an easy one. It is more of an art than a science, though understanding the stage of the market will help immensely.

Let's look at one difficult decision. One example that I was personally involved in was Tapjoy, which started its life as a mobile game company with such hits as *Tap Defense*, *Tap Sudoku*, etc. Tapjoy had moved into mobile advertising and had a unique model (called the incented install) that allowed advertisers to get lots of downloads, and mobile game developers to make lots of real money by offering virtual currency/points to users who were willing to install another app.

The model started to work really well in the fall of 2009. As we approached early 2010, each month brought with it increased revenue—$50K one month, $100K the next month, $150K the next month, then $200K, etc. And the trend showed no signs of slowing down. The two founders, Ben Lewis and Lee Linden, were happy with the growth but were worried about how long it would last.

The options were:

1. raise VC money (the top VCs in Silicon Valley were interested in investing in Tapjoy),
2. sell the company now, or
3. wait a few months to get to a higher revenue run rate, and then sell for a lot more money.

Lest you miss the point of the myths, each myth has an underlying kernel of truth. Since Tapjoy's revenues were climbing, they were sure to be worth more a year down the road. On the other hand, the market had passed the nascent stage and was in the growing stage, and multiples were starting to look like super-hot multiples (well over 3× to 5× revenues), but it was difficult to tell when the market would turn around.

Moreover, there were unquantifiable but significant market risks. The "incented install," which made most of the revenue, was a model whose life could be cut short by Apple, which was the dominant platform for mobile games at the time. This wasn't a theoretical risk—Apple was notorious for shutting down companies they didn't approve of in their ecosystem, and Facebook had literally shut down a similar model of revenue in social gaming not that long ago.

The founders decided to sell in March of 2010 to Offerpal, a company that had been doing quite well in the Facebook gaming space.

Should they have sold in 2010?

On the one hand, they got a great multiple on their revenues, and each of the founders received millions of dollars, and the company was less than a year old.

On the other hand, Tapjoy was growing rapidly, and that growth continued after the acquisition. The business went on to become a $100 million a year business (they were so successful that Offerpal changed its name to Tapjoy and became one of the largest mobile advertising networks!). So the founders and investors definitely would have made *more* if they had held on until then.

The answer seems obvious in hindsight, right? Well, not really.

The overarching message of the myths in this book is that things are rarely black and white. Selling when they did, they had a certain amount of money guaranteed—about a year and a half later, Apple *did* shut down the incented install business, and Tapjoy's revenue suffered as a result. By then acquirers weren't willing to pay nearly the same kinds of multiples for mobile advertising companies.

This is a great example of how holding on for a *little while* would make you more money, but holding on *too long* could have resulted in less money. This is obvious from looking at the valuation curve in Startup Model #9: Valuation in Secondaries: Common Versus Preferred.

Timing, as they say, is everything.

### *Sensing When the Market is Changing*

Although it's very difficult to predict the exact top of a market, there are usually signs in a market if that market is changing. Let's go back to another company, this one, curiously enough, also started by Offerpal cofounder, Anu Shukla, in the 1990s—Rubric Inc.

The company built a marketing automation solution to help enterprises manage all of their marketing campaigns, particularly as the internet was just becoming a key channel for marketing. Rubric had become one of the leaders of this new, emerging market ("marketing automation") since its inception nineteen months earlier.

Anu says, "We had a $30 million run rate, and I think we were the farthest ahead (in marketing automation). We had two competitors in the space that had emerged. We were the farthest ahead in terms of traction and in terms of product market fit for what we did, which was basically this lead generation thing that I had experience with. That was our focus, and we had twenty five customers, including Cisco, General Motors, and HP."

Traditional wisdom would say that if you are the market leader, you shouldn't sell, you should march on toward an IPO and define the market category. However, Anu and her cofounders decided to sell for $366 million in March of 2000 to Broadbase/Kana. Some of her investors were worried that they were leaving money on the table, getting only a 10× revenue multiple, while many of her peers in Startup Land turned down seven and eight figure offers during this period while they tried to build a billion-dollar company.

Keen observers will see that this was just before the dot-com bubble burst. However, neither Anu nor her investors claim that they knew exactly *when* the dot-com bubble was going to burst.

Anu explains that she could sense that the market for marketing automation was changing. When they had started selling the product, companies were willing to buy a marketing automation product from a startup. However, they started to notice that increasingly, the market was merging with sales force automation and customer support automation to become one big, maturing market, which started to be called "customer relationship management."

Anu says:

> A big factor is to consider the market—and this gets back to the issue of product market fit. I think that's what startups are all about—getting to the product market fit. If you get it, you're just going to keep going. You have to keep executing but you will keep going. In our case what was happening was that while we were selling marketing automation as a standalone solution, customers were starting to think of it as literally getting rolled up into CRM (customer relationship management).
>
> Companies were actually making decisions such as, "Look, I'm not going to buy marketing from one person, customer service from another, and sales force automation from someone else. I'm going to buy all three from Oracle or all three from SAP or all three from someone."
>
> In our case we either had to build out those other functions, which would require a lot of money, or we would have to get incorporated into somebody else's solution. That's why BroadBase/Kana were going for a full suite—customer service, analytics, marketing, etc.

Given the subsequent crash and the merging of the various "customer-facing" markets into CRM, selling for $300 million rather than going for the billion-dollar outcome seems like a prescient decision. It was made because the CEO/founder sensed that the market was already changing. If they had held on longer, after the market crashed, there is no guarantee they would have gotten that same kind of price (and as anyone who had a startup during that time can tell you, they could have found themselves suddenly worth significantly less, even as their revenue increased!).

## *Conclusion*

Entrepreneurs are tempted to think that the current trend will continue indefinitely, or at least for a few more years. This can make them hesitant to sell their companies when they're doing well, and then they suddenly find themselves anxious to sell when the market has crested or is falling. Unfortunately acquirers aren't as hot to trot when the market has passed peak.

The most important factor to figure out in trying to make a decision to sell is which market stage you are in.

You can tell this by looking at the valuation multiples that startups are getting from acquirers. If you are in the nascent or growing stages, this myth is probably true—your company will be worth a lot more in six months or a year, assuming the trend continues and you continue to execute well.

The valuation multiples for startups drop rapidly after cresting in the *super-hot* stage. It's important to try to keep this in mind when deciding whether or not to sell your company. Since it's difficult, if not impossible, to time the market precisely, you're usually either selling on the way up or selling on the way down—which would you rather do?

# Myth #16

## They're Buying Us Because Our Product is Awesome!

If you hang around Silicon Valley (or any hub for tech startups) long enough, you'll inevitably meet people whose companies have been bought (*acquirees*) and those who were in companies that did the buying (*acquirers*).

If you were to ask an acquirer why they went ahead with a particular acquisition, you'll hear some variation of the statement, "We bought company A because of *x*."

If you are really clever, and then go talk to the acquirees in the *same* transaction, you might hear them say them say something like, "Company B bought us because of *y*."

The funny thing is that while *x* and *y* should be the same, often they are not.

It's been my experience, in coaching entrepreneurs through multiple acquisitions, and having been involved on both sides of acquisitions myself, we (entrepreneurs) aren't always clear about why we're being bought, or why we're being valued as high (or as low) as we are.

In unpacking this myth, we will be asking some very important questions that you should answer before moving ahead with selling your company:

Why is an acquirer interested in buying your startup? Is it to get your awesome product? Is it the people? Or is it because of the underlying technology you've built? Maybe it's the customers or the revenues they really want?

## The Stated (Logical Reasons) for Acquisitions

The reality is that it is usually some combination of these reasons. Just as with investors, to maximize your value as an acquisition target, you should learn to put yourself into the shoes of the acquirer, and try see the world from *their* point of view.

I've found that the reasons usually fall into some broad categories. So let's look at these categories of "why acquirers buy startups" and how the valuations usually vary. As we noted in the previous myth, the valuation multiple you get on an exit will vary greatly depending on the stage of the market, as will the potential acquirers' reasons for wanting your startup.

***The Strategic Market Buy***. Some big companies will want to get a toehold in an emerging market that they know little about. To get there, they may buy a team that knows that market, but which does not have much revenue (let alone earnings). This is particularly true when the market is in the *nascent* stage, or at the start of the *growing* stage, when most big companies really don't know much about the market.

Although the purchase price in these scenarios may not be that high in absolute terms, acquirers are often willing to pay a premium for that knowledge in terms of a multiple on earnings (or more likely a multiple on sales, since a startup in a nascent market may not be profitable).

Sometimes, this leads them to buy a company with relatively little revenue for a multiple that seems outrageous; for example, a company with $1 million in sales is bought for $40 million. In a more normal situation, a 2× to 3× revenue multiple would be considered reasonable for software companies. A 5× revenue would be considered high. A 40× revenue valuation is off the charts but has been known to happen with high-tech startups during the *super-hot* stage of a market.

Let's look at an example of a strategic market buy that we mentioned in the last myth: in 2010, GREE and DeNA were the two biggest mobile game companies in Japan. They were making significant revenue and profits from their platform of mobile games, which ran on so-called feature phones (i.e., pre-smartphones) in Japan.

When smartphones, particularly the iPhone, started to be popular in the West, they realized that there was a huge market for mobile games here. They tried to build their own solution to become a mobile gaming platform in the West, but the market was moving very fast. Eventually, DeNA bought ngmoco for almost $400 million, and GREE decided to pay $100 million-plus for OpenFeint. OpenFeint, which was started by Jason Citron as part of Peter Relan's YouWeb incubator, had a very large toehold in mobile games—many developers used it for a single logon and for chatting and for leaderboards.

What multiple was this $100 million-plus on earnings? Infinite, because there were no earnings. What multiple was this on revenues? The total revenues in the twelve months before the acquisition were less than $1 million (significantly less), so the multiple was well over 100!

The DeNA acquisition of ngmoco, which was for more absolute money, was at a multiple that was over 10 times trailing revenue as well. In both of these cases, the companies paid multiples that might be considered outrageous in a normal market.

The reason? They both viewed smart phone as a strategic market that they really, really wanted to get a toehold in.

***The Geography Buy***. Sometimes an acquirer really needs to expand into certain locations, verticals, etc., and they have a straightforward need to have a team of people and a set of customers on the ground in that location. In traditional industries, this meant opening retail stores in new cities.

In high-tech startups, this usually means a sales organization in a particular area (say, in Europe for a U.S. company.) For a professional services company, or an enterprise software company looking to buy a services organization, it might mean the number of professionals you have that can easily be deployed to customer sites.

Let's look at some simple examples of the "geography" buys. When U.S. Web was building a leading "web development" company, they often bought smaller web development shops in different cities/states on the way to their IPO during the dot-com days. I remember the same happening when I was in the Lotus Notes consulting space. At that time, there was a small but well-known Lotus Notes consulting shop called DSSI in Los Angeles. Ernst and Young wanted to build a practice in this area, and ended up acquiring DSSI. They got physical geography (a team in L.A.) and market geography (experts in Lotus Notes and related technologies).

***The Technology/Product Buy***. Sometimes an acquirer really needs a particular piece of technology and they don't have time to build it themselves. More often, their customers need a particular piece of technology, and an acquirer wants to provide a "complete solution" to the customer. Why can't they partner with the company rather than acquire them? The truth of the matter is that they can, and often do, as a prelude to an acquisition.

During the "partnership period," the acquirer can validate whether the technology works well with the overall solution, and how easy/difficult the team is to work with. Then, at some point, the acquirer decides they would rather not have a piece of the pie owned by the partner.

Let's look at the case of Arbortext, which was founded from technology developed at the University of Michigan in Ann Arbor. Arbortext was an XML-based editing and publishing solution that was used for documentation of very large manufacturing and pharmaceutical clients—companies like Boeing and Toyota used them for documenting highly complex industrial processes and publishing manuals for their employees. The manufacturing companies of course bought many other types of software—namely CAD, and one of the leaders in this market was Parametric Technology Corporation (PTC). PTC found that Arbortext was a solution their customers almost always wanted integrated with their own CAD and documentation solutions, so they ended up buying Arbortext for $200 million.

This wasn't a purely technology-based valuation; Arbortext was on a run rate of over $50 million at the time of the acquisition, so it was a 4× revenue multiple, which was a good multiple, but not outrageous. The main reason for the acquisition was to expand PTC's product line to include the documentation editor.

***The Numbers Buy***. Sometimes an acquisition is done to get a certain amount of revenue (or profits) into the company, and is a straightforward piece of financial arbitrage—when you buy to take advantage of the price differences between markets. For example, a public company is valued at 5× revenue and they can buy your company for 2.5× revenue.

They profit just from making the deal, as they can buy you for 2.5× revenue and their market cap goes up 5×! These kinds of opportunities don't often last, but can be present in hot markets. The danger in this model is that if the acquired company's products or services don't fit very well into the rest of the company, then while there is a temporary benefit, it can be problematic in the long term when the valuations come back to earth.

In 2014–16, the Chinese stock markets were exploding, and many companies were being valued at what we in the United States considered crazy multiples. It was not uncommon for Chinese companies to see more than 10× multiple on revenues (with, obviously, a much bigger multiple on earnings), so they were willing to buy U.S. companies at 5× to 10× revenues, because it would increase their valuation by a proportional amount.

***The Acqui-hire***. The acqui-hire is a very common reason for acquisitions in a very hot market, particularly in Silicon Valley, one of the most expensive places in the world to live. Because the cost of living is high, and competition for talent is very high, when a market starts to grow and becomes super-hot, there is a shortage of talent in that particular space. For companies to meet their growth plans, they have to hire a lot of new talent, and that can be particularly difficult. So they will acquire a small startup that has the expertise they are looking for, and then get rid of the startup's product and have the team work on some project that is strategic for them.

As an example, Loki studios was a small but innovative game developer that came out of Stanford's StartX accelerator. Their game, *Geomon*, had some very interesting geo-location-type features, but it did not do well enough to support the team of seven developers in Silicon Valley. In 2013, Yahoo was looking to beef up its mobile development team and acqui-hired them (along with a slew of other small mobile development companies) to build its team in-house. They wanted a team with mobile and geo-location experience. They promptly shut down Loki's games and put the team on other projects. This is very typical in an acqui-hire; the acquired team's products are shut down but the team itself is put on one of the acquirer's other (important) strategic projects.

In another example, we had an educational software company that went through our accelerator. The founders were quite young, and weren't sure if they wanted to continue running the company after the accelerator. There was another educational software company that they were speaking to that was doing quite well. The second company was growing like crazy and because they were based in Silicon Valley, they were having a tough time finding enough talent. They offered to buy the startup that was in our accelerator to get a team that already understood the market. In this case, though, it wasn't an ideal situation because they viewed it only as a glorified recruiting effort and weren't really valuing the technology built by our startup.

This list is a useful tool to identify the primary (and if appropriate, secondary reasons) why an acquirer wants your startup, so it constitutes Startup Tool #4: Stated Reasons for Acquisitions that you can use to evaluate a particular acquirer's motivations.

## Startup Tool #4: Stated (Logical) Reasons for Acquisitions

Why is acquirer ________________ (X) interested in buying your startup?

Please rank from 1 (most important reason) to 5 (least important or n/a). Repeat for each potential acquirer.

___ Strategic market buy (expand into market)
___ Geography buy (expand to a specific location)
___ Product buy (product into their product line)
___ Technology buy (component of your product into theirs)
___ Numbers buy (put an X next to the number most important)
    ___ Revenue
    ___ Customers
    ___ Profits
___ Acqui-hire / Talent
- What will you work on after the acquisition?
- What will happen to your product?

Other comments:

______________________________________________

______________________________________________

## Real (Underlying, Emotional) Reasons for Acquisitions

Of course, in many acquisitions the reasons the acquirer pursues the transaction fall into multiple categories. Though the "buckets" listed above may be the broadly stated reasons for doing an acquisition, there are usually deeper reasons that are driving an acquirer to spend good money to buy other companies that go beyond the stated "logical" reasons.

"Emotional" reasons are rarely listed in a press release ("We were scared to death so we bought XYZ!") as the main reason for doing an acquisition. Still, any company, even a large public one, is run by people with personalities.

As I have pointed out before, in tech companies the culture of the company is very much influenced by the personalities of the founders, and the personality of the CEO in particular. This is true even for big tech companies like Oracle or Microsoft.

Just as you can categorize the "logical" reasons for an acquisition, I've found that if you dig deeper, you can also categorize the emotional reasons why acquirers jump into an acquisition (sometimes into an ill-founded one).

Here are some of the emotional reasons. If you can correctly identify the underlying emotional reasons, you can have a much more successful (and lucrative) acquisition and post-acquisition period.

***FOMO: Fear of missing out***. This is probably the most common emotional reason for doing an acquisition at a very high valuation—or for that matter, for many decisions we make in life. Startups are ephemeral, they come and go, as do the market opportunities that they represent.

In the days of the dot-com boom, this was definitely one of the major reasons why many web companies were bought. The traditional companies (more specifically, their management teams) were afraid of "missing out" on the next big thing. You could ascribe the AOL Time Warner merger to this fear of missing out on the internet age. While many people praised the deal at the time, it proved to be a disaster, since the Time Warner side of the business had real media assets and AOL didn't.

***Frustration/Headache:*** Another emotion that plays a very strong role in driving acquisitions is frustration. There are two types of frustration that can play a role. In one scenario, a big company is tired of losing customers to a smaller company, who may have better technology or may just be a nimbler team. The bigger company decides to acquire the smaller company to get rid of a competitor.

A more common type of frustration is when a big company tries to build a feature or product and repeatedly fails to deliver a viable or competitive product. The executives of the bigger company finally get to a point of frustration with their own employees/managers, and they say "screw it—let's just buy these guys, they know what they're doing and have already built a product that's better than ours."

It's important to note in both of these scenarios that timing is everything. Before the executive team gets to the "frustration" point, if you try to sell your company to them, you'll most likely get an answer such as, "We're building our own and it's going to be awesome! What do we need you for?" Then, the same company gets frustrated with its lack of ability to perform and comes back to try to acquire your startup.

***Checkbox:*** The checkbox acquisition is an interesting one—it's a subset of the "frustration" emotional reason. In the dot-com days, there were many examples of this.

A CEO was tired of being asked about their "internet strategy" and so he bought an internet company and was able to say (though not literally, of course), "that checkbox is covered." In the checkbox type of acquisition, it's not simply a matter of the acquiree's product or service or technology being better than the acquirers'; the acquirers want to check off the box and move on.

I saw this myself, when my company CambridgeDocs was acquired by Document Sciences, a public document publishing company. They kept getting asked about XML as a technology. I think they got to the point where they said, if we can just buy an XML company, that will check that box, and they bought CambridgeDocs. Later, Document Sciences was acquired by EMC's Documentum division, and our small product was lost within this larger division. Looking back, I'm not really sure they needed our product as much as they wanted to be able to say that the XML checkbox was covered because they had acquired the XML experts!

***Master of the Universe:*** Sometimes, when an industry is new, there are personalities that want to "dominate" the market space. Now, as we saw in Myth #2: Founders Start Companies to Make a Lot of Money, different founders have different kinds of primary motivations, and they are often not about money.

There is a particular type of founder who is very ambitious and wants to dominate. They will often buy companies to make sure that they are seen as the dominant force in this marketplace. This is often the case with roll ups: where a well-financed company will buy up, or *roll up*, a number of smaller, fragmented companies to build the dominant player in this space. Once upon a time, the hot new startups were auto companies—with names like Dodge, Chevrolet, and Ford. General Motors was founded on the idea that it could consolidate these medium-sized startups into one behemoth. GM became the number one car company in the world. There's a lot of emphasis in these organizations on "being number one."

***Shiny new toy!*** Sometimes a CEO wants to buy a company to trot it out as an example of the "future." Now, you might think this is the same motivation as the "checkbox" one, but it's really not. In the checkbox approach, the primary motivation is to check the box and "have it go away." When the shiny new toy is the motivation, it's to trot out the new acquisition as often as possible and spend time talking about the future, showing how the CEO of the acquiring company is a visionary. When Facebook bought Oculus Rift for $2 billion, many people scratched their heads. While there are some definite possibilities for virtual reality in a social context, the purchase price and the lack of immediate relevance to Facebook's business made it look as if Mark Zuckerberg wanted a "shiny new toy."

***Security***. Many times, a company has a relationship with another company, and wants to pull the employees and technology in-house—either in a small acquisition or even an acqui-hire. While the stated reason is to get the product/technology or the team, the underlying emotional reason driving it is often one of securing your supplier. Because the team and/or technology of the smaller partner are not "in-house," they could theoretically work with a competitor or do other things that are not related.

Usually this kind of acquisition happens when a relationship is going well and the acquirer doesn't want to take the risk that the relationship may end up going to a competitor. As an example, when my company, CambridgeDocs, was building an important component for Arbortext, they viewed us an important supplier. When Arbortext was acquired by PTC (as previously stated, for $200 million), PTC and Arbortext didn't want any risk associated with the component that we built for them (which was a way to take existing documentation and import it into XML). As a result, we got into acquisition discussions with them; we ended up not moving ahead with the acquisition, but it was a good example of "securing your supplier."

***Embarrassment***. Sometimes, a company's CEO (or management team or board) will realize that they really miscalculated the market. Their original product, while it may have been a good product, just isn't selling, or their original target market didn't work out. They look around for a pivot, not just to save the company, but also to save their reputation. Hence, they buy another company for the product to cover their own embarrassment. This is similar to the frustration argument, but in that case, the acquirer tries to build its own product; in the case of embarrassment, the company may have missed the market opportunity completely, or they may realize that their current product's life cycle is coming to an end, and they need a new, growing product to stay relevant.

Our next Startup Tool, Startup Tool #5, is a checklist that allows you to rank the underlying (emotional) reasons why a potential acquirer might be interested.

## Startup Tool #5: Real (Underlying, Emotional) Reasons for Acquisitions

Why is acquirer _______________ (X) interested in buying your startup?

> Please rank from 1 (most important reason) to 5 (least important or n/a).
> Repeat for each potential acquirer.
> ___ FOMO (fear of missing out)
> ___ Frustration
> ___ Checkbox
> ___ Master of the universe
> ___ Shiny new toy!
> ___ Security
> ___ Embarrassment

Usually, a combination of these emotional reasons underlie an acquisition; it's just that most CEOs or management teams aren't totally honest or forthcoming about these emotional reasons.

## The Secret

***Understand both the "logical," stated reason for an acquisition and the "emotional," unstated reasons for an acquisition, and use this to your advantage.***

You can use these two checklists, Startup Tool #4: Stated Reasons for Acquisitions, and Startup Tool #5: Emotional (Underlying) Reasons for Acquisitions, to compare and contrast what they "say" vs. what is really driving them.

Why is it important to understand the buyer's motivation? It will help you to understand where you can negotiate and where you can't. For example, when DeNA bought my company, Gameview Studios, back in 2010, we thought it was because our company was very profitable and had real revenue.

It turned out that DeNA wasn't concerned with our profit at all (which was a drop in the bucket in a billion-dollar company). What we didn't know was that they were (at the same time) negotiating a much bigger deal to acquire ngmoco as their "game platform." I would learn later that they wanted us because of our user growth, because of our ability to build games on their new platform, and as a hedge in case that (bigger) deal didn't go through. If we had known this, we could have negotiated a higher valuation, since they weren't really that concerned with our profit/revenue numbers.

# Myth #17

## The Best Way to Cash Out Is to Sell or Go Public

Most tech company discussions in Silicon Valley (and beyond) focus on two exit possibilities: acquisition or initial public offering (IPO).

The focus on acquisition makes sense because most tech companies have products that are interesting in the market for some period of time, but rarely does one product alone lead to a longer-term profitable business that could be public. I would suggest that more than 90 percent of successes in the tech world result from being acquired by a larger tech company, whether a really big public company like Microsoft, Google, Facebook, Amazon, or a midsize private company that is on its way to an IPO.

Because technology changes so quickly, some companies that go public are later acquired or "taken private" when they have stopped innovating and it's not clear that it can be an ongoing concern. Case in point: LinkedIn and Yahoo, which were public for many years and were eventually acquired by Microsoft and Verizon, respectively.

On the other hand, the popularity of IPOs waxes and wanes with the stock market. In the 1990s, during the dot-com days, the trend was to take companies public as quickly as possible. Most of these web companies had no profits (and some had very little revenue), yet they saw their stock prices bid up in the mania of the dot-com bubble. During the following decade, while there were IPOs, they weren't as crazy. In fact, some companies like Google (and Facebook later) tried to stay private as long as possible—at least until the SEC said they had so many shareholders they had to become a public company.

The IPO bandwagon was picking up steam again when the financial crisis of 2008 hit, resulting in many new regulations for public companies—a response to many Wall Street scandals—which made the requirements for a public company very restrictive. As a result, many companies decided to stay private longer, raising not just a series A, but series B, series C, series D, and sometimes even a series E financing at ever increasing valuations. This was what led to the term "unicorn," a private company that was less than ten years old and valued at more than $1 billion, which we spoke about in Myth #1: Build a Billion-Dollar Company.

While most of the myths in this stage are about selling your company (the most likely outcome) and many startup gurus focus on the IPO, this chapter is about an alternative that arose during the IPO dearth after the financial crisis, a new way of getting liquidity that has become popular in Silicon Valley. I encourage all entrepreneurs to look seriously at the private secondary sale at some point in their company's life.

That's right, you may not need to sell your company or IPO in order to cash out. In fact, with a secondary sale you can get a partial cash out, while still maintaining upside for an IPO or large acquisition down the road. Essentially, it allows you to have the best of both worlds.

## An IPO Is Not an Exit

Most of us involved in startups have fantasized at one point or another about our companies "going public." After all, going public is what made many of the early employees of Microsoft, Apple, Google, Facebook and many other well-known companies into multimillionaires (and in the case of the founders, billionaires). Microsoft reportedly created 12,000 millionaires (though this happened mostly because of the rise in its stock *after* the IPO). It is estimated that in 2019 alone, more than 5,000 millionaires will be created in Silicon Valley through the IPOs of companies like Uber. Of course, it's not just tech companies—McDonalds is known as the all-time champ in creating millionaires, with an estimated 25,000 millionaires created after its IPO.

When I cofounded my first startup, I mistakenly thought that the process of "going public" would actually put money in the pockets of the founders. That can happen, but an IPO is actually a financing event—just like raising money from venture capitalists or angel investors—and not an exit event at all!

This means that, just as with any other financing, there will be a set of "expectations" put on the company, and the investors will expect the company to "perform" to those expectations. The two main differences between a private financing and an IPO are:

1. the number of investors is much larger in an IPO ("the public"), and
2. the shares can then be freely traded on the open market (with some restrictions).

An IPO usually means that the company sells new shares to the "public," and the proceeds of that sale go into the company. It turns out that the making of millionaires and billionaires doesn't always happen at the IPO—instead, it gives the stock that founders hold a specific value on the open market, even though founders aren't allowed to sell their shares right away. For example, Bill Gates's shares in Microsoft at the time of the IPO were valued at $350 million. It was the company's performance after the IPO that turned Gates and his cofounder Paul Allen into multibillionaires.

This was of course part of the mistake that many entrepreneurs and VCs made when their companies went public in the dot-com boom. If a public company doesn't perform, or if the general stock market trend changes, then newly public companies are the first whose shares will crash. This happened often after the dot-com bubble crashed in 2000-01, and again during the financial crisis in 2008.

It wasn't just the founders of public companies that were affected. All of their employees (including founders of the companies they acquired for stock) were also affected. I recall a conversation with Michael Cassidy, who was CEO of Direct Hit, which sold to Ask Jeeves for $500 million in the height of the dot-com craziness. When the stock market crashed (and in particular the web companies crashed), the $500 million in stock they received had lost 90 percent of its value. Earlier, I gave the example of Exodus, which we sold to Service Metrics for $280 million at the height of the dot-com boom (in December 1999). Exodus subsequently lost 100 percent of its market value!

VCs generally don't have any restrictions on their stock and are allowed to sell at (or just after) the IPO. The founders' shares are usually locked up for at least 180 days (six months) and sometimes longer. Also, if you are CEO or founder of a public company, you can't just go and sell all of your stock at once. Why? It would be a bad signal to investors that you no longer believe the stock will go up!

Sometimes, to address this, a newly public company will arrange for a secondary public offering, which will sell not just shares from the company to the public, but will sell shares in a controlled way from founders, employees, and some investors as part of the offering.

The message here is that while an IPO will create, on paper at least, big fortunes, an IPO is a financing event. Here are some points to keep in mind:

- IPO trends require today's company's to have more revenue before going public (and in some cases, some amount of profit).
- IPO rules and regulations make an IPO unlikely for 90 percent of tech companies.
- An IPO is not an exit. It is a financing event, and the valuation will come with a set of expectations.
- You may not be able to sell your stock for some time after an IPO.

The benefits of an IPO are that public companies are generally valued much higher than private companies, you know exactly what your stock is worth, and you can (theoretically) sell it at any time.

As compared to an acquisition, the nice thing about an IPO is that you can potentially make a lot more money as your stock goes up after going public (assuming you continue to perform well as a company). Of course, if your stock crashes, you could end up making not very much at all, and you could end up wishing that you had sold the company instead!

There is a tradeoff between the "no-risk" approach of selling your company (assuming you sell for cash—we'll talk more about this in Bonus Myth #B-5: Upfront Cash is Better than Stock or an Earnout) versus the "risky" approach of going public in an IPO. An IPO can be much more lucrative but is much riskier. This is why the third option (a private secondary sale) is worth looking at.

### What Is a Private Secondary Sale?

A secondary sale is when a shareholder (typically one of the founders or an early employee or an early investor) of a private company sells his or her shares to another buyer. A "private secondary" is when the sale is to another private investor or group of investors (before the company is public).

A secondary usually (though not always) happens when the startup has achieved significant revenue or traction and is seen as a leader in their market space, on the way to an IPO or a major sale. Since the company is already doing well, most secondaries involve sales of millions or even tens of millions (and perhaps hundreds of millions) of dollars.

They are distinguished from a "primary" sale, in which the company issues new shares to investors, and the proceeds of that sale go directly into the company.

In both primary and secondary sales, investors are buying stock. The main differences between the two kinds of sales are:

1. where the proceeds go, and
2. whether the shares are newly issued or have belonged to someone else.
3. typically, the shares acquired in a secondary from founders or employees are common stock and have restrictions placed on them.

## What's Driving Secondaries?

As mentioned earlier, one of the main reasons why secondaries became popular in Silicon Valley was due to a dearth of IPOs after the 2008 financial crisis. Today, startups today typically don't go public until they have $100 million or more in revenue; in other words, they are staying private longer, getting more rounds of equity financing. Startups are becoming valued in the hundreds of millions or billions in these equity rounds of financing.

As the numbers get larger in subsequent rounds—from series A to series B to series C or D—the amount of money gets larger. Zynga, for example, did a $490 million round of financing before their IPO, and according to press reports, this included a certain amount set aside for the founder's shares and early employees who wanted to cash out their shares. Uber, Facebook, Twitter, Pinterest, Palantir—all of these are well-known companies whose valuations were well over $1 billion before they went public.

The main factors driving secondaries are:

1. *Supply and demand of the company's stock.* When a company is doing well, investors want to get stock in the company, but a startup may not need the financing or may not want to dilute its existing shareholders by selling stock, so its stock may be hard to come by.
2. *Liquidity for early shareholders.* Rarely do employees stay at one company for more than a few years, but it's possible that a successful startup may not have an IPO for five to ten years. That's a long time.

3. *Risk vs. upside (for founders).* From the point of view of founders and early employees, a private secondary sale offers the best of both worlds. You get cash out of the company, reducing your risk, and you still have significant upside—all of this without having to go through the laborious (and risky) process of taking the company public.
4. *Risk vs. upside (for investors).* Because startups are so risky, some investors in Silicon Valley and private equity funds have figured out that buying the stock of a company that is already successful and on its way to an IPO can end up being as lucrative as investing early on a risky startup. Although the return may not be as high by participating in one of these late-stage rounds, the chances are smaller that the company will collapse and you will lose your money.

## Who Buys Secondary Shares?

The first question I am asked by entrepreneurs when I tell them about secondary sales is: who can I sell my shares to?

The answer is, to the same people who invest in startups. Here's an overview of the different groups I've seen participate in buying secondary shares:

- **Existing and new investors in the company.** The most popular buyers of private secondaries are usually either existing investors or new investors who are part of a new round of financing. Why? Because these investors know the company well—they have done due diligence on it. If the company is doing well, then investors want to buy as much of the company as possible.

Some investors even have specific percentage thresholds they are trying to reach (or maintain)—for example, some like to keep a 20 percent ownership of their companies. I've seen term sheets that are structured like this (not actual numbers) in order to combine primary and secondary shares to get the percentage they want:

  - Primary: Investors x and y will put $18 million into the company and get new series C preferred stock (for 15 percent of the company).
  - Secondary: Investors X and Y will buy up to $6 million in common stock from existing founders, employees, and investors (for another 5 percent of the company).

- **Matching websites and microfunds.** There are a number of websites and organizations that specialize in secondary sales—three of these include

Shares Post, Second Market, and Micro Ventures. These sites are usually "matching" sites—either curated or uncurated. In the uncurated version, you post that you want to sell (or buy) shares of company X. If enough buyers (or sellers) match, then the organization puts together a limited liability company (LLC) to buy those shares, or just introduces buyers and sellers to each other.

- **Secondary-specific funds.** Thousands of startups are founded each year in Silicon Valley alone; very few of them make it to a series A, fewer to a successful series B or C, and even fewer make it to a late-stage series D or E or an IPO. A few years ago, investors realized that they could reduce their risk by investing in the handful of companies that have already made it onto an IPO track. They wouldn't make as much money as the early investors in those companies, but they would take considerably less risk. That is of course the logic of most late-stage private equity/VC firms. However, in recent years, a few funds have been formed *specifically* for buying secondary shares of startups that are taking off, such as Industry Ventures.
- **Private investors and SPVs.** In many cases, there are private individuals who are willing to buy your shares in a hot startup that's doing well. For example, when I was in business school at Stanford after the stock market crash of 2008, an early Facebook employee wanted to sell his shares, and I knew some people in Silicon Valley that were part of an initiative to buy his stock. Facebook was already at a $4 billion valuation at that time. This was considered an astronomical valuation for a private company that didn't have any profits. Of course, when it went public years later, its stock was valued at $100 billion, which was the largest valuation ever for a company upon going public! This was done through a special purpose vehicle (SPV), which was an LLC formed by investors specifically to buy the Facebook stock.
- **Investment banks.** In a special case, we once hired an investment banker to go out and sell our shares in a startup that had grown very big. Investment banks become interested in secondaries only when the dollar amounts are large enough that their fees can be meaningful, or to build a relationship with the sellers. Some investment banks are better at helping you negotiate the sale to a particular buyer, while other investment banks may be better at finding buyers because they have a spectrum of clients. Be sure to do background reference checks to find out what the investment bank is good at.

## What's in a Valuation, Part 3

So, the next question from entrepreneurs is typically, how much can I sell my stock for?

It's time to revisit the all-important subject of valuation. In my first financing, we had a pre-money valuation of $5 million for our startup, Brainstorm. Since my cofounder and I owned most of the company, I thought that meant we were multimillionaires, at least on paper. As we saw in Startup Model #5: The Four Quadrants of Hiring this was a result of not understanding what went into a valuation.

Here is another misconception of entrepreneurs who want to sell stock, which is just as important, if not more so: It turns out that founders have common stock and investors have preferred stock. That means that the price per share that investors pay is for preferred stock—whether it's series Seed, series A, series B, series C, series D preferred (or beyond). This is not the same price that you can sell your shares (which are common stock) for. Preferred stock means that investors get their money out first in any sale or liquidation, which is why it's worth more (a whole lot more in the early days of a startup).

Let's look at this dynamic and how it affects prices of secondary sales in a startup's lifecycle in Startup Model #9.

## Startup Model #9: Valuation in Secondaries: Common Versus Preferred

If the startup has had a recent financing, or is planning an upcoming financing that has been valued, you might assume that the price of your stock is the price that investors are buying it at. For example, if the company raised a series C financing at $100 million post money valuation, and has fully diluted 50 million shares, then the price in the last round was two dollars per share of preferred stock.

So how much is your common stock worth? It depends on the stage of the company and how close you are to an IPO. In fact, when the company does a 409a valuation for its options strike price for employees (who also have common stock), the valuation is kept deliberately low—often from 10 percent to 33 percent of the preferred price. This is so that employees get stock at the lowest possible price, and to account for the risk that common shareholders may never get any money back.

As a company matures and proceeds toward an IPO, the common stock becomes more and more valuable, approaching the value of the preferred stock, as shown in figure 17.1. Once the company goes public (or is just about to go public), the preferred stock and common stock are pretty

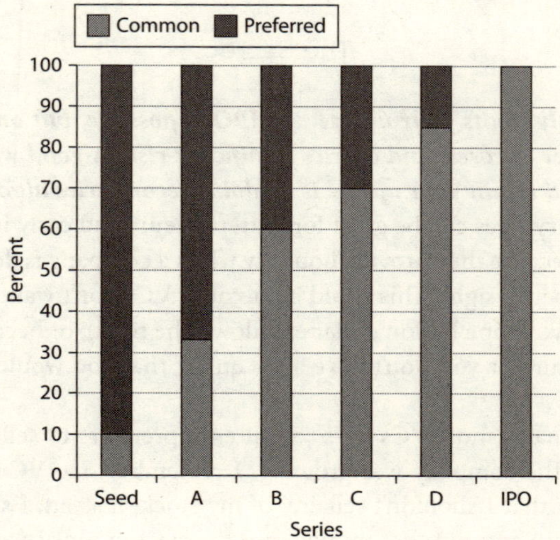


Figure 17.1
Value of Common Stock vs. Preferred Stock. Created by the author

much equal in value. Most investors will convert their preferred stock into common stock at the IPO, so that's why the ratio is 100 percent at that stage.

Correspondingly, as we see in figure 17.1, the graph starts from 10 percent in a seed financing. If you are in a financed startup, it's OK to ask how much money was raised, at what valuation, and what the 409a strike price is. The 409a price is set by the board (usually based on the recommendation of an outside valuation firm), and is the strike price used for options issued to employees. As the company gets to a series A financing, the risk in the company is theoretically less, but it's still risky. A good estimate is that ~33 percent of the series A price is reasonable. You can see the graph for rough estimates for subsequent financing rounds.

I saw a series D financing term sheet recently that included a secondary sale where the price of the common stock was 80 percent of the value of preferred stock. This is more of an art than a science, but in most secondaries I've seen, 60 percent of the value of the last preferred round is a pretty good rule of thumb for a series B, with that number going up or down depending on what stage the company is at, how hot the company is, and the specific preferences that the different series have.

## The Secret

***A sale usually limits your upside. An IPO is possible, but only in a very small number of cases, and carries significant risk. A good way to reduce your risk and retain your upside is by doing secondaries along the way!***

Secondary sales can be great for entrepreneurs and early investors and employees because they provide liquidity when a company is doing well but there is no exit in sight. This could be because VCs don't want to sell (they are pushing you for a billion dollar exit down the road), or because the IPO window is shut, or you don't have an acquirer that you would really want to be part of.

Traditionally, most VCs didn't want entrepreneurs to sell any of their stock while the company was growing. I remember one VC in the 1990s who told me that I shouldn't sell any of my stock; instead, I should mortgage my house and put that money into the startup too! I wondered why already having 90 percent of my assets in a risky, illiquid startup wasn't enough risk!

In recent years, secondaries have become more and more popular, particularly for startups whose stock is in demand. Also, VCs have become more understanding about founders selling shares in subsequent rounds of financing—and more sensitive to the personal and financial stresses that being in a startup can create. These days, saying you want to sell enough stock to buy a house is not seen as a bad thing. If you are feeling secure in your lodging, then you are more likely to continue to grow the company to get the billion dollar–plus exit that most investors crave rather than pushing to sell the company at some earlier stage.

Secondaries offer the best of both worlds, in my opinion; they let founders get security and peace of mind (that no matter what happens they won't lose all of their assets in a flash), and they retain significant upside (since they will still own the majority of their shares).

There are many different buyers for secondaries, but the most common are investors that are already in the company, because they know the company and can get comfortable with the price easily. There are, however, any number of ways for a secondary sale to get complicated, so be sure to know the specifics of your company's shares, investor rights agreements, etc., before committing to a secondary sale of shares.

# Bonus Myth #B-5

## Upfront Cash Is Better than Stock or an Earnout

So, you've been approached by a company that values what you have built from the ground up. They want to buy your company. The most important question, other than the total value of the deal, is how the consideration breaks down.

In an ideal world, someone will offer you, say, $20 million for your company, and all of it will be cash that arrives in your (and your cofounders' and investors') bank accounts on the day the acquisition closes, and everyone is happy.

Unfortunately, it rarely works that way.

During the dot-com days of the late 1990s, many companies sold for valuations that were pretty high (in the hundreds of millions of dollars) to public companies whose valuations were even higher. In these cases, the compensation to stockholders of the acquiree was usually 100 percent stock, usually public stock, which *theoretically* was as good as cash, but in practice was often restricted.

How happy these guys (the *acquirees*) were after the deal was usually a matter of the stock performance after the lockup period. Well, if that exit happened close to the crash of 2000, there's a good chance that stock significantly decreased in value (or in the case of some public dot-com-related companies, became *completely worthless*), before the acquirees had a chance to sell their shares!

▶ To read the full text of this **Bonus Myth**, including advice on the best way to structure your acquisition to reduce risk while maintaining upside, please download the Supplement to *Startup Myths and Models* from www.zenentrepreneur.com ◀

# Stage 6

## The Underworld and the Return
## *Myths About Life and Death in a Startup*

This is the hero's darkest hour. He must face his greatest fear, and draw upon all of his skills and experiences to overcome his most difficult challenge. Only through some form of "death" can he be reborn, experiencing a metaphorical resurrection that somehow grants him greater power or insight necessary in order to fulfill his destiny or reach his journey's end.[1]

The hero again traverses the threshold between the worlds, returning to the ordinary world with the treasure or elixir he gained, which he may now use for the benefit of his fellow man. The hero himself is transformed by the adventure and gains wisdom or spiritual power over both worlds.[2]

### Introduction to Stage 6: The Trip to the Underworld

For the final stage, I've borrowed and combined two phases of Campbell's hero's journey—the trip to the underworld and the return to ordinary life. Although startup gurus will tell you that success or failure is simply a matter of finding market/product fit and executing well, most entrepreneurs who have been through the journey will tell you that there's another, more personal element. This is the world of emotions—of hope, anger, fear, and greed—and how they surface during the "dark times" when things aren't going well.

1. Jon and Missy.com, "12 Stages of the Hero's Journey," accessed December 19, 2019, https://www.jonandmissy.com/12-stages-of-the-heros-journey-which-are-you-in-right-now/.
2. Wikipedia, "Hero's Journey," accessed December 19, 2019, https://en.wikipedia.org/wiki/Hero%27s_journey.

### *Overview of the Trip to the Underworld*

In most mythological adventures, the hero has to face some form of death. This might happen in a visit to the literal underworld, as is the case with Odysseus, who must travel through Hades to get to his goal; or it may be a physical "death," as almost happens to Frodo at several points in *The Lord of the Rings*; or it could happen through a trip to a metaphorical "underworld."

In startup adventures, there is a literal death that you must face, too. While it is perhaps less scary than death of a person, the death of a startup is always on the horizon when you are on this journey. Like Frodo and Sam traveling through Mordor, certain death may be around the next corner.

I've included this part of the book not to scare anyone away from going on the journey, but to help you realize that the real treasure of a startup adventure may or may not be financial reward. Instead, it might be the insights that you gain about yourself and your fellow humans during this journey and what you bring with you after the journey is complete. The elixir that Campbell mentions in the hero's journey is something that almost all entrepreneurs who go on the journey can bring back with them, regardless of the financial outcome.

Startup books that don't talk about the dark times, or the accompanying stress that comes with running a startup, are leaving out one of the biggest and essential parts of the journey. Much of that magic elixir—the wisdom and perspective I've gained from my startups—came from the times when I was facing imminent death and was terrified that I might "fail."

### *Overview of the Return*

Moreover, what you do after the startup adventure is just as important as what you do on the journey. Although a lot has been written about what it takes to make a startup successful, very little has been written about what you do at the conclusion of your entrepreneurial journey.

One of Tolkien's favorite parts of *The Lord of the Rings* was the scouring of the Shire, or the "return" to the ordinary world. In this chapter near the end of the saga, the Hobbits, having defeated the "big bad" (the dark lord, Sauron) and having helped Aragorn become the King of Gondor again, come back to their little corner of the world, the Shire, to find that they have changed and so has it. They now have to use the skills they acquired in the "big adventure" to their "little adventure," to clean house in their own little part of the world.

No matter what happens on your startup adventure, you will find yourself changed by the journey. Usually this is because of the trip to the underworld, which forces you to deal with your darkest, deepest fears and insecurities and overcome years of accumulated stress. Some entrepreneurs decide they don't want to do another startup—this could be because they've made enough money, or because they just don't want to deal with the stress again. Or you might decide, like I did after my first startup, that you don't want to do another venture-backed company. Or you may decide to become an investor and/or a mentor to help other teams of adventurers on their startup journeys.

You will then switch archetypes, from the hero to the mentor or the threshold guardian. This is entirely appropriate. Only then will the circle truly be complete.

# Myth #18

## Startups Are Hard Work

I first read that startups are hard work when I was still an undergrad at MIT.

Back then, there weren't as many books about startups as there are now; I recall reading about Steve Jobs pushing his Macintosh team to the brink, working them to create the "miracle" of the Mac operating system and hardware in a surprising fifteen months.

I also read about Bill Gates and Paul Allen's work on their first version of BASIC, which they finished just before Allen's trip to New Mexico from Boston to show it to Ed Roberts. Roberts was the founder of MITS, which made the Altair computer, one of the first PCs on the market. I remember being enthralled at how Gates stayed up late creating BASIC on an emulator, because they didn't have an actual Altair computer, the night before Allen's trip to Albuquerque to demo the product and show Roberts that Microsoft was a real company with a real product.

These stories of hard work late into the night weren't daunting to me. I remember thinking: I can handle long hours—after all, I was used to them as a computer science student at MIT. When I was in school, my classmates and I would work very long hours, often pulling all-nighters to get our assignments turned in by the morning they were due. Usually, we would wander in with that dazed look of someone who's had his head in a computer for many, many hours, and it was obvious that the other students who were handing in their assignments had been up all night too!

When we did our first startup, Brainstorm, shortly after graduating from MIT, our living room was our office. We were the proverbial "two guys and a garage" (without the garage—because garages are too cold in New England!). I wrote in my first book, *Zen Entrepreneurship*, about the long hours we spent building our first product, which was a link between Microsoft's highly popular Visual Basic and IBM's Lotus Notes platform. We stayed up until 3 A.M. regularly and built the product in eight weeks, and in a repeat of Gates's performance, we were working late into the night before our trip to our first conference to release our first product.

This period was stressful. Clearly, our first startup required a lot of hard work. And we weren't alone; most startups require hard work. So why is this myth not true?

## Why Startups Are Really Hard: Stress

Many of my colleagues from school went into investment banking and management consulting. Although they were employees of their respective companies and didn't have an ownership stake, they also worked very long, hard hours.

In fact, they would work well into the night, just as we would, with one very big difference: they had to be up early in the morning and in the office wearing a suit by 9 A.M. (or earlier!). After we stayed up until 3 A.M., we could get up whenever we wanted, and had to only wander to the living room to start work. No suit required.

As our startup grew from two to ten people in the first year, and we got our very own office space, I noticed that we weren't working nearly as much as we did when it was just the two of us in the living room. But I noticed something else: I was *more* stressed out, not less.

This stress manifested itself in my body and emotions. I was worried about the next payroll. I was worried about our next month's revenues meeting our lofty expectations..

Unlike myself and my cofounders, who were all single, many of our employees were married, with kids and mortgages. We were operating on razor-thin cash flow. One slip and we wouldn't be able to make payroll. If we couldn't make payroll, then my employees wouldn't be able to make their mortgage payments, rent payments, etc.

Later, as we raised VC money, the stress went away. We had enough money in the bank to make payroll for a year or more. I remember my cofounders, Mitch and Irfan, looking at our bank statement after we had raised our first million dollars and being amazed. We had never seen a seven-figure bank balance in our lives. The stress seemed to disappear. *For a little while.*

A few months later, I noticed the stress was back, and it again manifested itself as tension in my body. As I reflected on it later, I realized that it was manifested as emotions of fear, worry, and anxiety, which were just under the surface. I carried them with me wherever I went, even if I didn't talk about them publicly.

This time, I was stressed not so much about making payroll (since we had a good amount of cash in the bank), but about meeting our projections. When we raised VC money, we had put down very aggressive projections for growth. And we weren't meeting them. Slowly, as we were under more and more pressure to make up for the revenue shortage by having a big fourth quarter, the stress started to build. Then, as we missed those projections, and losses started to mount, the stress and worry increased.

Alarmed, I found a way to cut costs and get things back on track, and things were better. I was inspired, the team was trimmed and focused, and things were better. *For a little while.*

And then the stress came back. Each time we raised money or landed a new client or introduced a new product successfully, the stress would seem to go away for some time, and then after a few months it would be back!

The stress of running a VC-backed company was very different from the stress of bootstrapping, and in some ways subtler. As CEO, I felt a responsibility to make sure the company made money for our investors, provided jobs for employees, *and* met our crazy growth projections.

This was when I first realized that startups *are* hard, but not for the reasons that I had thought when I'd read about famous startups like Apple and Microsoft.

The real reason startups are hard isn't about the long hours. Many professions require long hours but don't cause the kind of chronic psychological and emotional stress that comes to founders of startups. Moreover, both successful and unsuccessful startup founders work long hours.

Rather, it's about the stress of *expectations*—these expectations are placed on us by . . . none other than ourselves! We put expectations on ourselves every time we pitch the company to investors, every time we take money, every time we hire an employee. Every time we do these things, there are *implied expectations*—that the company can build a product before it runs out of money, that enough units can be sold to support everyone's salary, that another round of financing can be raised before the money runs out, etc.

Although we can control the number of hours we work and whether a product gets built, it's much more difficult to control how the market will receive our product, whether investors will put money in, whether a certain customer will go your way, or whether a certain company will buy you. All of these things, which determine the outcome of a startup adventure, can be influenced by the entrepreneur, but they are not really under your control.

## A Different Kind of Culture

During that same startup, I took the train from Boston to New York one day to visit another well-known startup company in our market. It was called Kinderhook Systems, and it had been started by another MIT alum, Mark Hansen, who had more experience than we had at the time.

I visited his office in Manhattan toward the end of the business day, around 6 P.M. I knew that Kinderhook was one of the better-known systems integrators/consulting firms in our market space, and so I expected to see a room full of people ready to work late into the night.

Instead, I found a big, comfortable office that was mostly empty. Most of the employees had gone home, and it was clear that most of the others were on their way out. Mark welcomed me into his office and we sat and chatted about the industry. When I asked him about his plans for the company, he told me about a lucrative offer he had received from an acquirer, which he had decided to turn down.

I was amazed. First, by the fact that he seemed so relaxed; second, by the fact that his employees weren't working away in a frenzy; and finally, by the fact that he was turning down an offer to be acquired for many millions of dollars in cash.

He explained that he had decided early on in the life of the startup to hire people who were experienced, and who would want to go home by 5 or 6 P.M. to spend time with their families. These kinds of employees didn't want to travel, so he focused on clients who were in or close to New York City. He himself didn't do much of the consulting anymore, though he had been more hands-on when he first started the company.

I contrasted this with our own startup, which had clients all over the world. Of course, we were a product company and his was a service company, so that made us different in some ways, but that didn't explain the different culture. If a client in California asked us to do some consulting for them to customize our product, we would usually say yes, and my cofounder or I would get on a plane to California. Moreover, we were still spending long hours into the night working on our products ourselves.

Compared to our startup, Brainstorm, and many other startups I'd encountered and read about, Mark's startup seemed like an island of sanity in an ocean of startup craziness.

That's when I realized that it was possible to build a successful startup without having to work hard all the time. Now, don't get me wrong, Mark must have worked very long hours in the early days of his startup, but he built the company deliberately in a way that reduced his stress, rather than increasing it!

Mark told me that he actually *turned down* clients that, although lucrative, didn't meet his criteria. This made it easier to not put unnecessary stress on his employees. He had a different set of expectations for his company, ones that he didn't need to kill himself to meet, but he was still able to be successful. He also didn't have any investors, so he had no pressure to get the company to a certain size or to go public. Mark sold his company a few years later in quite a lucrative exit, especially since he owned most of the company. While the exit was small by VC standards and those of us trying to go public, it made him a multimillionaire many times over since he owned most of the company.

## So, Where Does Stress Come From?

The truth behind this myth is that startups *are* hard—but not just because they are *hard work*. By focusing on the right priorities, you can figure out ways to reduce the long hours. Even so, stress is *almost* unavoidable—it doesn't matter if you raise money from VCs or bootstrap your company.

So, let's ask again, where does this stress come from? Usually, it comes from your expectations about growth. You hire two developers to help you build your product, and one quality assurance person whom you expect to also help with customer support. You base your hiring decisions on the expectation that your product will make enough money to support the founders, two developers, and the qa/ support person. Suddenly, you've got the stress of making payroll, and the stress of your product having to be a success.

Let's suppose then that you raise $500K from angel investors to build your product. This is a very typical seed round (perhaps even small by today's Silicon Valley standards), and you use it to build a development team and a product manager such that your expenses rise to $100K per month. The inherent expectations are that you will release your product within five months, and will get some early traction so that you can raise a bigger series A round of financing to launch your product. If you can't raise a series A, you're now setting yourself up for more stress and facing the imminent death of the company. But suppose you meet those expectations and do raise a series A of $3 million to help you market your product.

Now you can take a breather, right?

Nope. Now you have to build a team and make your product successful in the market before that money runs out. This is easier said than done—at least building the product was under your control, but making it successful requires good sales, marketing, distribution, and more than a little bit of luck and market timing—which is why we call this phase "Stage 4: The Road of Trials"!

There's an old adage in startups that things usually take twice as long as you expect, and cost twice as much as you expect. Getting a product to be successful is no exception, and it's very possible that you will miss your projections, which are no doubt overly aggressive because you needed that to raise money.

The reason for this myth is that doing a startup is a stressful experience, and it's not the kind of stress that we as human beings are built to cope with. Our nervous system developed over many millenia to deal with stressful situations like encountering sabertooth tigers—a life or death situation—which triggers the "fight or flight" response. Our physiology is built to deal with acute stress, not chronic stress, the kind that doesn't go away once the tiger is gone.

How do you manage the stress of a startup? By understanding *explicitly* the expectations that you are setting up for yourself at each step. This is true with each hiring decision, and with each dollar of investment that you take from investors. As we found in Myth # 7: Take the Highest Valuation You Can Get, valuations are a form of *financial expectations*. But so is every other major decision you make in your startup!

## The Secret

***Manage Expectations, Watch* Star Trek, *Do Yoga, and Walk by the Bay***

While managing expectations can help you avoid stress, it's inevitable that you will feel some stress during your startup adventure—so how do you deal with it?

This is where having a daily exercise routine, or a yoga or meditation practice, helps immensely. My rule of thumb during stressful times has been: watch *Star Trek* and do yoga and take a walk by the bay.

I'm a big fan of *Star Trek*, particularly the *Next Generation*. Of course, there's nothing specific about that show that helps me relax; it's simply a TV show that I enjoy watching—it brings back good memories and lets me forget about my startup troubles. When we were building our first product at my first startup, Brainstorm, we would pause from writing code around 10 P.M. to watch an episode or two of *Star Trek*, which would then motivate us to keep coding into the wee hours of the morning.

Find something that takes you away but leaves your refreshed. A TV show is great because you can watch an episode at night when you're alone with your stress.

Many advisors will tell you that you should exercise regularly. Exercise can help, and you should do it, but it may or may not be sufficient in itself.

Yoga is particularly helpful in stressful times, and not just because it's a form of exercise. According to the ancient Yogic traditions, stress is actually held in the physical body and in one or more energy bodies (called *khosas* in Sanskrit). These clear light bodies get impurities and defects in them—called *samskaras*, which come from our reactions to everyday events in this (and, the yogis say, in other) lifetimes. In these traditions, it's not just the external circumstances that cause these impurities—it's our *reaction* to them. Sounds a lot like stressful situations—we all react differently to them, holding in more or less stress and taking a situation more or less personally than someone else might.

You don't have to believe in energy bodies or ancient Yogic traditions. You can usually feel knots of tension in your body when you're stressed out. Get a massage. Do a meditation. Or just do yoga and see how you feel afterward.

You will feel more centered and able to focus on the immediate tasks at hand (i.e., getting the next marketing campaign done) rather than worrying about the next stressful situation that always hangs over a startup (i.e., we'll be out of money in three months!).

After moving to Silicon Valley, I found that a walk in nature can have similar effect. There's a park next to Google in Mountain View called Shoreline Park, where I go to take a walk near sunset as often as I can. This park sits along the San Francisco Bay and makes me feel like I'm thousands of miles away—perhaps walking near the mountains in West Virginia or some such place—rather than in the bustling tech capital of the world.

These words (watch *Star Trek*, do yoga, walk by the bay) were my stress mantra—a phrase I could not just repeat, but actual activities I could do on any given day. One of these was a mental activity, one physical exercise, and one a physical location I could go to de-stress. You should come up with your own stress mantra—three things you can do on any given day of your startup adventure!

In any case, although the myth says that startups are hard work, which is usually true. But almost without exception, startups are hard because of the stress that startup challenges introduce into our minds and our bodies. The stress comes not just from long hours, but from our expectations of how the market will react to our product—the Road of Trials. If you are even a little bit sensitive and aware, you will no doubt feel the stress much more after your product comes out than before. When you do, find a routine that can help you get through it—remember your stress mantra!

### Dealing with The Dark Times, from a VC and an Entrepreneur

Startups can be very stressful. What is the best way to deal with the dark times? VC Brad Feld and entrepreneur Alex Haro give some valuable advice.

#### *VC Brad Feld*

Brad gives advice in a couple of simple categories:

1. *"One is, you are not alone.* Don't get confused with the idea that somehow this is happening to you and not to anybody else."
2. *"The second is, deal with reality, and deal with it every day.* Don't deny the reality of what's going on. It can be emotional, stressful, painful."

Brad continues: "Talk to people you trust, whether they're investors, board members, cofounders, mentors, whatever; make sure that you're open about the stress and struggle you're going through both functionally in the business as well as personally. Because if you hold it all inside, it just makes it worse."

"Make sure you get plenty of rest. People who are exhausted make shitty decisions consistently and it's easy to get emotionally into this thing. But you're going to have real hard decisions to make and you want to make sure you're making them deliberately rather than reactively."

*Entrepreneur Alex Haro, Life360*

Alex says, "Even with our success, even with our millions of users, there have been some really crappy points of our history. There were two different times we didn't have enough money to make the next payroll . . . for that month. We got really, really close."

Alex's advice includes:

1. *Communicate with the team.* "We were very transparent with the whole team . . . I think that's super, super key . . . You're convincing people to come join your startup that's completely unproven, for some equity that will probably be worthless. You owe it to them to be truthful about the state of the business, even if you go and lie your ass off to investors. I hate teams that are set up where they believe their own bullshit.

"It might mean saying, 'Hey guys! We've got two weeks of money left in the bank. We're really close on the seed deal, but if it falls apart . . . I'll be able to pay your last paycheck and then we all have to go find jobs.'

"When this happened to us, we had communicated the whole time around the status of the financing deal, and where it was going. At the time it's like, 'Hey, this looks good, but it might not happen.'

2. *Manage expectations.* "I think the more stressful part was just, I think any great entrepreneur sets up expectations for themselves that are very hard to meet. A lot of people talk about failing and failing fast, but it's still a sucky thing to go through to know that you have these great expectations and you're not hitting them, but even worse is just realizing that these ten people that took a bet on you . . . you're going to have to go look them in the face and say, 'Sorry. I, and we, failed at this.' Pumping yourself up for that conversation is definitely not easy.

3. *Explore all options.* "We were definitely talking through . . . all the options, really having an idea of every possible avenue. Maybe reduce the team to two people who don't pay themselves anything.

"Then there's a lot of just not blind faith, but we continued to try every possible avenue. No matter how bad or desperate it looks . . . continue to stay resourceful and try whatever. Even if it's a crazy idea, try it."

# Myth #19

## Whew, I'm Glad That's Over! No More Startups for Me!

Like many first-time startup entrepreneurs, I left my first company, Brainstorm, when our investors and board decided we needed to bring on a more "experienced" and "professional" CEO. We'd had four years of successful growth. When that startup failed a year later, I vowed I would never do another VC-backed startup again.

I also decided I didn't want to be CEO again. It was a stressful enough job, but to have it be one of my very first jobs out of college, and to go through both a meteoric rise and the disappointment and stress of seeing something you've built for years disappear was a bit much.

I needed time to decompress. I left Boston and spent six months in California. During that time, like many serial entrepreneurs, I decided to help others get their companies going, rather than starting another one myself, and I was fairly successful at this.

The funny thing is, despite my "heat of the moment" statement of this myth almost verbatim, I soon found myself in both positions again—as the CEO of a startup and raising money from VCs.

What gives?

## Groundhog Day for Entrepreneurs?

A few years after making my "vow," when we were building a company called CambridgeDocs, I found myself back in the CEO spot, even though I hadn't planned on it. I had helped the two other founders get the company going, and had planned to work only part-time at the startup. I had made a little money from my prior startups, and I was hoping to spend more time writing and doing other things—that is, things *other* than running a startup full-time.

We didn't have any outside financing, so it took a lot of effort to get this one going, and when one of the founders moved to another country to set up our off-shore office, I reluctantly agreed to be "acting CEO" again. Over time, as much as I enjoyed having no outside investors, I started to see how we were limiting ourselves by being so cash strapped. We couldn't hire many employees, and we couldn't pay the ones we had (including ourselves) very much.

Nevertheless, after a successful sale to EMC/Document Sciences, I vowed once again that I was done with full-time startups, I was done with being CEO of a startup, and I was (still) done with VCs!

Now I could finally get on with doing "other things"—namely, helping other entrepreneurs, writing, etc.

A few years later, when I was at Stanford GSB, a relatively well-known entrepreneur stopped by our class. His name was Lars Dalgaard, and he had started a wildly successful SaaS company, SuccessFactors (we didn't know it at the time, but SuccessFactors would be acquired a few years later). In his talk, he mentioned that he was the first CEO of a public company from his class at Stanford GSB, and I saw many of my classmates get very excited about that.

I could remember thinking: perhaps this is a goal that many in business school aspire to. In my own case, since I had pretty much started my career as a CEO, I was kind of burned out and wanted the exact opposite: a role with no direct reports to worry about, and well-defined responsibilities that I could dispatch while I was off doing the *other things* that I had been promising myself I would do for years. I figured I was done with startups—at least in running them.

Somehow, though, within a few years, I once again found myself CEO of a startup, even though it wasn't my intention to be. My cofounders wanted me to be CEO, for a variety of reasons, and we started Gameview Studios, which made the hit iPhone game, *Tap Fish*.

Once again, we contemplated raising VC money to help us grow. What was going on here? I kept vowing to do one thing, but kept ending up doing the opposite!

In the end, when we sold our gaming company to Japanese mobile gaming giant DeNA, I remember thinking, "OK, finally, I'm done. I've made enough money, I've proven myself, and even though I didn't want to, I took the CEO role one more time. Now I can finally get on to doing other things."

Of course, in Startup Land, there's almost no such thing as "done" if you have a certain kind of personality. After the success of Gameview, we had many VCs who were willing to invest in our next startup, with just a business plan. Within six months of my leaving DeNA, since I had the relationship with the lead VC, I ended up a CEO again, this time of another mobile gaming startup—and now I was doing the other thing I said I didn't want to do: dealing with VCs again!

It wasn't until I sold that startup that I finally got busy doing the other things I'd been talking about doing for years—namely, writing books like this one and helping other entrepreneurs with their startups through my accelerator Play Labs @ MIT.

My story might seem like an entrepreneurial case of the 1993 movie *Groundhog Day*, in which actor Bill Murray must relive a single day over and over again until he "gets it right"! Yes, it's not that uncommon in the startup world.

The point is that we all have patterns in our careers, whether we see them or not, and these patterns are usually driven by our personality, our strengths, and our weaknesses. Some of us just have startups in our blood.

## Digging into this Myth

It's worth noting that most people who end up being serial entrepreneurs say, "I'm done with startups," at some point, *whether their startups were financially successful or not!*

Most startups have two possible outcomes:

1) the startup fails (very common), or
2) the startup is sold.

There are, of course, other outcomes, which involve the company going public or becoming a profitable business. The percentage of startups that go public is so small compared to those that are either sold or go out of business that I haven't focused on IPOs as much in this book. So if you are a founder of a startup, you are most likely to end up in one of these scenarios.

Let's dig into each of them.

### *When Your Startup Fails*

When the startup is a failure and goes out of business, many entrepreneurs find themselves stressed out and not wanting to do another startup, at least not for a while, which is the sentiment behind this myth.

This is not always the case; there are those who say, "OK, let me jump back in to prove how I can do better." In Silicon Valley in particular and Startup Land more broadly, failures are not always viewed badly. John Glynn, one of our experts and a legendary venture capitalist, says, "Silicon Valley is built in such a way that failure is OK."

Whether you're likely to jump back in immediately after a failure usually comes down to how much decompression you need. Sometimes, it's the founder/CEO who holds most of the stress in the founding team. While startups are stressful for all founders, there is nothing like being the one to whom investors have entrusted their money.

Most likely, especially if you were the founder/CEO, you will need some time to decompress. This is a great time to do some traveling and self-discovery.

I recall a gaming company executive who decided to jump into the mobile gaming market. Like many who started their own companies, he got in after the market had gone through its super-hot phase and was maturing. His startup didn't work out, and he told me afterward that he just wanted to curl up in bed and not go outside for six months. Instead, he ended up getting a well-paying job at one of Silicon Valley's best-known giants (i.e., Google, Facebook). His experience was valuable enough that they made him an offer he couldn't refuse.

The good news is that after a startup experience, you are usually very qualified to get a reasonably good job at any number of tech companies in adjacent markets. If they are in Silicon Valley, they will probably value your startup experience for a key position.

This myth is a myth only in the sense that it's something that many of us say in the heat of the moment after our startup hasn't gone well: "Whew, am I glad that's over. I'm not doing another one of those soon!"

If you are married or have a family that you are responsible for financially, this becomes an even more emphatic sentiment. After the dot-com crash of 2000, the joke in Startup Land was that b2c meant "back to consulting" and b2b meant "back to banking," two industries where you could earn a stable paycheck to pay your mortgage and family's expenses!

Sooner or later, after some period of rest (yes, working for a big company can be stressful, but it can definitely provide a period of "rest" compared to bearing the entire burden of a startup), most entrepreneurs will once again find the energy that got them into Startup Land in the first place.

They might start to feel that "call to adventure," and as in most great stories, might feel like there's room for a sequel.

The sentiment usually changes from "I'm definitely not doing another one" to "Well, I didn't know that much last time; I know a lot more now, so why not do it again—but do it *right* this time?"

Of course, there is no way to be sure you are "doing it right." Every startup is different. As Winston Churchill is said to have observed about the Second World War, they wouldn't repeat the mistakes of the previous war (i.e., World War I), but they were likely to make a completely different set of mistakes!

### *When Your Startup Succeeds*

Let's look at the other scenario, in which your company sells for a good amount of money. What's a good amount of money? That depends on you. When I was 23 and starting my first company, $1 million seemed like all the money in the world. Today, you wouldn't even be able to afford a house in Silicon Valley with "only" a million dollars!

Still, the temptation to say, "Whew, I'm glad that's over, and I hope to never have to go through that again!" is also usually very strong if the company was successfully sold. If it was sold for quite a bit of money, you may find yourself suddenly financially independent. What could possibly drive you to do another startup?

I've also seen the exact opposite reaction after a successful startup exit. Some entrepreneurs forget all the pain and stress and want to do another one right away, thinking they will be able to make the same (or more) by selling the company again in just a few years. This isn't always the best decision, either!

Let's take the example of Trip Hawkins, who was the founder of Electronic Arts, one of the biggest game companies in the world. Trip went back into gaming and started 3D0. Since he was a successful entrepreneur, he was able to raise lots of money for 3D0, which ended up failing. This "overconfidence" and people willing to shower you with money often happens in Startup Land, after you've started something that went on to a substantial exit.

## Where's the Market?

Often, when a startup adventure has gone well, I've seen entrepreneurs who want to jump back into the market that they just exited. After all, he or she knows the market and knows that it's super-hot, so why not jump back in and do it again?

After we sold Gameview, which was a relatively easy startup compared to some of my other startups (i.e., our product took off and although we struggled with growth and management issues, we didn't really have to worry about the biggest thing startups get wrong—product/market fit), the market for mobile gaming was hot. So we thought it would be wise to jump back in while the getting was good and do it even better the next time around.

But the one enduring truth of startups that I want to make sure you understand is that no market stays static. Markets evolve, as shown in the Startup Market Lifecycle, and the opportunity for entrepreneurs changes with the market.

If you jump back in too quickly, you might be at the end of the "growing" or "super-hot" phases, and entering the "maturing" stage. If this is the case, you may find yourself competing with many entrenched competitors, competitors that you didn't take that seriously the last time around, and needing a lot of money.

This happened when I jumped back into mobile gaming in 2012. The market was moving from "super-hot" to "maturing," and although there was still consolidation, it became very difficult for new startups to compete without a lot of money.

Also, when I had done my first mobile gaming company in 2010, mobile games were made very quickly: the average game was built in a few months for a small amount of money.

By 2013-14, that had changed. Mobile games were becoming more expensive to make, users were expecting more polished user experiences, and user acquisition was even more expensive, to the point of being prohibitive. Many developers were now seeking publishers who had the money to market their games, and I found myself wishing I hadn't jumped back into gaming so quickly.

As the market evolves, the strategies that you have to use to enter the market may change considerably as well. Even if you were successful, you might find yourself not enjoying the new phase the market in as much as you did the early phases of your target market. This is where a little bit of self-knowledge comes in handy (see Myth #2: Founders Start Companies to Make a Lot of Money). What was it that you wanted out of your startup adventure?

## The Secret

***Give yourself and the market some time to decompress before jumping back in.***

If you've completed a startup, whether it went out of business or was sold for lots of money, or even if you left it on its way to a stellar IPO, there is no one right answer as to when to do another one.

One thing I can guarantee is that even if you vow never to do a startup again, you will probably hear the call to adventure again at some point. You might even do what many heroes in the ancient myths did when they heard the call—refuse the call, but it may be too tempting.

I usually recommend that all would-be serial entrepreneurs take a little time off in between startups. I don't think I've ever met an entrepreneur who regretted taking time off, if they could afford it financially (and even if they couldn't, there was always time to get a job later!).

Startups are tough, and even if you don't feel like you need to decompress, I can guarantee that you need to go through *some* decompression. The entrepreneurs who say they don't need to decompress are the ones who usually need it the most.

Taking some time off—even if it's just a month or two or six, also gives you some time to read where the market is going. Tom Higley, cofounder and CEO of Service Metrics, told me that he took almost five years off, to focus on music and family. That's a lot of time, but it all depends where your priorities are, and what options you have available (after a successful exit like Service Metrics', which sold to Exodus for $280 million at the height of the tech boom, he definitely had the option).

One benefit of taking this much time off was that Tom completely missed the "bust" years after the boom!

If there's one concept that's central to this book, it's that startup markets evolve. If you understand the Startup Market Lifecycle, you can easily figure out where the next wave is coming and have multiple successful startups.

If you do feel, after you've had some time to decompress, that it's definitely time to jump back in, then welcome to the "serial entrepreneur club"—or even the "parallel entrepreneur club"!

Those of you who hear the call to adventure more than once will realize that Startup Land is not just some faraway mythical place after all.

It's in your nature. You can't stay away.

Welcome home.

# Bonus Myth #B-6

## If My Startup Fails, My Life Is Over!

When I was trying to grow my first company, Brainstorm Technologies, we hit a point where our business was still growing, but we were low on cash. We had a good number of employees (I don't remember the exact number—it was probably in the neighborhood of thirty), and our payroll came to several hundred thousand dollars every few weeks.

We were working on arranging a round of financing with our investors, who had promised to put in the money. But, for whatever reason, the full investment got delayed. This is one of those near-death experiences that startups face, and a near-death experience in startups can really give you some insight into yourself and the company.

In this case, we were staring into the abyss, but we had a term sheet in hand for a new round and it was going to close eventually. We asked our investors to front us the money as a bridge loan.

▶ To read the full text of this **Bonus Myth**, including the Four Quadrants of Passion, please download the Supplement to *Startup Myths and Models* from www.zenentrepreneur.com ◀

# Bonus Myths

There were a number of important "bonus myths" that didn't make it into this version of the book, but which you will find valuable on your startup journey.

To download the latest bonus myths free (in PDF form), please go to the author's website, www.zenentrepreneur.com, and fill out the form for Bonus Startup Myths!

# Appendix A

## The Startup Market Lifecycle and Curves

This is a quick overview of the model that was introduced in Startup Model #1: The Startup Market Lifecycle, and which was further developed throughout the stages of the startup journey. Understanding this model is very important to understanding many of the "secrets" behind the myths. Because startup markets evolve quickly, understanding the Startup Market Lifecycle—the stages that a startup market evolves through—can help you to make decisions about when to start, how to fund, and when to exit your startup.

A quick overview of the stages:

- *Nascent*. Most markets begin in the "nascent" stage, which means that it is "new technology," typically the domain of super hackers and hobbyists and researchers. During this stage, it's great to get into a market and become a thought leader, but you have to be able to support yourself doing something else, as VCs probably haven't yet decided if there is a real market to invest in or not. *Valuations are nonexistent. Funding is from family and friends and some forward-thinking angels.*
- *Recognized/Growing*. This happens when VCs and the "echo chamber" across Silicon Valley recognize a market as one of the "next big things." Many companies that eventually become dominant players in

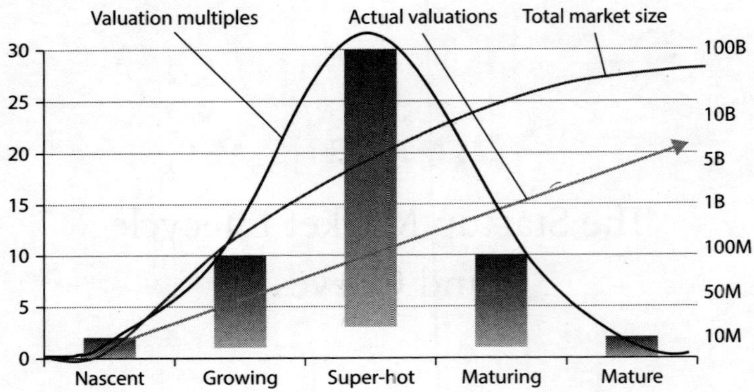


Figure ApA.1
Market Size Evolution with Stages. Created by the author

markets are actually started during this phase. There is, in the second part of this phase, a rush from big companies and VCs to put money into this space or to plug the hole in their product lines. *Valuations are typically in the range of 3×–5× revenue, peaking just before the next stage. The surest sign of this phase is that multiple VCs are looking to invest in this space.* The forward-thinking VCs have usually already invested by the time this stage gets going.

- *Super-hot*. Some markets make it to the mainstream quickly, some do it over a longer period of time. But there is an unusual period, which happens in high tech startup markets, where big players and VCs alike realize that they are "behind the curve" and need to get into this market. This is when outsized valuations happen, in both financing and acquisitions. I have seen one hundred–plus multiples on revenues during exits in this stage. *VCs are still investing and companies are buying at ridiculous valuations because of fear of missing out.*
- *Maturing*. During the maturing phase, the valuation multiples start to come down, there are several players that have emerged as leaders, and some level of consolidation is already under way. There is still an opportunity to make money during this stage, but it is very difficult and the capital requirements have gone up. Since valuations are going down, investors and acquirers can wait. *Valuation multiples go back down to 3× to 5×, and then lower, and projected profits are starting to become important. Very few new startups are getting funded at this stage,*

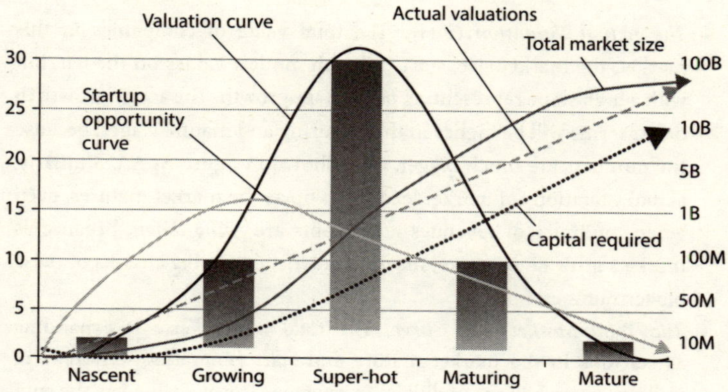


Figure ApA.2
The Startup Market Opportunity and Related Curves. Created by the author

*though the successful ones are raising large amounts of private equity.* The leaders in the market at this stage are achieving very high valuations in absolute terms.

- *Mature.* When a market matures, the emphasis shifts from growth to profitability in a given market. Companies start to be valued more on profits than revenues, and there are several established players who have made names for themselves as leaders. Most of what we learn in business school is tailored toward companies that are in this stage of the market. Unfortunately, the rules of big companies don't always apply to startups until this stage. Valuations at this stage are based on profits, and VCs no longer invest in this market space unless there's a new technological innovation.

When I was at Stanford's GSB, our economics professors would always draw curves for supply and demand and tell us how markets set prices based on the intersection of these curves.

The shape of the curve, they would say, is more important than the actual numbers. The same is true of the curves in this model, which we will return to again and again in looking at startup opportunities.

The shape and direction of the curves is what's most important, not the exact values on the axes. While it may be difficult to predict the exact timing of any specific "multi-billion dollar market" you can watch it go through various stages.

- *The Actual Valuation Curve:* The total value of companies in this market, the market size, starts off with modest values on the left, but with a high slope representing percentage growth. The actual growth in dollar terms will be higher in the maturing and mature stages, because the numbers are much bigger, as as shown in figure ApA.1. Similarly, actual valuations of market leaders go up as the market matures, even when multiples of revenues and profits are *going down*, because as markets grow and mature, market leaders take up big chunks of these bigger numbers.
- *The Total Market Size Curve.* The total market size is expanding as startups in the market mature and start generating hundreds of millions, even billions of dollars in revenue. This is defined as the sum of the revenue for all the startups in this market. You'll notice that the market size starts off lower than the valuations, but it grows and crosses at some point.
- *The Capital Required Curve.* As the market matures, more and more capital is usually required to make an impact on the market. When a market is small, the proverbial "two guys in a garage" can make a significant impact on the market. As it enters the maturing phase, there are startups that have hundreds of millions, if not billions of dollars in revenue, and so it's very difficult to catch up.
- *The Startup Opportunity Curve.* A corollary to all the other curves, this curve shows the time to get into a startup and how easy/difficult it is for a small team to make an impact. You might get in super early (nascent), but the market might never actually become the "next big thing." The best time to get into a market is at the beginning of the "recognized/growing" stage, before it has gotten too hot. When the market hits supernova valuations, then it's usually too late to get in (but not always).

# Appendix B

## Meet Our Cast of Characters and Startups

Every great adventure has a cast of characters. In this book, we refer to many characters representing many of the archetypes from multiple startup journeys—entrepreneurs, advisors, and investors whom you can learn from.

This section gives an overview of the many examples of startups that appear in this book. It also gives an overview of the VCs and entrepreneurs—the "experts"— whom I interviewed while writing this book.

This list is divided into three sections—Investors and VCs, Entrepreneurs and Companies, and the Startup Cheat Sheet. If a company is referenced only once, it may not be included in this list. To make this list a little more interesting, I've included some of the more colorful advice from each expert here.

### Experts: Investors and VCs

#### *Brad Feld*

Brad is a partner and cofounder of Foundry Group, a well-known VC firm in Colorado. Though Brad is not physically in Silicon Valley, he has written extensively about startups and is one of the most well-known VCs in Startup Land.

Brad sold his first company a few years out of MIT and then became an angel investor and cofounder in multiple companies during the dot-com boom. He has invested in many successful companies, including Zynga, FitBit, Service Metrics, Gnip, and many others. He was also a cofounder of TechStars.

Brad coauthored a number of startup books, including *Startup Communities*, *Startup Opportunities*, *Startup Boards*, and *Venture Deals: Be Smarter Than Your Lawyer and Venture Capitalist*.

Notable quote from Brad: "I'm not looking for entrepreneurs that are passionate; I'm looking for entrepreneurs that are obsessed!"

### *Randy Komisar*

Randy is a partner at Kleiner Perkins Caufield & Byers, one of the most well-known and respected VC firms in Silicon Valley. Prior to joining KPCB, Randy was a "virtual CEO" for many startups, and is the author of *The Monk and the Riddle*, one of the most beloved business books of all time, as well as *Getting to Plan B*, a book about management and innovation. Before becoming a VC, Randy was cofounder of Claris Corp, and CEO of LucasArts Entertainment. He has invested in a number of successful startups, including Nest, RPX, and Pinger.

Memorable quote from Randy: "I am in the failure business. Of course there are successes, but VC is one of the few industries where you can build a very good business and make a very good living by failing more than you succeed."

### *John Glynn*

John is the founder and managing partner at Glynn Capital Management. John has been described as a "veteran" of Silicon Valley—he has been a VC investor longer than anyone I've met (since 1970). John's list of investments reads like a "Who's Who" of Silicon Valley: Intel, Electronic Arts, Peet's Coffee and Tea, Silicon Graphics, Visicorp, Sun Microsystems, and Vertex Pharmaceuticals. John has taught courses on entrepreneurship at places like Stanford Business School and Cambridge University, which is where I first met him.

Notable quote from John: "We are looking for entrepreneurs who are looking to build a significant company, rather than those that are out to cash out quickly."

### *Sarah Downey*

Sarah A. Downey is a principal at Accomplice, focusing on early stage investments in frontier tech. Previously, she was an operator at two venture-backed consumer startups. Sarah received her JD degree from the University of Connecticut School of Law, and a BA in psychology from Hamilton College.

### *Jeffrey Bussgang*

Jeff Bussgang is a venture capitalist, entrepreneur, and professor at Harvard Business School, where he teaches Launching Technology Ventures, a popular class for MBAs starting or joining startups. His firm, Flybridge Capital Partners, has over $700 million under management and has invested in more than 100 companies. He was previously a two-time entrepreneur (UPromise, Open Market). He started his career with the Boston Consulting Group, and holds an MBA from HBS and a BA in computer science from Harvard College. He is the author of *Mastering the VC Game*, an essential guide for entrepreneurs raising capital, and *Entering StartupLand*, an essential guide for those who want to join startups.

## Experts: Entrepreneurs and Companies

The entrepreneurs I quoted in the book include:

**Jud Valeski**, cofounder of Gnip
Jud was a cofounder of Gnip, which was a startup that provided a single API to enterprises that wanted to access public data about users of multiple social networks. They were funded by Brad Feld's Foundry Group, among others. After their original concept of approaching social networks to let Gnip be an outsourced API provider didn't work out, they shifted to focus

on enterprises that wanted access to social network data. Gnip was sold to Twitter for approximately $175 million in 2014.

Notable quote from Jud: "We were all very clear on the fact that we were going to try to manufacture an entire market and that it wasn't just a product that we were going to try to insert into another market . . . The upside to that is you kind of get to play with all the variables in the entire landscape and you get to pretend like you have the answers to everything. Then the downsides to that are pretty obvious, which are you have a lot of work to do."

**Alex Haro**, cofounder of Life360
Alex started Life360 when smartphones and apps were relatively new, and he and his cofounder focused on understanding the needs of families and providing a smartphone app to meet those needs. Their app, Life360, started modestly (on Android) but began to grow quickly after it became common for multiple family members to have smartphones. Alex describes Life360 as the first social network built for families, which happens to be mobile. As of this writing, Life360 had experienced exponential growth and has had over 100 million downloads, making it one of the most downloaded apps of all time.

Notable quote from Alex: "When we started Life360, everyone was trying to make Facebook for *x*—let's create Facebook for dog lovers, and Facebook for game lovers, and Facebook for families. I mean, we actually looked at Facebook and said this is everything families don't need . . . the big insight for us was location is key to a lot of the communication and coordination that families do, so we created an app."

**Anu Shukla**, cofounder of Rubric Inc., MyBuys, and Offerpal/Tapjoy
Anu Shukla is a well-known serial entrepreneur in Silicon Valley.

After being a VP of marketing at Compuware/Uniface and Versata, Anu cofounded several companies. These included Rubric Inc., one of the first internet marketing automation enterprise software companies, which was acquired for $366 million in 2000. She later started MyBuys, whose original business model was unsuccessful, and then she pivoted the company to its eventually successful business model. Anu was also cofounder and CEO of Offerpal Media, which she started with Mitch Liu. The company raised over $70 million and later renamed itself Tapjoy. Anu is currently CEO of RewardsPay.

Anu's career in Silicon Valley has been an inspiration for women entrepreneurs. She has served on the board of directors of the International Museum of Women (imow.org), Forum for Women Executives and Entrepreneurs (FWE&E), and the advisory board for the Leavey School of Business at Santa Clara University. She was named to the computer industry "dream team" by *Business 2.0* magazine in 2004, was awarded the YSU distinguished alumni award in 2005, and was named the Entrepreneur of the Year by the Washington D.C.–based Dialogue on Diversity organization in 2005.

Notable quote from Anu: "I think there's a great deal of luck involved in everything. It's not that I'm discounting the fact that there's clearly a gender bias in Silicon Valley or that VCs will take too much of your company, etc. . . . All those things happen. I think what people don't talk about is how much luck is involved in actually making a company successful. It's one of the most unpredictable things."

**Saurin Shah**, cofounder of Sift Shopping
A former executive at Digital Chocolate, Saurin started Sift Shopping with a long-time friend to try to capitalize on the coming trend of mobile shopping. His company started with an app that consolidated products from retailers that the user had purchased from. After releasing a consumer app, and having cofounder issues, the company shifted toward a new strategy, to use the emerging iBeacon standard to help retailers reach customers' mobile phones. Sift folded in late 2014 as it was unable to gain the traction it needed to continue, after raising more than $1.5 million.

Notable quote from Saurin: "When I was raising money in the Valley, a lot of questions were, 'What's your tech platform? What's your viral coefficient?' It was very different in New York. When I went to New York, it was more like: 'Well, of course shopping is going to be big on the phone. What's your experience? What's the UI going to be?' They focused on different things; things that we were better at."

## Startup Cheat Sheet

Many startups are referenced in describing the Startup Myths, models, and tools presented in this book. Of course, some of these are well-known successful tech companies, such as Microsoft, Facebook, Google, Twitter, etc., but many of the other successful (and unsuccessful) startups may not be known to the reader.

Here is a cheat sheet of startups that are mentioned more than once throughout the book:

*Arbortext* (b2b)—founded on research done at the University of Michigan in the 1980s, Arbortext provided a framework and set of tools for structured documents using XML; their products were used by many of the largest manufacturing and pharmaceutical companies in the world, including Boeing and Toyota. Arbortext was sold in 2005 to PTC, a public company in Boston.

*Assured Labor* (b2b, b2c)—founded by David Reich and his colleagues from the MIT Sloan School of Management, Assured Labor provided a unique job-finding platform for developing economies, which was based on mobile phones more than desktop web pages.

*Brainstorm Technologies* (b2b, enterprise development)—my first startup out of MIT. We built tools for groupware applications for big companies. Notably, we built bridges between Lotus Notes and SQL platforms and client/server development environments like Visual Basic, etc.

*CambridgeDocs* (b2b, enterprise documents)—my startup, which made XML document processing software. Started with my brother, Irfan Virk, and Kedron Wolcott. The company was sold to EMC Document Sciences in 2007.

*Gameview Studios* (b2c, mobile games)—my startup (with cofounders Mitch Liu and Irfan Virk), which made *Tap Fish*, one of the most successful iPhone and Android games in the early days of smartphone mobile gaming. The company was sold to DeNA.

*Intelligize* (b2b, software as a service for law firms)—founded by Gurinder Sangha, a University of Pennsylvania–educated securities lawyer, who started a document management SaaS (software as a service) platform that came to be used by many of the leading law firms in the country. The company was sold to LexisNexis in 2016.

*CoinMkt* (b2c, Bitcoin exchange)—One of the first U.S.-based exchanges for buying and selling Bitcoin and other cryptocurrencies.

*Funzio* (b2c, mobile games)—Funzio was founded by Kenneth Chiu, Rick Thompson, Andy Keidel, Anil Dharni, and Ram Gudavalli, makers of the hit games *Crime City*, *Modern War*, and *Kingdom Age*. The company was acquired by GREE for $210 million in 2012.

*Gnip* (b2b, APIs for social networks)—founded by Jud Valeski and Eric Marcoullier, provided middleware for companies looking to tie into multiple social network APIs. The company was acquired by Twitter in 2014.

*Life360* (b2c, social app for families)—Founded by Alex Haro and Chris Hulls, Life360 is a "mobile social network" for families. Life360 went on to become one of the most downloaded apps ever, with over 100 million downloads, and went public in 2019.

*Offerpal/Tapjoy* (b2b2c, mobile gaming/advertising)—Offerpal was started by Mitch Liu and Anu Shukla, and Tapjoy was started by Lee Linden and Ben Lewis. At one point, Offerpal was the biggest ad network for Facebook games, and Tapjoy was the leading ad network for mobile games.

*Sift Shopping* (b2c, shopping app)—started by Saurin Shah, Sift was a shopping app that allowed users to browse and buy products across different retail stores.

*Service Metrics* (b2b, internet performance measurement)—a company I helped launch with a team of cofounders—Tom Higley as CEO and Neil Robertson as CTO—funded by IDG and Softbank, which sold to Exodus for $280 million in 1999.

*Zynga* (b2c, online and mobile video games)—cofounded by Marc Pincus in 2007, Zynga became one of the leaders in the emerging social gaming space. Zynga went public in 2011.

# INDEX

Page numbers in *italics* represent figures or tables.

# ACKNOWLEDGMENTS

This book is a result of my entire career—over twenty-five years of creating, advising, mentoring, and investing in technology startups. Because of this, it's difficult to acknowledge every one of my own mentors and entrepreneurs and employees who contributed (knowingly or unknowingly) to the lessons that I have put into this book. In some way, all of my startups and all of the entrepreneurs I've worked with have contributed.

Because my startup journey began even before my first startup in 1993, I'd like to acknowledge the folks at DiVA, the very first startup I worked for, which was a spinout from the MIT Media Lab. I'd like to give particular acknowledgement to my cofounders in my first (and many subsequent) startups, Mitch Liu and Irfan Virk, as well as Kirk Goodall, who joined us for part of that first adventure. I had many advisors during that first startup (and subsequent ones), but I'd like to acknowledge Dean Redfern and Brad Feld, who helped give me perspective during my formative startup episode. Even though I didn't always agree with the investors we've had over the years, I'd like to acknowledge them for believing in my ideas.

I also want to acknowledge all the startups that have gone through the Play Labs @ MIT accelerator—which gave me an opportunity to really drill down on these lessons and try them out in a group environment—and the folks at the MIT Game Lab, namely Scot Osterweil, Rick Eberhardt,

Sara Verrili, Philip Tan, and Andrew Grant, as well as the mentors, including Rajeev Surati, Irfan Virk, Durjoy "Ace" Bhattacharjya, and Ichiro Lambe, not to mention all of the great speakers who joined us.

On the writing of the book itself, I'd like to thank all the experts I interviewed and those who contributed to this book—they are listed in appendix B.

On the editorial side, I'd like to thank Susan Williams and Genoveva Llosa for looking at early versions of this book. At Columbia University Press, I'd like to thank Myles Thompson and Brian Smith for helping me bring the book across the finish line.

# ABOUT THE AUTHOR

Rizwan "Riz" Virk is a successful high tech entrepreneur, angel investor, best-selling author, video game pioneer, and indie film producer. He is the founder of Play Labs @ MIT, an accelerator for playful technologies (www.playlabs.tv), and manager of Bayview Labs (www.bayviewlabs.com). Visit his personal site and blog at www.zenentrepreneur.com.

Riz received a B.S. in Computer Science and Engineering from the Massachusetts Institute of Technology and an M.S. in Management from Stanford's Graduate School of Business.

Riz's entrepreneurial journey began at the age of 23, when he and his roommate grew their first company into a multimillion-dollar venture. Since then he has been a cofounder, investor, and advisor to many start-ups in Silicon Valley and beyond, including: Gameview Studios (sold to DeNA), CambridgeDocs (sold to EMC), Service Metrics (sold to Exodus), Tapjoy, Funzio (sold to GREE), Pocket Gems, Intelligize (sold to Lexis-Nexis), Moon Express, Discord, Disruptor Beam, Telltale Games, Sliver.tv/Theta Labs, and Bitmovio.

Riz has produced many video games that have been downloaded millions of times, including *Tap Fish*, *Titans vs. Olympians*, *Penny Dreadful: Demimonde*, and *Grimm: Cards of Fate*. Riz has also been a producer of many indie films, including: *Turquoise Rose, Thrive, Sirius, Knights of Badassdom,* and adaptations of the work of Philip K. Dick and Ursula K. Le Guin.

Riz is the best-selling author of *The Simulation Hypothesis: An MIT Computer Scientist Shows Why AI, Quantum Physics and Eastern Mystics All Agree We Are In a Video Game*; *Zen Entrepreneurship;* and *Treasure Hunt: Follow Your Inner Clues to Find True Success.* He has been profiled in *Tech Crunch, The Boston Globe, Inc. Magazine, Venture Beat, The Wall Street Journal Online, NBC News.com, Vox.com,* and has been on many radio shows including *Coast-to-Coast AM*, Fox News radio. He was even skewered on the *Daily Show with Jon Stewart*.